AFTER THE FINAL WHISTLE

THE FIRST RUGBY WORLD CUP AND THE FIRST WORLD WAR

STEPHEN COOPER

Foreword by
Jason Leonard, OBE

The History Press

First published 2015

The History Press
The Mill, Brimscombe Port
Stroud, Gloucestershire, GL5 2QG
www.thehistorypress.co.uk

British Library Cataloguing in Publication Data.
A catalogue record for this book is available from the British Library.

ISBN 978 0 7509 6422 7

Typeset by Donald Sommerville
Printed and bound in Malta, by Melita Press

AFTER
THE FINAL
WHISTLE

Contents

More praise for:
*After the Final Whistle: The First Rugby World Cup
and the First World War*

'In his award-winning *The Final Whistle*, Stephen Cooper concentrated on the extraordinary contribution his club Rosslyn Park made to the Great War by telling the story of 15 players who didn't come back. Now in *After the Final Whistle* Cooper broadens the scope massively and looks at the "rugby soldiers" of every Allied nation involved. It's an extraordinary and inspiring tale and concludes, after the Armistice, with teams from those military forces celebrating peace by going head to head in what many would describe as the first World Cup.'

Brendan Gallagher, *The Rugby Paper*

'A timely reminder of that fierce spirit which makes us all proud to be a part of rugby.'

David Sole, former Scotland rugby union captain

'As a rugby player and singer, it is impossible not to be moved by these powerful stories of rugby men in harm's way. It is comforting to know that they did not die in vain and their nations' anthems live on. There is silence in the stadium before I perform and then the eruption of sound in the thousands. Team-mates and supporters sing together, it is an incredibly powerful thing. Reading these stories now, gives each anthem a deeper meaning, it gives us our own identity.'

Laura Wright, internationally renowned soprano, rugby player and official RFU anthem singer

'A triumph: a proper accompaniment to the Rugby World Cup . . . further proof of the glorious civilising influence of Rugby Union.'

Justin Webb, journalist and BBC Radio presenter

Praise for:

The Final Whistle: The Great War in Fifteen Players, *Times* Rugby Book of the Year 2013

'This haunting and beautiful book . . . tells the story of men from one rugby club but it is a universal narrative of heroism and loss. He writes superbly and has produced a book of commendable scholarship. I cannot recommend it enough.'

Fergal Keane

'A fresh and fascinating take on the impact of the Great War, with a novel and moving focus.'

Ian Hislop

'Sensitive, original and profoundly moving'

Sir Anthony Seldon

'An inspired idea to link rugby and the Great War in this way – it brings home the pathos of these ardently lived lives . . . an original and illuminating approach to this endlessly fascinating subject.'

Edward Stourton

'Stephen Cooper has written a book of beauty and sadness . . . People use the word hero to describe sportsmen but the guys in this book are true heroes. A fantastic and inspiring read from the first page to the last.'

Jason Leonard, Lions & England

'. . . a book of stunning quality . . . a team-full of heartbreaking stories, each going in different and fascinating directions; poignant and powerful.'

Alan Pearey, *Rugby World Magazine*

'A fitting tribute not simply to 15 individuals cut down in their prime, but a paean to all those who died in the First World War.'

Mark Souster, *The Times*

For Clark and Ken Miller:
Men of rugby and flowers of Scotland, cut down early.

Foreword

by

Jason Leonard, OBE

This year we welcome the nations of the world to our country for the world's greatest celebration of rugby. England again hosts the Rugby World Cup for the first time since 1991, an occasion I remember well. Much has changed in our sport since then, not least the advent of professionalism; an event that started in the amateur era of 1987 is now the third largest sporting festival in the world.

But some things have not changed: I am pleased to say that rugby's values are as strong now as they were then. Those values of teamwork, respect, discipline, sportsmanship and enjoyment have always been there; they have made our game stand out, which is why we now talk about them openly and proudly.

For me, it was a revelation to find that those values were hardened in the most testing of times during the First World War, the great global conflict one hundred years ago that we commemorate today. It was a time of tragedy – and there are many tragic stories here – and it was a time of profound heroism and brave endurance. Rugby played its part at home, at the front and even in prison camps; it is no coincidence that once the horror was over, the instinct was to celebrate with a rugby tournament – the first ever team world cup.

This book demonstrates what all rugby lovers have known for many years, that there is more to rugby than what happens on the field. There is a way of life that comes with it; and a way of thinking that believes in honour, sacrifice, pain and love of team mates and country. We can never compare sport with war, but we can perhaps discover here the well-spring of those beliefs.

I am honoured to have won 22 of my England caps at four Rugby World Cups, including a memorable November day in 2003. I am privileged to welcome the rugby world to contest another great battle in 2015; but

I also ask you to remember the players from a century ago who made the ultimate sacrifice in that most brutal of wars. And remember too that, in the worst of times, they found enjoyment in our great game.

Jason Leonard, OBE
President, Rugby Football Union

On Rugby Fields the Whistles Blow

Twickenham: Friday 18 September 2015
A whistle sounds at 20.00 GMT at Twickenham to start England's first game of the 2015 Rugby World Cup against Fiji. It is heard around the world.

Let us go back 110 years.

Crystal Palace: Saturday 2 December 1905
Welsh referee, Mr Gil Evans begins the first meeting between white-shirted England and the All Blacks. He also officiates when Cardiff RFC successively play the All Blacks, the South Africans in 1907 and Australia in 1908; to celebrate this treble, Cardiff present Evans with an engraved sterling silver 'Acme Thunderer No. 58'. This passes on to countryman Albert Freethy, who uses it to referee the 1924 Olympic Games rugby final in Paris.

Twickenham: Saturday 3 January 1925
At the second encounter of All Black and all-white, Albert has the whistle again. When neither captain can produce a coin for the toss, he flips a florin lent by supporter Hector Gray, who later engraves it with a rose and fern; Freethy blows the Thunderer to dismiss New Zealand's Cyril Brownlie, the first player sent off in an international Test.

Eden Park: 22 May 1987
By now the sterling silver is nicked and worn with age; every surface is engraved with its history, like battle honours or a trophy. Australian referee Bob Fordham whistles for the start of the first modern Rugby World Cup. The florin has been tossed, and the trusty Acme has blown to kick off every one since.

RC Compiègne, France: Sunday 25 October 2009

On the edge of the Compiègne forest, where the Armistice was
signed in 1918, is a rugby field. Two teams of 14-year-old boys
surround a memorial bearing fifty-eight French names, all killed
in the Great War; the visiting side from England remembers 109
from its own club. On this Sunday morning, before their game, a
whistle signals a minute's silence.

These young tourists from Rosslyn Park, immortal in their
teenage rugby swagger, know little of the fate of Australia's Jim
Martin at Gallipoli, Horace Iles from Leeds or John Condon
from Waterford, Ireland, at Ypres: all died at their tender age of
14 in that war. But they listen solemnly to a French Army officer
who tells them that 'rugby and warfare share a common language,
but – *il nous faut souvenir, enfin* – they are very different'.

Rosslyn Park, London: Saturday 29 March 2014

A trench whistle starts a match of centenary remembrance, played
in baggy cotton jerseys, some splendid facial grooming and under
pre-war Laws. This whistle was taken in 1916 from the body of an
officer in the Yorkshire Regiment by a German soldier; it was later
returned to the regimental museum by his descendants and still
bears the scar of a shrapnel splinter.

⸿

The shared language of rugby and warfare still prevails today, a century
after the war which first connected them, as rugby's latter-day scribes
conjure the stark imagery of conflict. An untried England team under
new coach Stuart Lancaster opened their 2013 campaign away to an
experienced Irish side; unfancied, they came away from atrocious Dublin
weather with an unexpected 12–6 win. One journalist wrote: 'These are no
mere kids who need the roar of a Twickenham crowd to encourage them
to puff out chests. These are guys for the trenches, steely and trustworthy.'[1]
One hundred years later, the rugby field shares a common lexicon with
the battlefield.

My generation can still hear in its mind's ear the sonorous burr of
Bill McLaren, 'voice of rugby' and former artillery gunner, describing the
boot of Gavin Hastings as 'mighty like a howitzer'.[2] *The Times* reported
'aerial bombardment' when Wales played New Zealand in 1935; passes are

'fired', stand-offs launch 'torpedo' kicks, and scrum-halves 'snipe' round the blind side. Where did it come from, this language bond between rugby and warfare? And how is it that a century later the imagery born of the Great War is still deployed (see what I did there?) to add colour and drama to sports reports? It is not, heaven forbid, lazy journalism but something deeper, more intuitive, and an echo of shared values.

My conclusion is this. There are many sports that carry danger and physical risk for *individual* competitors, notably anything to do with horses and cars. Boxers, of course, willingly climb into the ring for a beating, and sadly even cricketers now face untimely death at the crease. Uniquely, however, in *team* sports rugby players deliberately and consistently, and without the protection of helmets or padding, put themselves in harm's way *on behalf of others – on behalf of the team and in its common cause.* This is what soldiers also do, and their comradeship sustains them far more than patriotic ideals or mission statements, or even Kevlar. Perhaps this explains the unconscious bond between rugby and soldiering and, in consequence, an almost symbiotic vocabulary.[3]

In a far better-qualified view, Australian Army chief General Sir Peter Cosgrove put it more explicitly:

> There are similarities between the harsh and lethal demands of warfare and the thrill we get from a full-bodied contact sport like rugby. The thing about rugby is that it does prepare people to keep going under severe stress when things they have to do are extraordinarily hard.[4]

Cosgrove was not the first military commander to draw the parallel. Admiral Lord Jellicoe, commander of the Grand Fleet in 1914, concurred:

> Rugby football, to my mind, above all games is one which develops the qualities which go to make good fighting men. It teaches unselfishness, esprit de corps, quickness of decision, and keeps fit those engaged in it.[5]

After the war, Field Marshal Sir Douglas Haig declared that team sport required 'decisions and character on the part of the leaders, discipline and unselfishness among the led, and initiative and self sacrifice on the part of all'. It was his belief that 'the inspiration of games has brought us through this war, as it has carried us through the battles of the past'.[6] *The Scotsman* reported the views expressed at the Scottish Football Union's AGM in October 1914:

The quick decision necessary to take an opportunity, the dash, the self-restraint, and the consideration for the opponent were most valuable training for both soldiers and sailors, and . . . was demonstrated by the fact that whenever this country has been at war Rugby men in large numbers went to the front.[7]

Paddy Moran, Australian captain in 1908, recalling the 'higher plane of organised roughness' of university rugby, noted:

When I read of [First Sea Lord] 'Jacky' Fisher's remarks while head of the British Navy, 'the essence of war is violence; moderation in war is imbecility', I thought his saying could well have been adapted to the Rugby Football of my own time. It was however largely a good-natured violence. Two commandments on which you were judged and condemned: Thou shalt not squib and Thou shalt not squeal.[8]

Rugby roughness gave them an appetite for the fight. The rugby writer, Edward (universally known as E.H.D.) Sewell recounts that one New Zealand officer 'lying smashed by Turkish bullets in hospital assured me that one of his chief troubles on Gallipoli was to keep back the Rugby players. Out of every twenty "first into" the Turkish trench, eighteen were Rugby men.' Even allowing for the popularity of rugby in New Zealand, this seems statistically unlikely, but we get the point.

In 1916, the *Arrow* in Australia paid tribute to rugby's wholehearted response to war:

The only bright spot in all this, apart from the fact that the Allies have the Germans hard on the defence, is that the response by rugby footballers has shown that their game is as fine a preparation for war as anything in the line of sport the world has invented. The response has come from all grades of players, from the juniors to the first graders of ordinary powers to the representative men, and to the men who have retired from play for many years. It is a great thing to dwell upon in this hour of the world's carnage.

Rugby and the military were already linked before the First World War. The Calcutta Cup, the oldest trophy in international rugby, originated from the army: stationed in India, the 3rd East Kent Regiment (The Buffs) and 62nd (Wiltshire) Regiment established rugby at the Calcutta Club. However, when The Buffs were posted out of India in 1876, enthusiasm for rugby waned and reduced membership forced the club to disband.

From the 270 silver Indian rupees left in the kitty, a cup was made with its distinctive design, three cobras as handles and an elephant atop the lid. In 1879, the Calcutta Cup was presented to the RFU to be competed for annually by teams from England and Scotland. The first match, in 1879, was a 3–all draw; it was on 28 February 1880 that England became the cup's first winners in Manchester.

Rugby, however, had to fight for its place in the British Army: in 1906, there were 578 army soccer teams, with 180 in the Royal Navy. The inauguration that year of the Army–Navy Cup, albeit for officers only, increased participation and rugby grew from its handful of military teams. Successive national tours by colonial teams, starting with the All Blacks in 1905, further developed interest and a steady influx of public school-educated rugby-playing officers into the Regular and Territorial armies meant that rugby was firmly established in the military by 1914.

Sport served a deeper psychological purpose at the front. Volunteer civilians who had dreamed of bloodless glory at the drill halls before August 1914 found the reality of warfare so hideous that they had to seek escape in order to survive. Humankind cannot indeed bear so much reality. Behind the lines, they took refuge from their trench terrors in games which offered a comforting return to a world before war, and an ordered 'other life' where war did not threaten to drive them mad. According to historian J.G. Fuller, the soldier 'sought intervals of pleasure to relieve the suffering, and exercised ingenuity to create islands of sanity in the midst of the horror'.[9]

Rugby was one such island. With its precise formations, set-piece confrontations, and disciplined rules, rugby restored a sense of order while its physicality and speed took men out of their troubled selves. Even 'Code Wars' served a purpose, as one Australian subaltern recalled:

> The relative merits of Rugby, Australian Rules and Association were debated as keenly on the battlefields and back areas of France and Belgium as they ever were under the sunny skies of Australia . . . the argument with the Kaiser was more easily settled than that one. The patronising manner in which a supporter of one particular game would ask another to 'come and see a real football match' was most amusing.[10]

As the French say more elegantly, the more things change, the more they are the same thing. In the 1916 diary of another Australian, Tom Richards, one can hear the yearning for yesteryear mixed with the joy of release. When his 1st Field Ambulance played the 3rd they journeyed eight kilometres by wagon and crossed the River Lys on a raft to a pitch with football posts,

> . . . but no other marks, neither goal lines nor sidelines as the grass was two feet long in patches . . . the ball could not be seen and the men kicked yards away from the ball . . . a fellow was laid out and none of our players noticed it . . . A jolly good experience second only to the first match I saw in England when a hailstorm stopped the play and a ball went into the scrum alright and burst therein; the players could not make anything out of it.[11]

Where indeed '*les neiges d'antan*' of the rugby field? On the October eve of their transfer to the Somme, he watched 'the 12th Battalion A Company versus the Bombers' in an elegiac setting that reminded him of home:

> The surroundings were almost Australian in their appearance. The playing field was roomy and the grass delightful both in its softness and colour. A rough hedge of hawthorn and fruit-bearing blackberry bushes protected one side and end, a row of tall majestic trees towered close to the other side and watercress banks of the river framed off the end.

The scene inspired in the soldier-players 'an unconscious undercurrent to urge on these valiant athletes to fight relentlessly for the honour, the prestige of each particular section'. And although reality will soon bite with the sharpest of teeth, there is a *carpe diem*. Inevitably in rugby – and without the need for Latin – there is also a whole load of banter:

> Tomorrow they will be en route for the Somme and the greatest Hell ever thought of, greater even than man's imagination is capable of conceiving. But what care they for the morrow, let's first find out who are the best footballers while there is still time in hand . . . No player dared make a mistake: in his mess he would obtain no peace for weeks should he fail to keep up his end.

Sport was a great equaliser between officers and other ranks, allowing both to forget themselves and their status for a brief while, yet maintain order and discipline through the rules and behaviour code of the game.

Even as prisoners of war, when they were no longer free to play in green fields, they improvised games in captivity on pitches far less attractive than Richards's water meadow. Douglas Lyall Grant, of

London Scottish, two years a PoW, broke a rib playing rugger on the cinder surface at Gütersloh *Offizierslager*, and moaned like a schoolboy: 'It's rotten, I'm off games for a bit.' At Schwarmstedt, the pitch was even more hazardous:

> The ground can hardly be called suitable, being only 50 yards long and 25 yards wide, while a pump and an electric light pole are obstacles to be avoided. However we had a good enough game with eleven a side and got hot dirty and scraped.[12]

Improvisation occasionally brought retribution. At Magdeburg, playing in a cobbled courtyard with no leather ball available, officers used a bread loaf; the German guards resented this insult to their *Brot* and gave them all eight days in the cells. Further proof, if needed, that Fritz was not a sportsman and did not understand the importance of games or fair play. Such shortcomings, in the eyes of soldiers and press barons alike, were directly responsible for the current hostilities. Rugby was played on neutral grounds too: in April 1916, 'Engeland' and 'Schotland' played '*het beroemde Engelsche spel, Rugby Football*'[13] at Leeuwarden, Netherlands. Teams came from 1,500 Royal Naval Division (RND) internees at Groningen, after the disaster at Antwerp had marooned them ashore for four years.

International players were celebrities at the front as at home. Lieutenant Chater writes in some astonishment at witnessing a spontaneous Christmas truce in his sector of the line; he is more impressed at sharing a dugout with David McLaren Bain, 'the Scotch Rugger international, an excellent fellow', who would shortly be killed at Festubert. Even generals were caught under the spell of rugby's stardust, as Henry Grierson[14] recounted of one corps commander who 'came to inspect our Battalion in the front line trenches' and found Edgar Mobbs, former captain of Northampton Saints and England:

> When the GOC saw Edgar, he corpsed the meeting by ejaculating, 'By Gad, it's Mobbs. The last time I saw you, my dear chap, was when you and Tarr scored that remarkable try for England against the Australians – let's go into your dugout and talk over old times.' And so they did, and the Lt Gen never went near the frontline at all, but talked Rugger instead, to the total amazement of the Divisional Staff. But they didn't know that General Fanshawe[15] was an old Blackheath player.

Just as Jonny is 'loved by the English, adored by the French', so too was Mobbs a century before, as rugby crossed the lines of language. Lieutenant Gurney, one of his Saints acolytes now serving under him, recounts a starstruck Frenchman exclaiming: 'C'est Monsieur Mobbs!' Gurney indignantly retorted, 'C'est *Colonel* Mobbs'. Back came the reply: 'Je le connais – rugby football – Bordeaux – I play against him.'

The cold statistics of war do not show a 'lost generation', a phrase coined by Gertrude Stein, not for those who died, but to describe the war-interrupted survivors drifting through the Twenties – the beautiful and damned of F. Scott Fitzgerald's novels. Over 8 million men served in the British forces and roughly 10 per cent of them died; this equates to between 1 per cent and 2 per cent of the population as a whole. Comparing census returns of 1911 and 1921 reveals a decline in the male population of military age of some 14 per cent. The influenza pandemic that raged globally through 1918 and beyond also took its own deadly toll of that generation,[16] unusually striking the young far more than its customary victims of infants and the elderly. Death in war does not spread itself evenly; like life, death is not fair, but indiscriminate.

Disproportionate blows fell on tight-knit communities who joined up together and fought in the same murderous battles: 'Pals' battalions from Accrington and Barnsley or the Tyneside Irish and Scottish were more than decimated in 1916. But other sections of the population not so easily tagged with local labels suffered as much. If 10 per cent of all combatant men died, the death rate for line officers was double at 20 per cent. A gruesome feature of Rosslyn Park's death roll of 109 names[17] is the number shot in the head. This is more than an occupational hazard of trench warfare, or the absence of top cover before the 'Brodie Bowler' helmet became standard issue in January 1916: it is because these were junior officers who led their men over the top and on patrol, peered over parapets, helped drag wounded soldiers to safety, only to be shot for their pains, or were picked off by snipers while checking on fright-weary sentries on their nightly rounds.

There is no statistical analysis of rugby players who died. Nor would it be possible to define the sporting allegiance of the 888,246 British and Commonwealth soldiers represented by a blood-red sea of ceramic poppies in the moat of the Tower of London. Those who both played and died for their country are the most celebrated. By my count, 137 capped players died in this war from Britain and its Empire, France, USA and even Argentina:[18] its side that played the British in 1910 lost forward Frederick

Sawyer at the Aisne in 1917.[19] But time and again, when photographs are shown, or stories are told of fifteen men together, or a game of thirty, there is a consistent fraction: ONE THIRD. Rugby players suffered a death rate between 30 per cent and 35 per cent.

Let us inspect the anecdotal evidence at school, club, or international level: Rosslyn Park lost 109 of some 350 who served, six from its 1910 XV photo; six of the XV of teenage Battersea schoolboys at Emanuel School in the 1914–15 season and six of their counterparts at Edinburgh Academy, or eight from its 1905 championship-winning side. Five Blues from Oxford's 1910 Varsity team perished, six of the French side at Swansea that year, and eleven from Scotland's clash with South Africa in 1912 (nine being Scots). Always a third or more.

The sorrowful roll call continues. Eight from Glasgow Academicals Football Club XV in its final pre-war season; six from that season's Liverpool FC, one of the greatest rugby club sides ever, with three national captains, two of them destined to fall in action; seven from 1913 French champions Aviron Bayonnais and from their Perpignan successors, five of the Barbarians side against the Royal Army Medical Corps (RAMC) at Richmond in 1915, including three international threequarters. And so on. Statistics are not everything in life – proverbially, they come a poor third to lies and damned lies. But in death, the 'killer stat' – ONE THIRD – will shake his bloody locks and haunt the many rugby teams of this book.

The Five Nations finale of April 1914 was poignant: it was the last peacetime international in Europe before the conflagration, with death's shadow hovering over eleven doomed English and Frenchmen. The March Calcutta Cup game in Edinburgh was even harder hit, with twelve gladiators about to die, a misfortune of 40 per cent: Scotland would lose seven of its flowers; five Englishmen would wither in the earth, including the tallest poppy, Ronald Poulton-Palmer. Most tragic is an unlucky thirteen scholars destined to die from a 1912 Varsity Match that featured nine internationalists and twenty-eight who fought.

Despite this litany of death and injury, rugby emerged reinvigorated; it got up off the floor after a multitude of crushing tackles and went at it again. After the fighting was finished, soldiers once more played rugby in 1919; they celebrated their victory and survival – and the memory of team-mates – with a unique festival: the first ever rugby world cup. This book tells that story.

During the war, the No. 58 Thunderer was the standard issue whistle for artillery crews, warning them to keep clear of the recoil, before it returned to its peacetime role on the sports field. For the record, when the whistle blew in 1905, the All Blacks won 15–0. Twenty years later, down to fourteen men after Cyril Brownlie's dismissal, they still beat England 17–11 to the silvery sound of Freethy's blast. In 1987, when the same whistle first blew for the modern Rugby World Cup, hosts New Zealand went on to beat Italy 70–6 in Auckland. This black pattern with a silver accent will be broken when England kick off against Fiji at Twickenham on Friday 18 September 2015. But the century-old whistle will add to the mystique of a sporting celebration that was first born out of a terrible war

In 2009, Rosslyn Park's U14 lads went on tour and played *les gars* from RC Compiègne; the result and score will forever stay on tour, as it must. And in 2014 at Roehampton, as we remembered 109 men who made the ultimate sacrifice, no one was counting the score – not even the actuary who ran touch.

Rugby won the day.

The Last of Peace

Oh, we don't want to lose you but we think you ought to go,
For your King and Country both need you so.[1]

It was an August Bank Holiday weekend.[2] As cricket-lovers at the
Oval watched a young Jack Hobbs stroke his way to 226 against
Nottinghamshire, the cries of the newsboys around the ground were
ominous: 'MOBILISATION OF THE FLEET', 'GERMANY IN THE
NORTH SEA' and – in Cockney tones – 'SPRECHEN SIE DEUTSCH'.
On Saturday morning, Ronald Poulton-Palmer had reported for duty
with his 4th Royal Berkshire Territorials as they prepared to leave for
their annual fortnight's camp near Marlow. But there was an expectation
of more news: France, Germany and Russia were already at war.

Just fourteen weeks earlier 'R.P.P.' had been at the Stade Olympique
at Colombes near Paris, captaining England to a successive Grand Slam,
and scoring four tries in the process. This was a flourish to the nominal
Home Nations 'championship' of those amateur days, as the French were
still finding their feet in international rugby. Indeed, France and Scotland
did not meet that year: their previous match in Paris had degenerated
into a riot, and the scandalised Scots declined to host the French in
genteel Edinburgh.

There had been little to choose between England, Wales and Ireland,
although the real thriller was the Calcutta Cup in Edinburgh when
the unfancied Scots ran England close, forcing them to hang on for a
narrow win by a single point, 15–16. England claimed the Triple Crown
and went to Colombes for the *coup de grâce*. Ireland and Wales contested
second place, each having beaten Scotland. The game in Belfast was
brutal, as the Welsh pack justified its reputation as 'The Terrible Eight'.
Several stoppages delayed play as bleeding men were treated for injuries.
A torrid private battle took place between Welshman Percy Jones and
Irish pack-leader William Tyrrell, which went way beyond Moran's 'good-
natured violence'; in later years, after bloodier slaughter put rugby brawls
in perspective, Tyrrell – by now Air Vice-Marshal Sir William Tyrrell,

a grandee of the Irish Rugby Union – specifically asked to sit with his erstwhile adversary Jones at a post-match dinner. They did not talk about Fight Club.

France, like Scotland, had lost all their games. But they scored first and were in the contest till the break when England led 13–8; in the second half the white shirts ran away to win 39–13. On top of R.P.P.'s four, Cyril Lowe, a wing considered too small by some at 5ft 6in, scored a hat-trick; he played twenty-five consecutive matches and was for long years England's record try-scorer. Of the thirty players who took the field, eleven were killed in the war. For England, surgeon James 'Bungy' Watson died when a torpedo sank HMS *Hawke*; Francis Oakeley drowned as a submariner; Jimmy Dingle fell at Gallipoli; Arthur Harrison earned a posthumous Victoria Cross for his action at Zeebrugge in 1918; Robert Pillman and Poulton-Palmer died in Flanders. On the French side the fallen were Marcel Burgun, who was shot down, Jean Larribau, Emmanuel Iguiñiz, Paul Fauré, and Jean-Jacques Conilh de Beyssac. Of the six Englishmen, four have no known graves, the bodies of three naval officers Watson, Oakeley and Harrison lost in the North Sea, and Dingle in Turkey. The pair with the dignity of a headstone, Poulton-Palmer and Pillman, are six kilometres apart at Ploegsteert, Belgium.

At 11 p.m. on 4 August, Britain's ultimatum expired and a state of war was declared with Germany. The next day dawned in Sydney twelve hours before it did on the Greenwich Meridian. The touring All Blacks played a Metropolitan XV at the Sydney Sports Ground. A message in stark capitals was placed on the scoreboard: WAR DECLARED. Ironically, the match proceeds were designated for sending an Australasian team to the Olympics planned for Berlin in 1916; many athletes, by then known as Anzacs, were still making strenuous efforts to get to Berlin in the summer of 1916, but were unavoidably, often permanently, detained by events at Pozières. Instead of funding an unlikely Olympic challenge, the New South Wales Rugby Union duly noted that 'much activity was devoted to the recruitment of members for the Expeditionary Force'. Ten days later, the kick-off for the last Test between the Wallabies and All Blacks was moved to 2 p.m. so the New Zealanders could board their ship home, which under new wartime regulations had to be out of Sydney Harbour by sunset, or be made to wait at the dock until next sunrise.

British rugby's first act of war on 5 August, within twelve hours of its declaration, came from Birkenhead Park: it was the first club to offer its ground and pavilion to the military. That morning the decision was steered through committee by former England captain Percy Kendall, who then promptly rejoined his former local Liverpool regiment in the afternoon. Another England cap at Birkenhead, RFU selector James 'Bim' Baxter, 'went afloat in the RNVR and served afloat to the end.' E.H.D. Sewell wrote: 'For instant patriotism, Birkenhead Park RUFC stands out as the most brilliant example of record.'

Across the Pennines, in Yorkshire's Wharfedale, Jack King was hay-making on his farm at Ben Rhydding with fellow Headingley forward, Thomas Lumb, an agricultural student whose 'boundless energy and high spirit' at Leeds Grammar School had earned him the nickname 'Busty' (no, me neither). Out in the field, Tommy, an 'enthusiastic Territorial in the Yorkshire Hussars of some years standing',[3] was handed his mobilisation papers: 'Sorry, Jack', said he, 'but I'll have to chuck now, pack up and make a bee line for headquarters – we are called up.' His friend enquired about the procedure for joining the Hussars, 'for I intend to come with you'. It was a *Boy's Own* adventure.

Jack left his home on Thursday 6 August, 'without fuss or show or noise, and with a few instructions to his sisters as to the management of the farm' (so far so Yorkshire), never dreaming that he would do anything but walk straight into the Yeomanry. But Jack King was rejected by King's Regulations: he was an inch short of the 5ft 6in required for military service. He grew remarkably quickly and three days later became a trooper in His Majesty's Army: it was 9 August, the same date he would die two years later at the Somme. His friend Corporal Busty Lumb died in May 1915 at Ypres, aged 22; his body could not be found, but his name can – on the Menin Gate Memorial. Major Lane-Fox of A Squadron wrote of him: 'I had only recently promoted him to Corporal, and no promotion ever gave greater satisfaction throughout the Squadron, for there was no more rightly popular man.'

Frank Mellish, still at South African College School in Cape Town, was summoned to the headmaster's study. Although he could not recall committing any heinous crime, the 18-year-old took the precaution,

> to slip my atlas inside the seat of my pants and unwittingly adopting the gait of a stiff-legged cowboy, did as I was bid. In the tense, curt Scots manner of our Headmaster we were told that Germany had declared war on Britain and that automatically meant on South Africa as well. We, being members of the Union Defence Force, were to report immediately to the Drill Hall, collect our uniform and be sent wherever we were required.[4]

Once Bank Holiday Monday was over, a total of 8,193 men enlisted between Tuesday 4 and Saturday 8 August. Many of the most eager were rugby players: one who signed his attestation papers on Wednesday at the Artists' Rifles' HQ was Rosslyn Park's Eric Fairbairn, an Australian-born oarsman and Olympic medallist; another was clubmate, Robert Dale.[5] Charles Alvarez Vaughan, a Middlesex and Barbarian winger of rare pace, working in Colombia on his family tobacco estates, received a cable requiring him to take up his post in the Reserve. On 17 August, poet Nowell Oxland took his army medical in Oxford, where he was studying. The number of volunteers climbed exponentially: by the third week of August, it was 49,000, by the fourth 63,000, and in the first week of September, it reached almost 175,000.

In Scotland, on 10 August, the SFU donated £500 to the National Relief Fund, offered the Inverleith ground to the military, and asked club members 'to do something for which the training in discipline and self-control given by our Game has fitted them'. By the time of its 8 October AGM, many attendees were in khaki. President Dr James Greenlees, a Lorettonian and four-time Cambridge Blue with seven Scots caps, sent apologies – he was with the RAMC in an army field hospital in France. Twenty-four clubs provided figures – out of 817 players, 638 had enlisted. In Ireland, the Irish Rugby Union Volunteer Corps was established before the British Expeditionary Force (BEF) had landed in France. England's RFU, wrong-footed at holiday time by the threat posed to the forthcoming season by this national emergency and by players' headlong rush to join up, did not immediately cancel fixtures but issued a circular to clubs on 13 August:

> The Rugby Union are glad to know that a large number of their players have already volunteered for service. They express a hope that all Rugby players will join some Force in their own town or county.

Nine days later scrum half Gordon Bayly of Rosslyn Park and his pilot Vincent Waterfall, another 'keen sportsman', were the first British airmen to be shot down by enemy fire on 22 August, as they reconnoitred German columns moving on Mons. The unimaginable scale of the mechanised slaughter to come was measured by the death of 27,000 French soldiers on that single August day.

Gloucester Football Club reservists like Boer War veteran and hooker Fred Goulding, 'A' team full back William Hancock and centre Bernard

Roach had been immediately recalled to the Colours; Hancock and Roach were dead by Christmas. It was clear within days that a New Army was needed and Kitchener's famous finger was pointed; on 28 August, at a recruitment drive at Gloucester's Shire Hall, Major Collett called for twenty-five enlistees to join the territorial 5th Gloucestershires, to bring the battalion up to strength. Between 300 and 400 men rushed the platform, led by a rugby player:

> . . . a tremendous cheer went up when Sid Smart, the Gloucester footballer and English International took his place on the platform and similar demonstrations were accorded to the Captain of the Gloucester football team, [Lionel] Hamblin and his colleagues, Albert Cook and [William] Washbourn.[6]

Most Gloucester FC players joined the 5th; faced with its players marching to war, the club had little choice. On 2 September, it issued a statement:

> . . . practically the whole of the playing members have enlisted but in any case the Committee would not have felt justified in fulfilling the fixtures even if the players were available owing to the rapid change of the situation in connection with the war.[7]

Local newspaper *The Citizen* announced that its sporting edition would no longer be published; any games played would be considered unpatriotic and would not be reported in its pages. Yorkshire's Committee met on 31 August for the first time since the declaration and passed a resolution that 'all football in the county be suspended during the continuance of the war, and we strongly appeal to our players to join some unit for the defence of the country'.

On Saturday 5 September, with most players and clubs already ahead of them, the RFU cancelled all matches for the 1914–15 season. In Glasgow that Saturday, instead of preparing for an afternoon match, the Honorary Secretary of the Academicals, John Macgill, was typing a flurry of urgent correspondence. In his haste, secretarial accuracy deserted him. He replied to Dr James Nicoll, who had offered funding in the current crisis:

> As I expected, the Meeting on Thursday decided to cancel all Football fixtures. The Meeting thereafter considered what could be done in the club to further recruiting. It was resolved to try to raise an Academical Company to form part of the battalion of commercial men which is being got up by the Chamber of Commerce. So far I have got about 35 names. With regard to

your very kind offer to contribute to any expense which might
be incurred in connection with the formation and equipment of
an Acamedical [*sic*] Corps, of course with our present scheme we
do not anticipate any outlays, but at some future stage there may
be some scheme of training Acamedicals for which funds will
be required.

He wrote next to A.D. Lawson, his 'oppo' at Gala Football Club to cancel
their forthcoming fixture. He then confirmed to one of those '35 names',
William Mercer Alexander, that:

I have your wire and confirm in reply that I have entered your
name in the Academical contingent being formed for services in
Kitchener's Army. The idea is that our contingent, the members
of which will be kept together, forms a unit of the Battalion of
Commercial men.[8]

As Second Lieutenant Alexander, 17th Highland Light Infantry, William
would lose his life on the first day of the Somme; he rests in name only on
the Thiepval Memorial.

In Ireland, Harry Magrath, of Cork Constitution, younger brother
of Irish cap Dickie, was elected captain for the 1914–15 season. When
war was declared, it was agreed to play charity matches only: the last
played was the Charity Cup final against University College Cork on
19 December, which Constitution won 5–3. Thus Harry had the pleasure
of captaining his team to its last success before all rugby activity was
suspended for the duration. Serjeant Magrath, 24th Royal Fusiliers, met
his death at Beaumont-Hamel on the Somme in November 1916.

Football, meanwhile, attracted nationwide derision and critical column
inches in equal measure for its 'unpatriotic' stance. Professional clubs
saw no good commercial reason to cancel players' annual contracts for a
war that would assuredly be over by Christmas, and kept the turnstiles
clicking; the players just wanted to earn a crust – the first Lamborghini
was not built until 1963 so what else was there? Not only players but
spectators too were accused of shirking:

Every club which employs a professional player is bribing a needed
recruit to refrain from enlistment, and every spectator who pays his
gate money is contributing so much towards a German victory.[9]

Recruiters were frustrated in their September efforts outside football
grounds where 'the results were grievously disappointing':

There is apparently something about the professional football match spectator which makes a recruiting appeal a failure. At the Chelsea ground . . . not a man was induced to join. At other football grounds appeals were made, and with equal ill-success. This failure contrasts strongly with the wholesale volunteering which has distinguished the performers and the devotees of other forms of sport. Rugby Union clubs, cricket elevens, and rowing clubs throughout the kingdom have poured men into the ranks. The dismal story of Saturday's recruiting is relieved by *one* man who volunteered at the Woolwich Arsenal ground.[10]

You can almost hear them chanting, 'One-Nil to the Arsenal'. When Saturday came, women with white feathers were the only ones who did a roaring trade, often mistakenly picking on soldiers in mufti simply hoping for some afternoon entertainment while in training, recuperating from wounds or (less likely) on leave.

Bolts of fury were hurled at football from press and pulpit alike. On 30 August, the Reverend Youard, clearly a Christian of the muscular persuasion, addressed his flock at St Swithun's. He considered the balls of the battlefield, how they roll not, neither do they spin, except in oval shape, and urged:

> . . . every able-bodied young man in East Grinstead to offer yourself without delay in the service of your country. The Welsh Rugby Union Committee has passed a resolution declaring it the duty of all football players to join immediately. Blackheath Rugby Football Club has cancelled all its matches for the same reason. That is the right spirit. I hope it will be imitated by our own clubs. Go straight to the recruiting officer and offer yourself. That is the plain duty of every able-bodied young man today.

A letter from 'A Soldier in France' complained that 'hundreds of thousands of able-bodied young roughs are watching hirelings play football while others are serving their country'. On 6 September, Sir Arthur Conan Doyle, in a recruiting speech, borrowed liberally from Ecclesiastes when he addressed footballers:

> There was a time for all things in the world. There was a time for games, there was a time for business, and there was a time for domestic life. There was a time for everything, but there is only time for one thing now, and that thing is war. If the cricketer

had a straight eye let him look along the barrel of a rifle. If a footballer had strength of limb let them serve and march in the field of battle.

They did not turn: a propaganda poster lamented 'When will they ever come?' Another man of God, the Bishop of Chelmsford, preaching a pointed sermon:

> ... in an address on Duty, spoke of the magnificent response that had been made to the call to duty from the King. All must play their part. They must not let their brothers go to the front and themselves remain indifferent. He felt that the cry against professional football at the present time was right. He could not understand men who had any feeling, any respect for their country, men in the prime of life, taking large salaries at a time like this for kicking a ball about. It seemed to him something incongruous and unworthy.[11]

You might very well think that, my Lord Bishop; I couldn't possibly comment.

Frederick Charrington, scion of the brewing family, accused West Ham United players of being effeminate and cowardly, getting paid to play while others fought. Celebrated all-round sportsman, C.B. Fry, Corinthian legend and FA Cup finalist with Southampton, called for football to be abolished: all professional contracts should be annulled and no one below forty should be allowed to attend matches.

In December, William Joynson Hicks[12] established the 17th Battalion, Middlesex Regiment, which quickly became known as the 'Football Battalion'. Within weeks he had a full complement of 600 men; few were footballers, most being fans who wanted to slope arms with their idols. Mr E. Cunliffe Owen wrote to the *Daily Telegraph* from the Hotel Cecil, under the heading 'The Footballers' Chance':

> Sir – Without entering into the controversy as to whether football should cease or not, may I point out that there is an honourable alternative for the man who ought to serve his country and yet must play and talk football – namely, to join the 2nd Sportsman's Battalion Royal Fusiliers, the battalion which is now recruiting at this hotel. The corps already contains well-known footballers, and friends joining at the same time, who have interests in common, can be kept together, live in the same hut, and so on. They need

not altogether sacrifice their love of sport while training for the great international now being played in northern France.

But as late as March 1915, only 122 of 1,800 registered professional footballers were reported to have joined the Colours. The public voted with their feet and gates fell by more than half; the Football Association finally bowed to popular pressure and suspended the game on 23 April, the suitably patriotic St George's Day.

Amateur rugby by contrast rushed to war: 90 per cent of players were in uniform by the end of 1914. Mr Edward Roper of Liverpool FC proudly told the *Daily Post* on 1 September that 'between 50 & 60 of the club's players had joined and there was not a player left'. By December, recruiting posters hailed the 'Rugby Union Footballers Doing Their Duty' as a 'Glorious Example to British Athletes'. *The Times* thundered: 'Every player who represented England in Rugby International matches last year has joined the Colours.' Indeed they had, and twenty-six England men would die over the next four years, with a twenty-seventh a week after the Armistice. Leonard Tosswill, of Bart's and Middlesex, ever-present in England's 1903 side, an RAMC medic and later eye-surgeon, declared that a man 'who had learned to "play the game" on football grounds might be trusted to do no less in the greater game of war [and] answered the call of his country as he would to the whistle without questions'.[13]

The approbation of rugby's patriotic leadership by War Office propagandists and opinion formers in the national press was even extended to the enemy. Or at least to one representative of the otherwise 'vile Hun' who showed himself to be 'a jolly good sport' of the right sort. The German cruiser SMS *Emden* had sunk 74,000 tons of shipping in the Far East; one night HMS *Yarmouth,* escorting a merchantman out of Singapore, reportedly received an unexpected signal:

> 'Captain von Müller of the *Emden* and the ward-room mess send their compliments, and would be obliged if the *Yarmouth* would let them have the result of the inter-regimental Rugby Football match.' The result of the match, which had taken place that afternoon, was duly given together with the intimation that it would not be long before British Sportsmen in the East had the pleasure of the Captain's company at all field and track events.[14]

When *Emden* was finally sunk by HMAS *Sydney*, her captain was mourned: 'It is almost in our heart to regret that the *Emden* has been captured and destroyed; we certainly hope that Commodore Karl von

Muller, her commander, has not been killed, for, as the phrase goes, he has shown himself an officer and a gentleman.'[15]

There never was a Rugby Battalion, as there was a Footballers' or Sportsman's (17th and 23rd Middlesex). The reason was simple: all the rugby players had already joined up and were dispersed among the Regular and Territorial regiments. Nonetheless representations were made, and on 9 September, RFU Secretary C.J.B. Marriott issued another letter:

RUGBY FOOTBALL UNION AND
LORD KITCHENER'S ARMY

On reference to the authorities, the Rugby Football Union find it is not feasible to form a separate battalion of Rugby men. They have received, however, answers from various Commanding Officers saying that they will gladly accept for their Regiments a company about (120) of Rugby men, who could be enlisted together.

A very large number of our players have already responded to the previous letter of my Committee and joined some Corps, but it is probable there may be some others ready to enlist. I will therefore enter names sent in to me, and as soon as I have enrolled sufficient to form a company, will send them on to a Commanding Officer for enlistment as a Football Company in Lord Kitchener's Army.

Marriott's company was never incorporated; the workings of committees may be tolerated as a necessary evil in peacetime, but rugby players preferred to follow charismatic leaders to war. One such leader was Edgar Mobbs.

If one man epitomised rugby's contribution to the war effort, it was Edgar Roberts Mobbs. This tall, powerful winger with seven England caps had captained his country once ('the Ultima Thule of any Rugby player's ambitions', he told the *Boy's Own Paper*) but held his home town crowd at Northampton Saints in thrall for seven years and 177 tries as its leader; Saints were not the power they are now, and many viewed Mobbs as 'carrying the team on his shoulders'. His East Midlands Counties was the only provincial side to beat the touring Australians and he had the personal satisfaction of England's first try against Australia.

Too old at 32 for a commission when Kitchener made his first call for 100,000 men in August 1914, Mobbs enlisted immediately as a private soldier. Like some energetic feudal squire, he set about raising a company of 264 like-minded local sportsmen, which became D Company,

7th Northants, known as 'Mobbs' Own' – readers may remark the thread of rugby-playing D companies woven through these pages. 'On 14 September, he marched away from the Northampton barracks at the head of the company he had raised, to entrain for a military camp', wrote Sewell. Despite the private taking a presumptuous lead, he was not formally commissioned until the end of training.

George Percival, fourteen years a diminutive Saints scrum half with 'attitude' (goes with the job), played under Mobbs and followed his call. The recruiting sergeant thanked him politely, but pointed out he was too short. Percival protested: 'My captain said to come and join up, so here I am.' The language became more Anglo-Saxon, and when the sergeant threatened to kick him out the door; George turned on him: With ____ like you running this war, you'll soon kill off all the tall men, and then you'll have to come for me, 'cos I won't come willing.' Two years later they had killed off the tall men, lowered the height restrictions, and sent George his call-up papers, which he ignored. Eventually two redcaps came to his house, only to find him packed and ready to go: 'I told you ____ in 1914 you'd have to come and fetch me, and now you have. Let's go to war.'

Mobbs was a one-man recruiting machine; when he wasn't recruiting, he played rugby and often combined both. He sat on the wartime committee of the Barbarian Football Club (along with England's Bruno Brown, Cherry Pillman and Harold 'Dreadnought' Harrison). In training at Shoreham Camp, he captained a team against his own Baa-Baas in a December match 'in aid of Lady Jellicoe's North Sea Fleet Comforts Fund'. As 1915 dawned, he switched to the famed black-and-white hoops at Leicester, 'for encouragement of recruiting and in aid of patriotic funds'. The improvised nature of these games can be seen on the team-sheets. At Leicester both sides were one short: Shoreham's full back, James Urquhart, was a Grimsby Town amateur footballer and Northampton teacher who had never played rugby before, nor belonged to a club, but sailed under the Rosslyn Park flag of convenience on the irresistible advice of his gigantic team-mate, John Rosher, of the Durham Light Infantry.

Mobbs was prime mover in a 'Scotland versus England' challenge played at the County Ground, Northampton, on 30 January 1915. The match programme left spectators in no doubt of the serious purpose of the game, exclaiming: '90 PER CENT of the Rugby Players of our Empire are serving their King and Country. Will you join them!' No question mark was used or needed. The local hero was star of the show: Lieutenant Mobbs as 'the English Captain' is pictured in uniform with Colonel Fawcett at the Northampton Barracks. The same photograph would reappear in a changed world after the war. Edgar skippered the side from the centre against Lieutenant Ian Moffat-Pender's[16] line-up of Scots in khaki; they were actually lent Scotland's official blue jerseys for the occasion while 'England' played in the green and white hoops of Mobbs's East Midlands. The team was essentially the Shoreham Camp side, peppered with Saints and Counties men from D Company. Programme notes confide that 'Lieutenant Mobbs will be pleased to interview any new recruits in the Dressing Room after the Match or at the Plough Hotel after 7 o'clock in the evening.' Kitchener is quoted: 'We must have more men and still more men if we are to crush the enemy.' As chilling for an English crowd as these words and the January weather was the announcement tucked away in small print: 'The Scotch Pipers from Bedford will be in attendance and play Selections.' 'England' restored the peace of a day in the shires, 'winning by about 50 points'.

Mobbs's Barbarian rugby caravan reached Richmond's Old Deer Park in April to play the RAMC, its ranks swelled by a glittering array of eight international stars; they faced another six caps in the Medics' red jerseys. Billed as the 'Great Rugby Service Match' in aid of the Red Cross Fund, this was one of the first Services charity games organised by Rosslyn Park's Harry Burlinson, which sustained rugby through the war in the absence of clubs. A week later, on 17 April 1915, Mobbs captained the Baa-Baas at Cardiff Arms Park in what was termed a 'Military International' between Wales and 'England', designed to boost recruiting for the newly formed Welsh Guards and to raise funds for local military charities. The match raised £200. Wales fielded a near full international team with only two uncapped players, Dan Callan of the Royal Munster Fusiliers, and Tom Parker. The Barbarian side had twelve Englishmen, two Irishmen and a Welshman (Joseph 'Birdie' Partridge) who had been capped for South Africa.

Even Barbarian historian Jock Wemyss found the 26–10 victory 'one of the greatest surprises imaginable, as not for one moment was it expected that the scratch Barbarian Service XV stood any possible chance of beating the Welsh side'. Scratch was the word. At Paddington, they were a man down and counted only seven forwards; on the train, they discovered centre John Birkett of Harlequins, who had been independently invited by the Cardiff organisers to turn out for 'England'. At least they now had a XV, but played with an extra back instead of a full pack:

That the seven forwards not only held, but actually got the better of the Welsh eight was the most astonishing feature of the match, but it must also be said that Birkett and Mobbs displayed such wonderful form and ran so hard and straight, that the Welsh centres were quite unable to cope with them.[17]

On that day, Wales wore white, which everyone knows is not right; just as in 2007 grey was not All Black against France. (In the 2011 Final, the French nobly conceded a colour change out of respect to the hosts; how might that result have changed if New Zealand had played in their all-white second strip?) In the end, Wemyss concluded that victory belonged to the 'visitors [who] were remarkably fit owing to the fact that fourteen of them were then training for Active Service'. On the same day, at Hill 60 east of Ypres, Alec 'Fin' Todd, British Isles and England forward, twice wounded in the Boer War, returned from home leave, stood tall in his trench and was again wounded, in the throat: third time, not so lucky.

Services rugby came to an abrupt end when they crossed the Channel. Initially war was one big game and the boys from schools and clubs relished the outdoor life, the physical exertion and the bonds of male company. In fact, it reminded them exactly of school life (with dreary diet to match). Scotland's Freddy Turner, 'somewhere in France' with the Liverpool Scottish in late 1914, wrote to his old master at Sedbergh:

> It is a man's life out here and it agrees with me splendidly. I have never felt fitter in my life; in fact, I could very nearly run the whole length of the old footer field at school uphill without breaking down, which, you will admit, would be a performance of some merit.[18]

Henry Grierson, Mobbs's friend, rugby team-mate and comrade in D Company, recalled: 'To France we went in August 1915, did a lot of training for open warfare, and suddenly walked sixty miles to Loos to take part in that appalling mess-up. No orders, no rations, no water, no nothing.'

In early September 1914 after the RFU cancelled the season, *The Times* reported that 'rugby football is temporarily and honourably dead.'

More permanently, no less honourably, its players would be next.

3
Scotland

When will we see your like again?
That fought and died for
Your wee bit hill and glen[1]

The Scots were spoiling to fight: some 690,000 served, of whom 65 per cent willingly joined the Colours in the two years before conscription, a higher proportion than the overall 53 per cent of British volunteers.[2] And that's without reckoning with the 'Jockish diaspora' across the Empire who rallied to the cause. By November 1918 Scotland topped another dismal wartime table: the flower of its rugby men – thirty-one capped players – had been hacked down, the highest score of all the nations.

Scots took the early hits in 1914 when the trained regulars of the BEF tried in vain to stop the swinging arm of the Schlieffen Plan punching into France. They would be the early casualties at the First Battle of Ypres, whose frozen bodies dug into the parapets would thaw and reek in the spring of 1915, as the Second Battle began. They would wilt in the June heat of Gallipoli, in a disastrous campaign of mismanagement and misadventure. In September 1915, kilted regiments charged with braveheart cries at Loos, just as the Tyneside Scottish would at the Somme in 1916. With players to the fore as natural leaders, Scottish rugby suffered early blows in the first half of the 'Greater Game'. The first was Lieutenant Ronald Simson, aged 24, capped just once for Scotland against the 'Auld Enemy', and killed by a new foe after just forty days of war. He was lionised by friends and the cheerleading British press as the first international sportsman to die for the Colours in this new war.[3]

Edinburgh-born Simson was an all-round athlete who captained the Royal Military Academy XV at Woolwich. His impressive showing in the first of his three Army v. Navy games at Queen's Club secured him selection at centre for Scotland at Twickenham in 1911. He 'picked up a bad pass, ran clear to Williams [the English full back] kicked over his head and after nearly colliding with a goalpost, managed to get the touch down'. His wing that day was London Scottish team-mate

Lieutenant Stephen Steyn (originally Stephanus from Cape Province), a Rhodes scholar, capped before he won his Blue. Like Simson, he joined the Royal Field Artillery (RFA); Steyn died in Palestine, the day before General Allenby took Jerusalem in 1917. Despite his try, Ronnie was never picked for Scotland again. Perhaps he lacked seriousness: he was always 'bubbling over with mirth . . . if he was stamped upon by the opposing forwards, he came up shaking with laughter'. He was not laughing on 14 September; as he reconnoitred on horseback for his battery, a shell burst under his mount, killing man and beast instantly.

Two days later another London Scot, James Huggan from Jedburgh, Edinburgh medical graduate and RAMC lieutenant, was the second to fall. His game was one of 'all-out dash and energy'. He had scored one of three tries[4] in the last close-fought Calcutta Cup at Inverleith; on 13 August, just nine days into the war, he dashed to France with the Coldstream Guards in the force hastily despatched to repel Germany from neutral Belgium. After Mons, the 25-year-old Huggan's war became a desperate fighting retreat.

Newspapers were feeding public bloodlust by painting all Germans as barbaric, nun-raping Huns, library-burners and child-murderers laying waste to 'poor little Belgium'. They even accused them of melting down British corpses for candle tallow. James Huggan, doctor and professional soldier, calmly did what he was trained to do and showed a sense of fair play nurtured on the rugby field and in his Hippocratic Oath; in doing so, he gave his own life to save his enemy. His CO, Lieutenant Colonel Fielding described the action on the Aisne to Huggan's brother:

> There were in a barn about sixty wounded Germans; they were all cases that could not move without help. The Germans shelled this barn and set it on fire. Your brother, in spite of shot and shell raining about him, called for volunteers to help him save these wounded men from this burning building and I am glad to say it was greatly in consequence of his bravery that they were all saved. After he had run this great danger successfully he moved many of his wounded men to a quarry in rear, when a big shell came into it and killed him and many others. He was buried where he fell. The whole battalion regretted his loss, as we had all got very fond of him, and admired him as a really brave man, always ready to sacrifice himself for the good of those who should happen to come under him for treatment.[5]

As troops staggered back in headlong retreat before the relentless German push, his field hospital of broken and bleeding casualties 'in rear' had often found itself closer to the enemy than the fighting line. His previous coolness and bravery under fire had commended him for the Victoria Cross, but his compassion for his fellow men, regardless of whether they wore khaki or field-grey, was not the story the War Office – or editors – wanted in the press. His commendation is as lost as his body; only his name remains, on the La Ferté-sous-Jouarre memorial and in Sir John French's despatches.

Scots also led the charge of the citizen-soldiers: the 14th (County of London) Battalion, London Regiment (London Scottish), were the first Territorials to cross the Channel to Le Havre on 16 September. Six weeks later, on All Hallows' Eve, they were the first into action near the Belgian village of Messines. The London Scottish Football Club (LSFC) mourns 103 men on its enamelled bronze memorial at the Richmond Athletic Ground; nineteen were internationalists, the red lion's share of Scottish rugby's honour roll, with Huggan the first.

Forty-five of those men were mythologised in *London Scottish (1914)*, the elegy by poet and 1978 Magdalen College XV skipper, Mick Imlah[6] from Milngavie:

> April, the last full fixture of the spring:
> 'Feet, Scottish, feet' – they rucked the fear of God
> Into Blackheath. Their club was everything:
> And of the four sides playing that afternoon,
> The stars, but also those from the back pitches,
> All sixty volunteered for the touring squad,
> And swapped their Richmond turf for Belgian ditches.
> October: mad for a fight, they broke too soon
> On the Ypres Salient, rushing the ridge between
> 'Witshit' and Messines. Three-quarters died.
> Of that ill-balanced and fatigued fifteen
> The ass selectors favoured to survive,
> Just one, Brodie the prop, resumed his post.
> The others sometimes drank to 'The Forty-Five':
> Neither a humorous nor an idle toast.

There is artistic licence here: Scottish did not play on the last weekend of the season, nor did all four sides play the same day, or even against Blackheath, and Brodie is a mystery. But his poem has a hard core of fact: in 1919, pre-war Territorial and club member John King wrote to the regimental *Gazette* stating that of the sixty in the four XVs playing at the end of the season forty-six had been killed. So what if Imlah chose instead to rhyme 'survive' with 'five', for this is what poets do. A toast to 'The Forty-Five' with its distant Jacobite echo will always make Scottish hearts beat faster.

The 14th was no 'Pals' battalion, joining up in an autumn rush of patriotic fervour. Eight from LSFC were already serving with the regiment; all eight were at Messines. On 31 October, they were ordered to plug a gap in the Ypres Salient to withstand a German attack. Requisitioned 'Old Bill' buses, still hawking Pear's Soap and Fry's Chocolate, shipped 800 London Scots in distinctive hodden grey kilts,[7] sporrans and glengarries, to Wijtschaete ('Whitesheet' to Tommy, 'Witshit' to Jock).

From midday till the next dawn breaking over the 'wee bit hill' at Messines, their Hallowe'en vigil held off the enemy and averted the threatened breakthrough. But they paid the butcher's bill in full, with more than 300 killed, missing or wounded, and were forced to retire. LSFC's price was heavy: Oxford Blue Charles Farquharson was wounded and missing in action; Kyle and James Ross (capped for Scotland in 1905) were killed; B.D. Tod survived Messines, but was dead before Christmas; Robertson, Jebb and Mather were commissioned in other regiments but did not see the Armistice. Private Kinross was back – briefly – on the rugby field in December: the 6ft 1in forward wrote in his diary, 'Beautiful day. Played Rugger in the afternoon, game stopped in second half as we had to parade and march off.' He was later commissioned and survived the whole four years. Messines remains a battle honour of the London Regiment; a dinner every Hallowe'en at its Horseferry Road depot commemorates the first horrors and heroism shown in October 1914.

Six hundred kilometres north of the Exiles' ground, in Britain's then second city, Glasgow Academicals played arch-rivals West of Scotland in the last game of their season on 28 March 1914. 'Accies', a club of former schoolboys from the city's Academy, were reigning Scottish champions. 'West' were founded in 1865, a year before the Glasgow Academical Football Club – no need, it was felt, to include the word 'Rugby' as Association did not arrive in Glasgow until the formation of Queen's Park in 1867 (and why on earth mention some wee English school?). The fixture, first played in 1867, is an ancient tie that still binds the clubs to this day. On this occasion, the 'junior' club ran out winners by 27 points to 8, although the championship would elude Accies, despite their season of 500 points scored and only 76 against.

Football under both codes had prospered in Scotland, despite an unpromising early ban declared at Perth by King James I way back in May 1424, (and reiterated by James II, III and IV, presumably to little effect): 'It is statute and the King forbiddis, that na man play at the futeball under the payne of xl.s [40 shillings] to be rasit to the Lord of the land.' By the late nineteenth century, a cabal of high-minded Edinburgh schools and clubs had set a forbidding and Presbyterian tone for Scottish rugby, with particularly severe views on amateurism and any form of expenses or payment. The Scottish Football Union (SFU) opposed any 'alterations designed to make the game faster, more interesting to spectators and so beneficial to gates'. Even shirt numbers reeked of professionalism: when King George V complained that he could not identify players at the Calcutta Cup he was rebuked: 'This is a rugby match, not a cattle-sale.' The SFU refused the touring 1905 All Blacks a guarantee, offering instead the gate, net of expenses deducted: the Southern Hemisphere had the last laugh on and off the field, carrying away a 12–7 victory and £1,700, four times what a guarantee would have given them. This naturally scotches any scabrous rumours spread by Englishmen that Scots are anything but the most generous of people.

Edinburgh's Academicals may have been the first Scots rugby club in 1857, but their Glasgow namesakes were the first to send a team south, to Liverpool and Manchester in 1870. Two years later they crossed the sea to Belfast to defeat North of Ireland FC. In the absence of a Scottish governing body until 1873, Accies joined the English RFU. After an Association 'International' against England had been played at the Oval in 1870 (not officially recognised as most of the 'Scots' players were Londoners[8]), Accies' J.W. Arthur signed a challenge to the English for a proper game of Rugby Football. It has all the bristle of the thistle, softened by the promise of a dram, as is the rugby way in Scotland:

> Sir, There is a pretty general feeling among Scotch football players that the football power of the old country was not properly represented in the late so-called International Football Match. Not that we think the play of the gentlemen who represented Scotland otherwise than very good – for that it was so is amply proved by the stout resistance they offered to their opponents and by the fact that they were beaten by only one goal – but that we consider the Association rules, in accordance with which the late game was played, not such as to bring together the best team Scotland could turn out. Almost all the leading clubs play

by the Rugby Code, and have no opportunity of practising the Association game even if willing to do so.

We therefore feel that a match played in accordance with any rules other than those in general use in Scotland, as was the case in the last match, is not one that would meet with support generally from her players. For our satisfaction, therefore, and with a view of really testing what Scotland can do against an English team we, as representing the football interests of Scotland, hereby challenge any team selected from the whole of England, to play us a match, twenty-a-side, Rugby rules, either in Edinburgh or Glasgow on any day during the present season that might be found suitable to the English players. Let this count as the return to the match played in London on 19th November, or, if preferred, let it be a separate match. If it be entered into we can promise England a hearty welcome and a first-rate match.

The English took up the challenge and a first ever rugby international was played in bright sunshine at Raeburn Place, Edinburgh, on 27 March 1871, in front of 4,000 spectators. Teams were twenty-a-side (six Scots being Accies, including Arthur) and two halves of fifty minutes were played. Scotland's winning try was only awarded after a ten-minute argument; referee Dr H.H. Almond declared 'when an umpire is in doubt, he is justified in deciding against the side which makes the most noise. They are probably in the wrong.' The good doctor's wisdom resonates loudly today.

By 1914, forty such 'first-rate matches' had been played, with Scotland three ahead in victories. The Saturday before the West clash, Accies' Eric Young had won his only cap for his country with Huggan in the narrow Calcutta Cup defeat; trailing 6–16, Scotland fought back with a drop goal (then 4 points) and a converted try (5) to thrill the Inverleith crowd, but lost by a single point. By close of play that year, three players who took the field in this last international on British soil were already dead. In total, eleven men would not survive; there's that 'killer stat'.

There would be no next meeting for the two Glasgow rivals for a long while. On 7 September, West's Honorary Secretary, Hugh Harper, announced that,

as so many members owing to the war are not available for football, the Committee have decided that all fixtures for the coming season be cancelled. The Committee also strongly urge upon all other members who are eligible, to promptly offer their services to some branch of His Majesty's Forces.

The Accies' own battle cry has been lost, but one distinguished Academy former pupil would take Harper at his word, serving in *two* branches of HM Forces and offering service to more than one King George.

Half back Louis Greig had not only captained club and country, but won three caps in the centre on the 1903 British tour of South Africa. In 1905 the All Blacks arrived; Edinburgh doctor Alfred Nelson Fell (an Otago University graduate born in Nelson, South Island) declined to play against his countrymen,[9] and Accies' Billy Church refused, so Greig stepped in as third choice – and third half back to counter the black pack of seven forwards and a rover. They strove to little avail, as they were 'unaccustomed to playing this formation and the Scottish back play and defence were disorganised'; they lost 7–12. The following November, however, brought triumph when Louis skippered the Scots to victory over the visiting Springboks in front of a record 32,000 at Hampden Park.

By now Greig was serving in the Royal Navy as a surgeon-lieutenant, and playing his rugby for United Services and the Navy; he was a try-scoring fly half against the Officers of the Army in 1910. Perhaps this was when he was first noticed by King George. The Glaswegian was famed for his swearing; it was said that people did not go to watch him play, but to hear him. He dropped a pass directly in front of the royal box and, precisely aware of his position, exclaimed 'Oh b . . . other!' returning the king's amused glance in full.

He met the teenage Prince Albert at Osborne Naval College, and became friend, mentor and later personal doctor to the shy and diffident stammerer. The grateful king saw to it that the pair served on the same ships – HMS *Cumberland*, then HMS *Malaya*. When war came, Louis joined the Royal Marines; he was captured at the fall of Antwerp in September 1914, spending eight months as a prisoner of war. Released in an exchange, he was summoned to Buckingham Palace on his first day back in Britain; the Court Circular shows that King George saw only one other visitor – Lord Kitchener.

After the king abandoned the House of Saxe-Coburg-Gotha for Windsor, Greig also dropped his middle name, Leisler – given in honour of his father's German business partner. (Fellow Scot, Douglas Schulze, capped thirteen times under that name, changed to his mother's maiden name of Miller; England's Frank Steinthal became Petrie.) Greig's friendship with the prince grew: Louis became his equerry and they both joined the RAF, flying to France in a Handley-Page bomber as the war neared its climax in 1918. After the war, he played both Cupid and Wimbledon tennis partner to the now Duke of York and future George VI, his influence on him arguably greater than that of Lionel Logue, the Australian speech therapist; it was Louis who encouraged his courtship of the true 'Kingmaker' – Lady Elizabeth Bowes-Lyon, the future Queen Mother.

The Glasgow Academicals XV from that final hurrah against West before the holocaust joined up to a man. Of those willing Glasgow warriors, eight were killed, six wounded and only one returned home unscathed. The catalogue of deaths, wounds inflicted and decorations awarded to this single band of brothers is extraordinary. Of the six try-scorers, Thomas Burton was twice wounded at the Somme and invalided home in January 1917 with a mention in despatches and an MC. Glasgow Highlander Arthur Russell (a pre-war coach in France) died of his wounds in July 1916. William Barras of the Argyll & Sutherlands was awarded the Military Medal, but died of his wounds in March 1918, on the first day of the German *Kaiserschlacht*, an all-out gamble to win the war before the might of the Americans arrived.

Charles Andrew, who dropped a goal that March afternoon, was wounded three times, mentioned in despatches three times and won an MC and Bar. Scotland's John Warren, who had faced Ireland in February drizzle at Lansdowne Road, also earned three wound stripes on his Royal Engineers sleeve and the MC on his chest. Skipper Arthur Laird joined the Highland Light Infantry (HLI) and was one of 19,240 men killed on the first day of the Somme; his was a one-way trip to Blighty Valley Cemetery. John Smith of the HLI was wounded in March 1917. John Sandeman was twice invalided home, from France and Palestine; his brother Frank fought in Mesopotamia and returned wounded from France in 1918. Robert Arthur of the Royal Glasgow Yeomanry earned six mentions in despatches and was awarded the MC and Belgian Croix de Guerre. George Spiers fought with 6th HLI in Egypt and France, was wounded earning his French Croix de Guerre and finally killed six weeks short of the Armistice in 1918. George MacEwan of the same battalion died of his wounds in July 1915 at Gallipoli. George Warren, who had scored four tries, was the sole survivor to return to the Accies' Anniesland ground.

In an echo to the east, all of the 1914–15 Edinburgh Academy team of schoolboys, playing their final season while war raged, would go from sixth form into uniform. They suffered four wounded and six dead, all of them with Highland regiments, although one – Ian Gilmour Cameron

– had taken to the air with the Royal Flying Corps (RFC) before being shot down by Richthofen in 1916. The last of the six survivors, Gurkha Captain George Alexander Bain, remained in the army and died in Devon in 1982. Their team photograph, taken at the end of the season, shows boyish young men, their faces serious in expectation of harder matches to come. Their autographs on the facing page, all underlined with the defiant manly flourish of the 1st XV, are a handwritten memorial. The 'Athens of the North' saw many of its brightest sons die before their promise could be fulfilled: just four Edinburgh schools (Academy, Fettes, Loretto and Merchiston Castle) nurtured eighteen of the fifty-five Varsity Blues who were to die in the war.

Glasgow Accies' first loss was Stuart Bulloch-Graham, 2nd Gordon Highlanders, on 31 October, his name inscribed on the Menin Gate; the club would suffer another 326 deaths of its 1,375 former pupils who served. Newly capped Scottish flanker, Eric Templeton Young had joined the Territorial Force as early as 1911 and was promoted to captain in August 1914. After training, he joined the 8th Cameronians (The Scottish Rifles) who drilled at Accies' original Burnbank ground, a green 'oasis in a growing desert of red sandstone'. He was reported 'missing, presumed killed' at Gallipoli, fifteen months to the day after the victory over West. Aged just 23, he was not alone on that terrible June day in 1915: three of his Glasgow team-mates – Archie Templeton, Tommy Stout and William Church would also die in a disastrous attack at Gully Ravine.

A proud photograph of Eric Young in December 1914 with ten smiling fellow Cameronian officers, all 'Old Glasgow Academy Boys', records that eight would die that same day, with a ninth killed elsewhere. For many years, his body lost, Young was wrongly commemorated with the 6th Battalion at Le Touret in France but his name is now rightly carved alongside his club comrades on the Helles Memorial, as well as at London Scottish where he also played. He was, wrote a fellow officer, 'a man of sincere and straightforward character, absolutely downright and one of the most fearless. He took great interest in his men, and was much loved by them.' His LSFC clubmate and Scotland flank partner from March, the solid and experienced Freddy Turner, was already dead, shot by a sniper near Ypres, in January.

The Scottish Rifles were in the 52nd (Lowland) Division of pre-war Territorials, which took heavy losses even before leaving home turf. On the way to Liverpool for embarkation to Gallipoli in May 1915, 210 men died and 224 were injured (mainly 7th Royal Scots) in a fiery train crash at Quintinshill, near Gretna, to this day Britain's worst rail disaster. It briefly delayed their departure for the Dardanelles and more slaughter under a blistering sun. Lieutenant Francis Wishart Thomson, aged 24, of the Royal Scots, Edinburgh Academy and Oxford, survived the crash, but met the same fate as the Glaswegians at Gully Ravine; his younger brother, Lieutenant Eric Thomson, aged 22, died in the same action. Lieutenant Tommy Stout, aged 23 but looking more youthful than Young in the photograph, never got that cherished Scotland cap. He came close, as an international reserve (not a substitute – such a notion was scorned), but was never called up; instead he joined the Colours on another field.

Major James Findlay, took command of the Cameronians a week after landing at Cape Helles in June and, another week later, led his inexperienced battalion into action at Gully Ravine. Where there was ammunition for artillery support, the Turkish trenches were easily taken; more often there was none and waves of frontal attacks were exposed to withering machine-gun fire in the bright glare of daylight. The men had small metal triangles sewn on their backs to aid identification by their own troops. As the bombardment lifted, the ground sparkled, 'as if someone had quite suddenly thrown a big handful of diamonds onto the landscape' wrote Sir Ian Hamilton, a cerebral commander and lyrical diarist. Those diamonds would be dulled in scrub fires which reduced bodies to ashes and left only bones. Over 10,000 Turks were killed too in their desperate counter-attacks. Fifty years later, a historian found 'piles of grinning skulls' and kicked 'clouds of bones scuffling through the dust' as he walked.[10] Findlay recalled:

> I do not think that many of us got much sleep . . . but dawn came at last, cool and beautiful, with a hint of the coming heat, and the dried-up sparse scrub had been freshened by the night's dewfall. One was impressed by the good heart of all ranks, but, whether it was premonition or merely the strain of newly acquired responsibility, I could not feel the buoyancy of anticipated success . . . The artillery bombardment which took place from 09.00 to 11.00 was, even to a mind then inexperienced in a real bombardment, quite too futile, but it drew down upon us, naturally, a retaliatory shelling. Centuries of time seemed to go by. One became conscious of saying the silliest things, all the while painfully thinking, 'It may be the last time I shall see these fellows alive!' Prompt at 11.00 the whistles blew.[11]

His men were met by deadly fire from all sides. Findlay sent back for reinforcements and advanced with his Adjutant, Captain Bramwell, and Signals Officer, Lieutenant Tommy Stout, to establish a forward headquarters:

> We soon arrived at Pattison's bombing party, which I had sent up this sap. He had been killed, and those of his men that were left were lying flat; they could not get on as the sap rose a few yards in front of them to the ground-level, and the leading man was lying in only about 18 inches of cover. Bullets were spattering all around us, and we seemed to bear charmed lives, until just as we arrived at the rear of this party Bramwell fell at my side, shot through the mouth. He said not a word, and I am glad to think that he was killed outright. I made up my mind that the only thing to be done was to collect what men there were and make a dash for it. I told this to Stout, and stooping down to pick up a rifle I was shot in the neck. At the moment I didn't feel much, but when I saw the blood spurt forward I supposed that it had got my jugular vein. I stuck a handkerchief round my neck and tried to get on, but I was bowled over by a hit in the shoulder. Up came young Stout and said, 'I am going to try to carry you back, Sir!'

His wounds were serious, but Findlay was obsessed with his objective and the next attack. Tommy Stout ignored him:

> I told Stout to send another runner for reinforcements. A few minutes later he came back and took me by the shoulders and some other good fellow lifted me by the feet, and together they got me back some 10 yards, and though a bullet got me in the flesh of the thigh, I was now comparatively sheltered while they were still exposed. It was then that a splinter of shell blew off Tommy Stout's head, and the other man was hit simultaneously. Gallant lads! God rest them!

Findlay finally staggered back to the lines, with seven major wounds. His battalion had suffered over 470 casualties in its baptism of fire, including twenty-five of its twenty-eight officers. A chaplain described the valley 'with its heaps of rotting refuse, its burning pyres and sickening stench' as 'a veritable Gehenna'; General Egerton, inspecting the ravaged remains of his 52nd Lowland Division, was enraged when General Hunter-Weston blandly remarked that he was pleased to have had the opportunity of 'blooding the pups'. Major Findlay wrote to Tommy Stout's parents in Kelvinside: 'Tom was a good soldier and a great favourite with all of us. I do not suppose there was an officer in the Battalion who knew his job better than he did.' 'No more', wrote the *Glasgow Chronicle,* 'shall we see Tommy Stout scoring a try for the Accies, with that wonderful swerve of his and with his hair flying in the wind.' His body was never identified; Tommy and Eric Young share the Helles Memorial with 20,868 others.

Thirty-nine from Bill McLaren's beloved Hawick RFC did not return to their Mansfield Park ground in the border country. The blackest day for the 'Greens' was 12 July, once again in the furnace of Gallipoli, when the 4th King's Own Scottish Borderers were caught in a 'friendly fire' bombardment and took over 350 casualties, eighty-six of them from Hawick and District. Five died from the rugby club: Privates William Beatson, Cairns and Cranston, Eli Cunningham and Thomas Farmer. The 'weel-kent' internationalist Major Walter 'Wattie' Forest from Kelso, capped at full back in eight successive Scotland games from 1903, survived that day, and would win the MC on the Somme. His charmed life ran out at Gaza, Palestine, in April 1917, in his second crack at the Turks, when he was killed leading an assault.

Another Hawick son and hero, Walter Sutherland, or 'Wattie Suddy', not only won thirteen caps on the wing for Scotland, but was national sprint champion and wore the Scottish athletics vest. A Seaforths subaltern, he was killed on 4 October 1918, five weeks short of the Armistice and seven weeks before his 28th birthday. According to Sewell:

> such was his anxiety to be with his men after a period of rest, he hired a bicycle to cover the distance separating him from them. Passing through the village of Hulluch, a stray shell from the enemy reached his vicinity . . . and he was killed, not leading his men as he would have desired, but nevertheless in just such a manner as he lived, doing his duty.[12]

Off Cape Helles the waves would also swallow Scots captain David 'Darkie' Bedell-Sivright. A surgeon in the Royal Naval Division, he worked ceaselessly in the charnel-house conditions of insanitary field hospitals and ships in that baking summer, first operating on Royal Scots Fusiliers, then Royal Marines. For a man renowned in Australia for his aggressive rugby which verged on outright violence, this was often to his frustration: 'It makes me swear that I am a medico. I'd be ten times more useful with a parcel of jam-tin bombs and a few Turks in front of me, than a sort of qualified vet.'

Twice a British Isles tourist, once as captain, with four Cambridge Blues and twenty-two Scotland caps (his debut at age 19 against Wales), Darkie was brought down by septicaemia after an insect bite in September. No little irony here for a man who was, in Sewell's view, 'the hardest forward who ever played International football',[13] and once reportedly rugby-tackled a carthorse on Edinburgh's Princes Street after a match dinner. This after he had stopped the Edinburgh traffic for hours by lying across the tram rails; the police knew his reputation and dared not intervene. But man against mosquito is not an equal fight: RND lieutenant and poet Rupert Brooke, one half of a gilded but doomed centre partnership at Rugby School with Poulton-Palmer, had died the same way at Skyros, en route to Gallipoli in April. Bedell-Sivright, as is traditional for sea burials, is on the Royal Naval Memorial at Portsmouth; less traditional but as well-deserved is his 2013 place in the World Rugby Hall of Fame.

Brave are the hearts that beat beneath Scottish skies. Many more would be broken.

4

Australia

In history's page, let every stage
Advance Australia Fair.

As the Greeks knew, there is drama in the unity of time and place. For Australians, one single day in the Great War has grown to be the defining symbol of nationhood: 25 April 1915, commemorated as ANZAC Day. It is a day that remembers one place, a tiny patch of sandy beach, then called Gaba Tepe, now officially renamed Anzac Cove. In all 8,141 Australians died in the misbegotten Gallipoli campaign out of a total wartime death toll of some 60,000.

Such is its significance in the Australian mind that ceremonies from Canberra to London, from Villers-Bretonneux to Bullecourt, where many more Australians later died, commemorate one day when battle raged thousands of miles away on a remote peninsula, not far from the site of ancient Troy. Myths are powerful; they are rarely the whole truth but they can make nations. Gallipoli is Australia's war myth. For a country where sport is an obsession, its nation-building military exploits are entwined with sporting mythologies. Myths also need grand Homeric figures and two of Australia's greatest rugby warriors were on that beach that day: Tom Richards and Blair Swannell.

New South Welshman T.J. 'Rusty' Richards is the only Australian-born player to represent both Australia and Britain; in his honour, the Wallabies and Lions contest the Tom Richards Trophy every dozen years. In a globe-trotting career, he also represented Transvaal, Bristol, Gloucestershire, East Midland Counties, Toulouse, Biarritz, Queensland, the Waratahs and Manly, and coached France. When he won Olympic gold for Australia *The Times* departed from its customary reserve to proclaim: 'If ever the Earth had to select a Rugby Football team to play against Mars, Richards would be the first player chosen.' In war he served from Gallipoli to Bullecourt and was decorated with another medal, the Military Cross.

Tom was a wandering rugby troubadour. This early pioneer of the fine antipodean tradition of 'going walkabout' introduced surfing to France and felt 'expanding one's horizons to be more important than money'. In 1905 his miner father took the family to South Africa, looking for work in the goldfields. Tom joined a Mines team full of Cornishmen like Redruth's Jim 'Maffer' Davey, later of England; both turned out for Transvaal in the Currie Cup. The South Africans planned to tour Britain in 1906; not yet eligible to play for the Springboks, Tom decided to play *against* them. He sailed from Durban to England, climbed off the boat and joined the nearest club, which happened to be Bristol.

Residency qualifications in Britain were less rigid when it came to outstanding rugby talent; Tom was duly selected for Gloucestershire against the South Africans, who were somewhat disconcerted to see him. Hearing of plans for a first Australian tour of Britain in 1908, he hurried home to win selection for what would be called the Wallabies.[1] After impressing for Queensland, Richards won his place on the tour, playing against Wales and England, and scoring the maiden Test try by a Wallaby. The British press had tried to christen them the 'Rabbits', but they rejected the nickname of a pest introduced by the British.

Rugby's popularity in Australia was demonstrated by the crowd of 52,411 at Sydney Cricket Ground the previous year, who watched New South Wales play New Zealand. National identity was now being asserted on overseas rugby fields in the 'green and pleasant land' of the Mother Country. The famed green-and-gold shirts were a long way off[2] and Australia played in light blue with a waratah flower on the left breast. Captain Herbert 'Paddy' Moran noted that when the scrum was under pressure against Wales, 'the pack would encourage each other with cries of, "Australia! Australia!"' But he lamented the pressure to perform an Aboriginal war-cry, *haka*-style, as the 'Wallabies' gravest affliction'.

The tour coincided with the London Olympics, at which rugby was an event. When defending champions France withdrew, the only teams were Australia and Great Britain, represented by reigning county champions Cornwall, the county of Tom's father's birth. Aussie victory by 32–3 in the 'Final' at a foggy and half-empty White City stadium, meant that the miner's son had struck both gold, in the form of his Olympic winner's medal, and another blow for Australian sporting pride. He might have compared medals over a beer with his mate Maffer Davey, but the Cornish had just one silver medal to share between them.

The British press were admiring:

> It is only fair to the Australians to speak of their play in terms of unqualified praise. The ground was very slippery and very heavy

and as a result of several hours of continuous rain the ball was very greasy. The excellence of the play of the Australian backs therefore surprised the spectators. They gave a display of football which would have done credit to a Welsh international side at its best.[3]

They stood the test of comparison with Wales in a close defeat by a penalty, 6–9. The *Daily Mail* selected Richards for a 'World's Greatest XV' from those watched by its correspondent over fifty years. His individual contribution to the 'First Wallabies' brought him acclaim as:

> the greatest player seen during the season, whose pace, tackling, cross-kicking and resourcefulness stamps him as one of the finest forwards who ever put on football boots. Throughout the tour he was the best man on the field in every match, and how many tries he gained for his side indirectly would be difficult to say.[4]

On their return to Australia, eleven of the 1908 Wallabies defected to Rugby League in search of a living from the game; Union crowds declined and the echo of their parting shots is still heard today.

Back in Queensland's gold-mining country, Richards remained true to Union. He captained and coached Charters Towers, but his wanderlust soon took him back to Africa, where Dr Tom Smyth's 1910 British Isles team would soon arrive. With the sureness of destiny, Richards was invited to join the injury-stricken tourists and made twelve appearances, listed as a Bristol player, including two Tests. In 1912, he was once again Australian, touring North America as vice-captain and in the side for the 'All-America' Test. He returned to England, touring France with Mobbs's East Midlands Counties in 1913. He helped train France for their match against Wales in Paris and guested for Toulouse. The prodigal then hiked with his swag-bag and £50 to Biarritz, where he surfed and picked up a game or two, before returning to Sydney.

In August 1913, Tom retired from rugby and became a writer for the *Sydney Morning Herald* and sports paper *The Referee*. When he enlisted in 1914 – with such alacrity that his service number was 25 – his given occupation was not journalist but 'traveller'. The adventurer would sail forth again with the first Australian Imperial Force (AIF) on 1 November, on the troopship HMAT *Euripides* – a portent of tragedy if there ever was one. He railed against the deity in his diary:

The whole business seems almost unbelievable. Thirty-five ships laden with men and weapons, some 30,000 in number, including some of the country's very best men and most valuable assets . . . There is something wrong with the world. This is how we sailed out from Albany, in mournful procession, for a destination unknown, and enshrouded in mystery, making a course westerly. Church service was held at 11.30 when the Chaplain tried to justify the Allies' position and asked God for protection and deliverance. The irony of it all! What hypocrisy! Surely this great God, if he had the power to influence victory in any particular way, would also have the power to prevent it at the very first and before lives were sacrificed.

So it came to pass that on 24 April 1915 he found himself off the Turkish coast. With the lofty perspective of an Olympian and potential interplanetary sportsman, Richards was sceptical of the area's antiquity ('Achilles, is buried here, or at any rate there is a place described as the "Tomb of Achilles"') but conscious of new history being made. That evening he listened to an officer's final briefing aboard ship:

His speech was full of fine humour, dealing chiefly with our likely fear. It was hardly the kind of speech one would expect on the eve of big doings, as there was plenty of ridicule, nonsense, but no hard facts or detailed information. It seemed more as though we were preparing for a pantomime instead of grim warfare. I don't mean for one moment that he should have made us melancholy and miserable but he could have given us something like an idea of what to expect.

Humour, much of it the deepest black, was a survival tonic for trench-bound troops in the war, but the Australians had irreverence down to a fine art. The 'leaning virgin' atop the Basilica of Notre-Dame de Brebières at Albert on the Somme, battered by artillery fire till she hung horizontal, inspired soldierly superstition in German and Briton alike: both sides believed that if she fell, the war would be lost. The Australians simply christened her 'Fanny Durack', after their famed Olympic freestyle swimmer diving off the block.

Richards recorded his four years of war in an articulate and consistently kept diary and even took seven photographs as he came ashore on 25 April. He faced his day calmly: 'I don't feel the coming danger any more than I have felt anxious the night before an international football match.'

On the morning of the landings at Gaba Tepe he was able to write:

> No bugle call to wake us this morning, but most of us were astir
> before the sun rose – a brilliant and pleasing red glow. It was just
> the same as sunset last night – a stage setting with the flashes and
> booming of the cannon to enliven matters.[5]

A field ambulance stretcher-bearer, Tom was one of the first to land, was
mentioned in divisional orders in July for 'acts of gallantry', and was one
of the last to leave the peninsula.

After the evacuation of January 1916 – the only bright spark in a dismal
campaign – he returned to Egypt and then departed for the Western Front,
where he reconnected with his rugby network. On 3 May 1916 he wrote:

> I heard that Capt Johnnie Williams, the Cardiff wing three-
> quarter was about – I called on his men, he was absent, but the five
> Welsh officers compelled me to sit down and wait for his coming,
> and produced wine, whisky, cigarettes and Perrier. They were not
> long in finding out my name and my footer performances and a
> cheery welcome followed until I left at 9.20pm . . . Football was
> not much dwelt upon as Williams has retired and Welsh football
> having gone back so much of late years. I had but little to say as
> Australian rugby is professionalised and dead.
>
> My pass was only to be out until 8pm and it was 9.20pm when
> I left the mess. It was dark and lonely with a picket every now and
> then shouting: 'Halt, who goes there?' It was easy to pass them.
> I usually swore at them and one at least apologised for interfering.
> I got home safely but the flare shells and roar of bombs, cannons,
> rifle and machine guns was thick and continuous.[6]

Corporal Richards was commissioned second lieutenant, 1st Infantry
Battalion; Johnnie Williams, whom he had faced in 1908 at the Arms
Park, would die at Mametz Wood in 1916.

There are periods in Tom's account of war in spring 1916 where he
seems to do little more than stumble across rugby games and mates; this
is the eagerly seized escape to pre-war normality that sustained many
through the man-made hell of mechanised warfare. But Richards did
not shirk the tough stuff: in May 1917, he led a nineteen-man bombing
party near Bullecourt – a gap in his diary as he was a trifle busy – and
was promoted and awarded the MC. Twice evacuated with wounds to
England in 1917, and again in May 1918, when his back and shoulders were

damaged by a bomb, he also survived a gas attack which would cause him respiratory problems till his death of tuberculosis in 1935. He never played rugby again after 1918.

If Richards was Odysseus, Blair Swannell was Achilles, a more complex hero, whose rugby voyage was in the opposite direction. Australia claims him, for he died in its uniform and had represented it against New Zealand on the rugby field. But he was English-born, had fought for Britain in South Africa and played rugby *against* Australia for two British touring teams in 1899 and 1904. A formal notice of his death portrayed a charismatic pillar of the 'great and good':

> It has been said that he played rugby in more countries than any other player except T.J. Richards. In 1909 and 1910 he was Secretary to the Metropolitan Rugby Union. During the past few years he occupied the post of [Armed Forces] Area Secretary at Darlington and was one of the first to volunteer.[7]

He coached hockey as well as rugby at St Joseph's College, and refereed for three years, earning a reputation for his ability to control a game; he was vice-president of the Sydney Swimming Club and trained military cadets in surf lifesaving. So far, so stalwart, but reaching deeper into his history, it is clear that his life was tainted by controversy, much of it self-made, even down to his last moments on 25 April 1915. Paddy Moran, paid loyal tribute, but also acknowledged the Marmite stain in Swannell's character:

> In the end, he wore an Australian uniform as stubbornly as he had worn an Australian jersey. He was early in the field and found his end storming the goal on that April morning at Gallipoli. He is still there holding on. When his death became known to his troops, it was rumoured that his own men had shot him down. They did not like his domineering English manner or the way that, in speaking, he clipped off the end of his words. But the story of his being shot from behind was just somebody's canard.[8]

This wasn't the only stain: Swannell was notorious for wearing the same pair of unwashed breeches for every game, which may explain why – perhaps by team vote – he made his way to the back of the pack, as number eight for Australia. And also why he never married?

Born in Buckinghamshire in 1875, Blair Inskip Swannell was schooled at Repton and played his club rugby for Olney, Western Turks and Northampton Saints, where he was known as 'good old B.I.' After leaving school he qualified as a seafaring second mate and embarked upon a life of swashbuckling adventure, not all of it plausible or verifiable, but all part of the legend. His first visit to Australia, in whose colours he would play, fight and die, was in 1897 aboard a schooner; his second was with Matthew Mullineux's British tour party of 1899, when he played seventeen matches and three of the four Tests. The jerseys he faced were maroon in the Queensland Tests and blue in New South Wales.

How Swannell's abrasive style went down with the Reverend Mullineux is not recorded; the scrum half had toured South Africa in 1896, so was presumably hardened in Christian tolerance. The churchman was both humble – dropping himself from the Test team after playing badly – and obtuse, preaching an after-dinner sermon to the losing Australians after the third Test in Sydney on the poor quality of their play. Serving as a wartime chaplain in the Boer and Great Wars, he would win the MC in 1918, taking command of an aid post (after the medical officer was wounded) under twelve hours of shellfire. He would later found a charity to fund war-grave visits and led pilgrimages to Gallipoli in the 1920s.

Back in Britain, Swannell also enlisted, serving in South Africa where he was commissioned in the field as a lieutenant with the 35th Imperial Yeomanry. If his own claims are to be believed he also fought alongside insurrectionists in Uruguay, hunted seal in Chile and Labrador and played rugby in France, Germany, South Africa, India and both North and South America, even representing Wales (probably New South) and Argentina, by one newspaper claim.

To that list can be added with certainty Australia and New Zealand. His second British tour in 1904 saw him play all fifteen games, including three more Tests against Australia (with his first and only international try scored at Sydney) and one against the neighbours across the Tasman Sea (his first defeat). Swannell stayed on in Australia, as did skipper Bedell-Sivright and doctor Sidney Crowther. In an era before air travel, rugby adventurers often used a paid tour passage to build new lives: Irishmen Tommy Crean and Robert Johnston stayed in South Africa after the 1896 tour. Both won VCs four years later in the Boer War on the British side; but they did not wear new colours, as Swannell did in his adoptive land. In 1905 he played for the country he had already defeated six times, and ironically lost in his only game – against New Zealand on Australia's first overseas tour. For all his travels he never played a Test on home soil.

At just over 12 stone and 5ft 10in he was no giant by modern standards, but made up for it with his aggressive play. Moran's memories of his youthful game against Swannell at Sydney's Cricket Ground show grudging admiration for a hard but complex man:

> My back was black and blue from his attentions. He looked across at me, a much younger player, to see how I had taken it all. 'Are you satisfied?' 'Perfectly,' I replied. After which he invited me to have a glass of beer with him, a signal honour, for he was not given to treating. In life as on the football field, Swannell gave no quarter and asked for none. We, less mature men stood somewhat in awe of him.

For Moran, who served at Gallipoli and in Mesopotamia as an RAMC surgeon, there is mixed fascination and repulsion. His praise is the more generous when we consider his open disapproval and low rating of Swannell as a player, considering him,

> a bad influence in Sydney football and also incidentally a greatly overestimated player. His conception of rugby was one of trained violence. He kept himself in perfect condition; this alone enabled him to conceal his slowness on the field. In appearance he was extremely ugly but, like Wilkes in the eighteenth century, he could talk away his face in half an hour. He was popular with the fair sex; men, generally, disliked him.[9]

Aware of his reputation, New Zealand man-marked him with a 'vigorous Maoriland scrummer' known as 'Angry':

> At the conclusion of the game in which no quarter was given or asked for, the Welshman [sic] who could hardly see out of a pair of lovely black eyes walked off the field with his shadow and ventured the remark that the match had been 'a bit rough'. 'Rough?' retorted 'Angry', who had not come out of the fray unscathed; 'that's nothing. You should see a North v South Island match.'[10]

The combative Swannell liked to have the last word, as 'FullBack' reported in the *Otago Witness*,[11] claiming he was 'quiet as a lamb until his opponents began to deal it out to him, and then skin and hair fly':

> In New Zealand where the forwards with the large feet come from, he made them cry a go first, although they started the rib-kicking tactics. He left the Dominion with black eyes extending down to his neck, with his mouth torn at the corners, and minus

many molars, but he still had the smile that could not be kicked off, and he expressed the hope in a sucking-dove-like voice that when he returned they would have learned to play a good hard game – that he never could stand the parlour game anyhow. I have a photograph of his boots and judging by the boots, there were safer places in the field than in front of a pack of Swannells.

Moran's comment on that game was that 'he got there what he had often given elsewhere. There was no preciosity in his workmanship. He was a hard virile unsympathetic type, but a man.'

Private Harry Cavill, in his D Company (always D as we shall again see) at Gallipoli, later wrote in open admiration of his officer:

> Never shall I forget the look on his face when we first got within striking distance of the enemy. 'Fix bayonets! Charge!' rang out his order. There was a flash of steel, a wild hurrah, and the boys dashed straight at the wall of fire, heedless of the frightful slaughter. They were not to be stopped. It was in this charge that Major Swannell was killed. He had seized a rifle, and with dauntless courage was leading his men, when a Turkish bullet, penetrating his forehead, ended his career, thus depriving the First Brigade of one of its finest officers.[12]

Lieutenant Colonel Kindon revealed another facet of his 'rough diamond' major, promoted on New Year's Day, whose 'personality impressed itself on all who came in contact with him':

> He was a fatalist and firmly believed he would not come through. When, after the landing, we dumped our packs before pushing up to the heights, he said to me: 'There's a bottle of whisky in my pack. I leave it to you. I shan't come through today.' Opposite Baby 700 a few hours later he took it through the forehead whilst looking up trying to locate the enemy. I never got the whisky.

Moran's final verdict, still shot through with the awe of the younger man, but delivered on behalf of the country they both represented – and loved – is in effect 'Well played, Aussie':

> It was always said of a Roman emperor that he should die on his feet. Swannell, no doubt, thought a footballer should perish following on. His hard-visaged comrades said he died with the ruling passion strong upon him; still putting in the boot. Through

sacrifice, he passed to transfiguration. The hard porcelain of his spirit had richer glaze than we had previously perceived; it was love of country. For me who knew him well, this is his epitaph: he never hung out of a ruck.[13]

Another rugby man killed that day was Ted Larkin, a former policeman who played hooker versus New Zealand in 1903. He had crossed the rugby divide to become NSW Rugby League's first full-time secretary after the 1908 breakaway from Union and his hard work saved the new code after a rocky start. He was also MP for Willoughby, declaring in Parliament in August 1914: 'I cannot engage in the work of recruiting and urge others to enlist unless I do so myself.' He joined the same 1st Battalion, AIF, as Swannell; in Egypt, Sergeant Larkin organised rugby in the shadow of the pyramids. At Anzac, the battalion landed at dawn and fought to take the dominating height of Baby 700 above the cove. The Turks counter-attacked to drive them from the high ground; Ted Larkin died in a hail of machine-gun rounds. Harry Cavill again remembered:

> Wounded and dying he lay, yet when the stretcher-bearers came
> to carry him in, he waved them on, saying 'There's plenty worse
> than me out there.' Later they found him dead.

Larkin's older brother Martin, aged 37, also lost his life that day. Though their bodies were recovered in a 24 May burial truce, their names are recorded on the Lone Pine Memorial commemorating 4,934 Australian and New Zealand troops killed in the sector who now have no known grave. Ted was one of only two serving members of an Australian parliament to fall, both at Gallipoli, the other being the Member for Armidale, Colonel G.F. Braund, who played for NSW against the British tourists in 1888.

Private Clarrie 'Doss' Wallach, Eastern Suburbs forward and five times a Wallaby, landed at Anzac Cove in August. He wrote a letter to *The Referee* about his time in 'Hellopolis' and the fortunes of his rugger comrades:

> We have been in pretty solid work but expect the real stuff next
> week. All the rugby union men are well here, from the Major down
> to the privates. Twit Tasker told me how Harold George died a
> death of deaths – a hero's – never beaten until the final whistle.[14]

The Major was James MacManamey, NSW Rugby Union President, who played in the first interstate game against Queensland; he died a few weeks after Wallach's letter was written. He was 57 and had served in the Sudan in 1885. 'Major McManamey stated that if it was right for sons to go to the front it was also right for those fathers who had had military training to go also to be of what service they could in protecting those sons.'[15]

Private Harold George was a clubmate and fellow internationalist with eight caps, of whom *The Arrow* wrote: 'It is hard to imagine anyone playing a harder, tougher game than he did. Perhaps never super-brilliant, he always played himself out to the last ounce, and was an awfully hard man to beat for the ball in the front rank of a scrum.' He had also been one of the 'first-dayers' on 25 April with the 13th (NSW) Battalion, as they tried to consolidate the beach-head. He was wounded at Pope's Post and died of his wounds on a hospital ship on 10 May, from which he was buried at sea. Tom Richards wrote that George,

> . . . got the axe for a very brave action . . . he was one of five to go at midday and locate a machine gun and Turkish trenches. The sergeant got a rough time and was finally shot. Harold after a while found the corner too hot and taking the sergeant's body he made it back under heavy fire to the trenches. When he was preparing to get into the trench himself a bullet passed through his body low down.[16]

He is commemorated with the Larkin brothers at Lone Pine.

Another Wallaby in the unlucky 13th Battalion was back-rower Fred Thompson, whose death is mentioned in the same letter. Thompson sailed from Sydney on HMAT *Seang Choon*, the same transport ship as George and Tasker, on which a rugby ball was reportedly thrown about on the crowded decks. Thompson has the rare Gallipoli privilege of a named grave in Shrapnel Valley.

> He was shot through the head, and dropped in the trench. To someone who wanted to move him, he remarked that he "hadn't far to go", and died very soon afterwards. To everyone who knew them, Harold and Fred have always been known as men, good sports who 'played the game' good and hard, and never shirked. By their noble and gallant conduct when they doffed the jersey and donned the King's khaki they have proved their manhood, and shown the world that the Australian Rugby Union player is a man right through.[17]

All three Eastern Suburbs men had played for Metropolitan Sydney against the All Blacks on 5 August, the day that Australian newspaper placards and the Sports Ground scoreboard screamed 'WAR DECLARED'. Nine of those Wallabies enlisted during the war, four were killed in action.

The League code also suffered losses at Gallipoli. Rugby League kept its main competitions going in wartime, and claims have been made that 75 per cent of unmarried League players did not enlist.[18] But many did heed the call of NSW Premier W.A. Holman in July 1915: 'Your comrades at Gallipoli are calling you. This is not the time for football and tennis matches . . . it is serious. Show that you realise this by enlisting at once!' Ten of the 1914 Newcastle RL team served, including star player and captain Stan Carpenter; he was joined by Horace Brown, district secretary. Like Ted Larkin, both enlisted within ten days of war being declared; both fought at Gallipoli, with Carpenter reputed to be the first member of the AIF to be recommended for a VC. He received the Distinguished Service Medal (DSM) instead. George Duffin, 18th Battalion, a League Kangaroo against the Kiwis in 1909, was killed at Hill 60 in August 1915. Charles Savoury, one of several New Zealanders who toured with the second Kangaroos to Britain in 1911, landed with the Auckland Infantry on 25 April and was killed on 8 May.

By the end of the campaign, five Wallabies and various Kangaroos would not leave the peninsula. For the fallen Scots, Kiwis, English, Welsh, Irish and French whose bodies or unidentified remains lie in Turkish soil, there's a cracking ghostly Sevens tournament to be played on a moonless night. If they can find a patch of ground level enough.

The Australians moved to France where the Western Front saw a veritable rugby reunion, as Tom Richards testified. A ball of some description was always a big factor in the life of the AIF in the field, and the pursuit of sport knew few bounds. 'There was always a game of some sort as close up to the front line as was permissible and sometimes closer,' wrote Lieutenant Goddard in laconic style:

> The ball that had the biggest vogue was that of the .303 Mark VII SAA [Small Arms Ammunition] but the 'game' played with that particular variety was not always the most enjoyable. In fact the number of players who were hurt made it the most unpopular of all. Men came and men went, but King Sport reigned during the whole of the time.[19]

George Pugh, who won his single cap for Australia against the USA in 1912, wrote in March 1916: 'Have met lots of old friends, including Rugger men. It puts you in mind of a football tour, as they all seem to be here. No omissions by the selectors on this trip.'[20] Pugh was killed by mortar shrapnel on 5 September 1916 near another infamous Hill 60 in the Ypres Salient and is buried at Railway Dugouts Cemetery. It was then an Advanced Dressing Station at Transport Farm, where the 1896 British lock Alec Todd, fatally wounded in the throat, smoked his last cigarette in April 1915.

Clarrie Wallach, who 'went right through Gallipoli without a scratch', fought on the Somme at Pozières, was commissioned captain and awarded the MC. In 1918, during the bitter resistance against the German Spring Offensive, his luck ran out near Villers-Bretonneux. On a cold and rainy 7 April, an attack on Hangard Wood was to go in at 0455 supported by a barrage. Something misfired and no barrage fell in front; Wallach nonetheless led his company across 400 yards of open ground. German machine gunners in the wood, untroubled by shelling, opened up; one man in four was hit and Wallach fell with wounds to both knees. Lieutenant Percy Storkey took command and pushed into the undergrowth with eleven men; they took an enemy position by surprise, killing and wounding about thirty, and capturing three officers, fifty men, and one machine gun. Storkey received the Victoria Cross; Wallach had both legs amputated in a desperate attempt to save his life, which ended on 22 April. The five rugby-playing Wallach brothers make a terrible casualty count in one family: two were killed (Neville a month after Clarrie), Arthur was wounded, Henry shell-shocked and Rupert taken prisoner.

William 'Twit' Tasker, who told Wallach of the deaths of George and Thompson at Gallipoli, was a fly half, 'powerful and fast with one of the finest swerves in the game'. He and Pugh had toured North America with the woeful 1912 Wallabies: they lost all but the single Test against the USA, a performance ascribed to serious partying in college fraternity houses and a lack of disciplined tour management. The indiscipline spread to the pitch with Tasker the first Wallaby to be sent off in a Test. Having landed at Anzac Cove, Tasker was severely wounded by a shell fragment at Quinn's Post. Manly's H.A. Mitchell wrote home that: 'A bomb loaded up Tasker's ankle and leg with about seventeen pieces of shot. It will be some time before he can do any of that sidestepping he used to do.'

So severe were his wounds that he was evacuated to Melbourne and discharged from the army in December 1915. A newspaper review revealed his survivor-guilt after the deaths of George and Thompson:

Somehow it does not seem right, that we three should go away together, and these two not come back, while I am here alive to-day. Perhaps I should have been where they are, and if it comes to my lot to go back I would like to go out leaving something accomplished behind me comparable with what they did.[21]

Intent on getting back to the fray, Tasker repeatedly tried to rejoin. While the infantry refused him, the artillery relented: he went to France in September 1916 with a howitzer battery. He was wounded twice more and gassed, before dying of further shrapnel wounds four months after Wallach, at Amiens. This decisive victory of 'all-arms' warfare in 1918, combining infantry, artillery, tanks and aerial support was brilliantly led by Australian General John Monash, who had been at Gallipoli. For the German Army, their 'Black Day' of 8 August was the beginning of the end; for Tasker, the 9th was simply the end. He is buried at Villers-Bretonneux, another destination for Australian pilgrims in these centenary years.

Herbert Moran, writing defiantly thirty years later in his memory of the jeers and catcalls of the 1908 Wallaby tour, said with pride of Australia's contribution:

At Loos, in a hard match, an Irish battalion dribbled the ball towards the enemy lines. My people too joined in that rush, forming up again and again in their drive towards the goal. There was then no prig who dared to shout out from a self-righteous crowd: 'Play the game, Australia!'[22]

Of some 332,000 Australians who served in the Great War, 212,000 were casualties including 60,000 dead, the highest casualty rate of all the Allied combatants at 64 per cent. The fallen are remembered on ANZAC Day, and all who served are named on their war memorials. Australian fighting men were always willing volunteers (in Tasker's case, a bloody-minded and determined one) as conscription, introduced in 1916 in both Britain and New Zealand, was twice defeated by referendum. An estimated 5,000 rugby players from both codes went on active service between 1914 and 1918, representing well over 90 per cent of senior players in New South Wales and Queensland.

Some thirty-five Union Wallabies served in the armed forces, and ten died. It is for someone else other than a Union pommie to tell League's war story; it was controversial at the time and still sparks periodic outbursts. But Rugby Union in Australia would struggle on a hard road from war, before it found its feet and ran with the ball again.

New Zealand

From the shafts of strife and war
Make her praises heard afar.

New Zealanders were alongside Australians on the beach that April day at Gaba Tepe, consecrating Anzac Cove in the national memory: 600 of the 3,100 who landed became casualties. Like the Canadians at Vimy, they stormed a ridge in 1917, this time at Messines, and matched signal success with fewer losses than the grim Western Front norm. They had days of bloody disaster with the British at Chunuk Bair on Gallipoli, suffered terrible reverses at the Somme and Passchendaele and paid back the Turks in Palestine. At the death in November 1918, they finished the war on a literal high as they scaled Vauban's fortress walls of Le Quesnoy using ladders borrowed from French firemen.

For New Zealanders, however, no single moment of wartime myth-making defined a young nation, as it did for Australians and Canadians, or even South Africans at 'Devil's Wood'. For that national legend had already been fashioned, ten years previously, by warriors who boarded a boat and sailed from the 'uttermost ends of the earth' to fight on peacetime playing fields in Britain, Ireland, France and the USA. The narrative that underpins New Zealand's national identity was written by a rugby campaign in 1905; the war simply consolidated that identity. Both stories cultivated the 'stereotype of the Kiwi male as a tough, uncomplaining, self-disciplined team player'.[1] Chief in this heroic saga was the captain, Dave Gallaher. That he would again shrug on his armour, reclaim three years of his youth with a lie in order to fight, and die aged 43, during an attack at Passchendaele merely sanctified his myth in New Zealand memory.

Born David Gallagher in Ireland's County Donegal in 1873, he became plain Dave Gallaher when, in May 1878, his parents James and Maria took their seven children on a 12,000-mile voyage ('Are we there yet?') on the *Lady Jocelyn* to settle in New Zealand's Katikati. This North Island coastal town would later strike an early blow for independent nationalism (and lure picnickers) by rechristening its St George's Bay as Anzac Bay in

January 1916, spurning the name of England's patron saint and king in favour of 'the letters of the word [which] would always remind us of those memorable deeds. "A" stood for Australia, "NZ" for New Zealand and "AC" for the Allies' Cause'[2] (actually Army Corps, but the speechmaker, also a George, knew what he was doing). The last troops on the Turkish peninsula left the following day; the small town would lose nine of its sixty menfolk who served.

Life was tough in Katikati for the Gallahers, with another seven children added to their brood, now one short of a full XV. Dave's teacher mother was the breadwinner and when she died of cancer, his father was already 75; the older children worked, Dave leaving school at thirteen, and the family relied on charity. Katikati held its first rugby game in 1880, and by 1904 supported three teams, even forming its own Rugby Union; Dave learnt his trade. Rugby was already widespread in New Zealand and the wellspring of an uncompromising character and pride. As the journal *Zealandia* asserted in 1890, 'there is now no danger of New Zealand rearing a nation of milksops, effeminate fops and luxurious dandies'.[3] Chris Laidlaw, an All Black at 19 and later skipper, before entering politics, argued that, 'Rugby became the medium by which New Zealanders would come to realise that they were different from the British.'[4]

The Gallahers moved in search of a living to Auckland in 1889. Dave worked as a foreman for the Farmers' Freezing Company and played his rugby for Parnell, then Ponsonby. By 1901 and his departure with the NZ Mounted Infantry for the Boer War in South Africa, he was the local hero:

> A very large crowd of the members and enthusiasts of the Ponsonby District Football Club assembled at the Ponsonby Club Hotel on Saturday night to say farewell to 'Dave' Gallaher, the well-known footballer, who left with the Sixth Contingent for South Africa this week. Mr. S.D. Hanna proposed the health of the guest in a very happy manner. Several other well-known members spoke as to 'Dave's' good qualities, and the chairman then presented him with a well-filled purse of sovereigns. Corporal Gallaher replied very feelingly, and thanked all his old comrades for the kind way they had treated him.[5]

He returned in 1902 with two stripes on his sleeve, three clasps on the Queen's South Africa medal and two on his King's, and ten games of army rugby under his belt. Playing for Auckland in its first Ranfurly

Shield challenge (lost to Wellington) was precursor to selection for the 1903 New Zealand tour to Australia; they won all twenty matches. Beginning the tour as hooker, Dave played the last five as a wing forward, perfecting the rover role and winning his first international cap in Sydney. A second winning cap was added at Wellington's Athletic Park against the 1904 British tourists, with Blair Swannell but without the injured Bedell-Sivright – what a clash that might have been. Dave was then selected as captain for a ground-breaking tour of Britain.

Aboard the SS *Rimutaka*, there was daily training as relief from the monotony of shipboard life: 'physical drill' started at 7.45 a.m., followed by separate morning sessions for backs and forwards, and afternoon sports including boxing, wrestling and conditioning with Eugen Sandow's bodybuilding apparatus. Gallaher (forwards) and vice-captain Billy Stead (backs) took training, with coach Jimmy Duncan sidelined. They held team meetings to discuss rules, tactics and styles of play; these innovative brainstorming sessions continued throughout the tour, as they refined techniques like passing 'at the moment of being tackled' – offloading skills are nothing new for New Zealanders. Other passengers watched and some, including women, even joined in the training. This approach was highly professional when you consider that Alec Todd, Tommy Crean and the 1896 British Isles tourists played deck quoits, ducking for coins and 'slinging the monkey' on their voyage to South Africa, and lost the tug of war to the ship's stokers.

Once docked at Plymouth, the men in black were 'in the pink' of fitness and signalled their intent with the 55–4 annihilation of reigning county champions, Devon. Five-eighth Jimmy Hunter scored the first of eleven tries in the third minute; his personal tour tally would reach forty-two. They were a sensation and set off round the country like travelling prize-fighters, taking on all comers in thirty-two matches, high-scoring and undefeated in all but one: against Wales, a hotly-debated try by Bob Deans, that would have tied the game, was disallowed. The twenty-three English games produced an aggregate of 721 points to 15. When they walked onto Cardiff Arms Park in front of 45,000, 'the crowd started from their seats and almost tumbled over one another in their eagerness to see the famous All Blacks'. Their virtuoso back-play, and forwards playing specific positions in an innovative 2–3–2 scrum formation, with Gallaher as rover,[6] created the legend of these 'Original All Blacks'. Their schedule paled by comparison with Joe Warbrick's 1888-89 Māori visitors, who played 107 games, often three a week.

The secret was in their 'system' and the scientific thought and constant practice put behind it. But it was no closely held trade secret: they even published a book to explain. Shoemaker fly half Billy Stead sat down during a London break and crashed out *The Complete Rugby Footballer in the New Zealand System* in just two weeks, with Gallaher drawing the diagrams. The system still works, but there's more to rugby than reading a manual. Few rugby tours have inspired award-winning novels as this 1905 epic has,[7] but that's how legends are nurtured. Poet and historian, Sir Keith Sinclair even claimed the Welsh defeat as 'New Zealand sport's equivalent of Gallipoli'.[8]

The famous nickname was also popularised on this tour, although it was hardly news, and certainly not the 'brand' it is today. Its origin has many elaborations: Wellington's 1889 team first played in black; in 1893, Thomas Rangiwahia Ellison, who pioneered the wing-forward position and scored forty-three tries on that first Māori tour, proposed at the first NZRFU AGM that the playing colours of New Zealand should be predominantly black, with a silver fern monogram, black cap and stockings and white knickerbockers. This was similar to the Māori team strip, and with a switch to black shorts in 1901, became the familiar national signature. So they were all in black before coming to Britain. After the first pummelling of the Devonians, a local hack depicted 'the All Blacks, as they are styled by reason of their sable and unrelieved costume'.[9] But such was this side's breathtaking interplay between pack and backs that reports reached London that they played as if they were 'all backs'. The typesetters at the *Daily Mail* (*Grauniad*, surely?) added their bit of 'l', and the rest is history – if not well verified.

They pioneered commercial endorsement: the team advertised 'Jason's Unshrinkable Underwear for Athletes'. An illustration of the England match at Crystal Palace, was captioned: 'The New Zealand Footballers Write, 4th Jan 1906',

> Gentlemen, It may interest you to learn that the 'Jason Underwear' has given general satisfaction to members of the New Zealand Football team, its general good qualities (especially the fact of its being unshrinkable) justify us in commending it to all Athletes and Sportsmen. Yours faithfully . . .

Facsimile autographs are appended of the whole New Zealand team except O'Sullivan, whose broken collarbone left him unable to sign. Copywriting has come a long way since in refreshing the parts, and the Adidas golden fleece is far richer than Jason's, but it was a comfortable start.

These specimens of colonial masculinity in their 'Unshrinkable Underwear' became a popular sensation throughout Britain; David Beckham is doing nothing new. In December, a *Daily Mail* columnist, tongue-in-cheek, described what possessed him 'body, soul and spirit: the all-conquering Blacks':

> Every word written in the newspapers about the colonials I have devoured . . . I know their Christian names, surnames, nicknames, birthplaces, pedigrees etc. and every stray biographical fact . . . I never wear anything but black now, and all my gorgeous fancy vests and the more brilliant ties have been given away for money . . . My life, dear reader, has become a perfect misery. Why, only the other day I made a long journey in a penny 'bus to the Cottage Tearooms in the Strand in order that I might see the girl there who wears a silver fern brooch.

Of course, as was customary in theatrical spectacle during the festive season, they also lived up to the implied villainy of their dark uniform. Gallaher was accused of gamesmanship, crooked feeding, and being constantly offside, obstructing the opposing scrum half; thus was he the spiritual forebear of celebrated open-sides to come. The *Manchester Guardian* pilloried the 'professed obstructionist' and Henry Grierson recalled that at Bedford:

> Gallaher played wing forward, wore his shinguards outside his stockings, shouted 'A-heave, A-heave', which annoyed the crowd, and did lots of good work in the obstruction line.[10]

His team-mates argued with referees, querying decisions when they were repeatedly penalised; their vigour in hurling men to the ground after tackles was even noted by the press back home. But it was all great box-office. No more so than in Scotland's bastion of amateurism, where the SFU's high-minded refusal of a guarantee, in favour of the tourists taking the gate, backfired spectacularly as 21,000 flocked to the spectacle. Despite their popularity, the British establishment did not invite them back until 1925, although they would return in uniformed guise – and triumph – in 1919.

On the way home via Paris, they summarily despatched France, who would take many years to perfect the mercurial hoodoo which they now spring on the All Blacks when they are not looking. The French were then emerging as a rugby nation: this international baptism was a daunting debut. They wisely treated the tour-toughened '*Noirs*' with the respect of novices, as George Smith told the *Herald*: 'If a Frenchman grassed one of our players at all roughly they would turn around and say "Pardon, monsieur".' In March France first played England in a friendly, but the new sporting *entente* did not admit them to a full set of Home Nations fixtures until 1910.

In America, the Originals played a nominal New York side (bolstered by six of the tourists) in a Brooklyn baseball park, then took the Santa Fe railroad via Chicago and the Grand Canyon to California, where exhibitions were played against British Columbia. In front of crowds new to rugby in San Francisco, they 'showed wonderful speed and skill . . . created enthusiasts, won over lukewarm spectators and silenced many critics'. Tour manager George Dixon made admiring notes on a stroll through the city's streets: 'understand no limit to hours pubs kept open – but have seen no cases of drunkenness'. He was optimistic too that 'our missionary work will bear fruit in the near future'; that is a chapter to come.

On docking in Auckland, they received a welcome fit for conquering warriors, and the native greeting '*Kia ora*' from Premier Richard Seddon who, like all politicians, missed no chance for a moment of national popularity. He personally escorted them off the ship and pronounced with pride that 'the triumph of the team is not only a credit to the colony but to the Empire'. He might as well have added, 'and I claim this game of rugby for New Zealand over all others and in perpetuity', but modestly refrained. The Auckland *Observer* noted: 'Their tour and its splendid achievements have not only added to the prestige of New Zealand football . . . but have also advertised the country in a way that a score of immigrant agents and half-a-dozen Tourist Departments could not have done.'[11] And this was well before the films of Peter Jackson.

Smug sportswriters predicted that the 'kindred in the Mother Country would, in all their important matches, employ the wing-forward, as one of the many things taught by the All Blacks', ignoring its Yorkshire origins in the 1880s. These conquistadors also brought with them untold riches: it was announced that tour receipts were £14,700, 'a sum beyond everyone's wildest dreams', with net profit after expenses £9,500, enough to put the national body on a sound footing ever after. The mould for the touring All Blacks was cast in gold. One dissenting and isolated voice was 'Sport', a correspondent to the *Auckland Star,* who bemoaned the 'banquet laid on for a team of men who have had expenses paid and even an allowance per day for a good holiday trip. Why should such a fuss be made of them?' He made pointed comparison with the treatment of earlier military returnees:

> When our gallant Contingent, the Seventh arrived from South Africa no reception of any sort was proposed . . . and the authorities had not even the common courtesy to present their medals, but advertised that they were available at the Defence Office.

We could perhaps infer that 'Sport' may have been one of the 'gallant Seventh'. Either way, the distinction between military and rugby warriors was soon to be wiped out, along with many thousands of New Zealand soldiers and sportsmen.

Gallaher had passed 40 when war was declared, but volunteered in July 1916 after younger brother Douglas was killed with the Australians near Armentières in June. Dave knocked three years off his age to be allowed to fight. In February 1917, he once again sailed for Europe, aboard the *Aparima*, and in June became a sergeant in 2nd Battalion, Auckland Infantry Regiment. His service number – 3229 in South Africa – was now 32513, sure sign of the scale of this new conflict. That Gallaher was already a national celebrity – and a confident one too – was soon clear, as the Official History described the voyage:

> . . . the only 'regrettable incident' being the stranding of two or three personnel at Colombo owing to a misunderstanding as to the hour of departure. As the last of the troopships left the latter port and was making good headway westwards, a small tug came racing out and signalled her to stop. There was much speculation as to the reason for this action, and the usual wild explanations multiplied as the tug was seen to lower a boat which pulled smartly over to the trooper. The gangway was put down, and up this majestically stepped a solitary Rifleman. This was the famous New Zealand footballer, 'Wing' David – a man much beloved by his comrades and something of a trial too, though secretly admired by his officers. Arrived on deck, he waved a haughty dismissal to the tug and a condescending signal to the bridge that the troopship might now proceed.[12]

From Dave to David: it seems he had lost his 'id' and gained an ego. He would die four weeks short of his forty-fourth birthday in 1917, shot in the face at Gravenstafel Spur during the struggle for Passchendaele. He died of his wounds the following day at No. 3 Australian Casualty Clearing Station, little more than a dugout scooped from a trench wall. His home city obituary was as imprecise as he had been (and the CWGC still is) on his true age:

> Mr. Gallaher was born in Belfast, about 46 years ago, and came to New Zealand, as a child. From his boyhood he was recognised as a capable athlete, his prowess being exhibited chiefly in Rugby football. Mr. Gallaher was for many years sole selector for the Auckland Rugby Union, and was the captain of the All Blacks team which toured England in 1905–6. He saw service in the Boer War and on the outbreak of the present war was eager to join the forces, but was for some time detained on account of family ties. Mr. Gallaher is survived by his wife and child, at present in Sydney.[13]

Another member of the Originals, Ernie Booth, who stayed in England and played for Leicester, wrote: 'Dave was a man of sterling worth . . . girded by great self-determination and self control, he was a valuable friend and could be, I think, a remorseless foe. To us All Blacks his word would often be "Give nothing away: take no chances".' Since 1922, the Gallaher Shield has been Auckland's premier club competition; the Dave Gallaher Cup is awarded to the winner of the first Test between New Zealand and France in any calendar year. Of the five Gallahers who served, three were killed in France. Dave is buried at Nine Elms Cemetery, Poperinghe, where his headstone bears the fern.

Twelve others who wore the black jersey in Tests would also die, four of them in a fortnight at Messines; with Gallaher, this made one in ten All Blacks from the previous decade. As a group, they present a telling picture, with many differences from their equivalents in other national teams. Of this thirteen who died, all but one were 'other ranks'. Nor were they callow youths in their teens or early twenties but grizzled veterans with an average age over 32, only four being still under 30.

When war exploded in Europe in August 1914, New Zealand's first act of war was bloodless, seizing German Samoa as a 'great and urgent Imperial service' to the Mother Country. Lieutenant Colonel Robert Logan and a 1,419-strong advance party of the New Zealand Expeditionary Force (NZEF), including six nurses, landed at Apia on 29 August without resistance. Logan proclaimed a New Zealand-run British military occupation and raised the Union flag. The new administration was later blamed for mishandling the 1918 influenza pandemic, which killed a fifth of the local population, and its eventual forty-eight-year rule was rarely popular. But it did provide a legacy of fine Samoan-origin players in black shirts, from Bryan Williams, Frank Bunce and Jerry Collins to Ma'a Nonu, Julian Savea, Jerome Kaino and Sonny Bill Williams of the current generation.

After Samoa, there were no easy games. New Zealand rugby's contribution to the 'Great War for Civilisation' was soon acknowledged by 'Quidnunc' of the *Canterbury Times,* who avowed in 1915 that 'the dash and ginger that characterised the bayonet charges of the New Zealanders in the trench-lined hills of Gallipoli were undoubtedly largely due to the rough-and-tumble training of the football ground'. He continues:

> It is certainly a fact that the football clubs of this Dominion have been first-rate recruiting grounds for the Expeditionary Force and its Reinforcements. All over the country . . . the call to arms has drained the clubs of their best men. From South Otago, not one club in that district can raise a team this season for flag matches. This is a matter in which the followers of the game may well take pride: the fewer players there are left while the war lasts the greater the honour for what may be called New Zealand's national pastime.[14]

This is not just the war-cry that 'Rugby Players are Doing their Duty', as trumpeted in the British recruitment poster; this is an entire population sacrificing its passionate devotion to their national sport to the pursuit of war. By 1916, rugby in New Zealand was at a standstill 'except for those games confined to players under military age and reinforcement drafts'.[15] New Zealanders already in Britain joined up immediately. George Chapman, Waitaki High and Otago University, won three Cambridge Blues, and played for the London Hospital and the Barbarians. As an RAMC medic he was killed, aged 27, by a shell as he attended the wounded in May 1915, at Ypres. He had already been decorated in December by the French *'Pour Courage et Dévouement'*, for saving a life in rough sea off Boulogne. Before the war, journals like the *Otago Witness* filled many column inches following the fortunes of New Zealand's rugby exports in hospital and club teams, and more than one international side – Adams and Palmer, Kiwis from Otago University, were both capped for England. For a small nation of 1 million inhabitants, already defined and united by love of rugby, it was inevitable when casualty reports started to wash over the news pages that whole communities would grieve for their rugby boys. In wartime, players who were revered celebrities were also personal friends or even relatives to writers, spectators and townspeople, and would be widely mourned.

There was deep sorrow in Wellington at the death of Roy Lambert with the Auckland Regiment at that fatal first landing. In the column by 'Drop-kick' there is heartfelt affection:

> To many members of football clubs in Wellington, the reality of war will be brought home with distinctness even greater than before by the death of Roy Lambert, a player admired and liked by all. This is the first death of a really prominent footballer in the New Zealand Expeditionary Force . . . he was not a graceful player, for he was tall and had an awkward appearance. In taking the ball he appeared uncertain, but he always managed to stretch his limbs to the requisite length and surprise the men who expected him to miss . . . Lambert's reputation for clean, sportsmanlike play was of the best, and this made him doubly popular.[16]

The same column also regrets the death of 'Private Day (Wellington Infantry Battalion) who died of wounds received in the Dardanelles fighting, and was a keen footballer in the Wanganui district'. Private Edmund Fahey, of the Otago Battalion, and 'a man of herculean build' is reported wounded at Gallipoli, as are 'Private McQueen, the Otago 'Varsity front-ranker of last season' and his fellow prop Lieutenant Nisbet, 'wounded practically in the same forward rush on the Turkish lines'. The language of rugby is already the language of warfare, as whole teams go to war like the 'Pals' battalions of England's industrial towns:

> First off the football ground and first into the field of battle, Pirates have sacrificed their first grade team to the nation's cause, and still more of the Blacks are going to the front to join those already there. E. Currie, A.E. Duncan and C. Jamieson left on Saturday with Lord Liverpool's Own for Trentham, where a number of Pirates have been in training for some time ready to depart with the next reinforcements. Prominent amongst these is the old Pirates forward Smeaton, who has received a commission in the battery, and Roy McKellar, wing three-quarter and brother of Gerald, ex-New Zealand, ex-Wellington and Otago forward.

Note here that the sacrifice is to the 'nation's cause': New Zealand was fighting its own battles, not those of some remote empire. They began by volunteering, but as in Britain (and unlike Australia) conscription was introduced in 1916. Some 124,000 men served – nearly half the eligible males – of whom 100,000 went overseas with the NZEF. Even the hats they wore were symbols of their home landscape (and prevailing climate): the 'lemon-squeezer' hat was modelled on the outline of Mount Taranaki, and allowed water to run off, as useful in Flanders as it was in New Zealand.

As with clubs, so with families: another famous rugby family was waved off to war. Billy Stead, the master tactician of the Originals tour, was Māori:

> The well-known Stead family of footballers in Southland will be well represented in the firing line shortly. N.L. Stead, a Southland representative, brother of W.J. Stead, the All Black, is the latest to enlist. A cousin of the once-famous New Zealand five-eighths is also about to join the reinforcements, while another member of the family is already at the front and reported wounded in the Dardanelles operations.[17]

The New Zealand Māori carried their traditions and heritage into the trenches: NZEF Captains Pirimi Tahiwi and Roger Dansey of the Ngāti Tūwharetoa tribe introduced the bloodcurdling *haka* '*Ka Mate*' to the Gallipoli trenches. Away from the front in Malta, Dansey and friends relaxed by vanquishing the British in trench-digging contests. Dansey was accustomed to bloody violence even before the war: he had been so badly spiked in the first game of the 1910 Māori tour to New South Wales – with All Black Māori Stead and George Sellars – that he did not play the rest of the series. The death at Chunuk Bair of Corporal Philip Manu Blake (another Māori Australian tourist in 1913) in the same action as Sergeant Albert 'Doolan' Downing (the first All Black to be killed), doubtless added edge to their *haka* performance. The 'cannibal war dance' struck terror into the Turks listening just yards away; if they had been foolish enough to watch, they would have been scared to death – or picked off by snipers. Just think of that when next inclined to dismiss the All Black *haka* as pantomime cabaret.

Downing, so passionate about rugby that he wore a tattoo of the Ranfurly Shield, played for the All Blacks thirty-one times, including five Tests. Early on 8 August, his A Company, Wellington Infantry, occupied a Turkish trench on the crest of Chunuk Bair and dug a supporting trench behind it. The Turks' dawn counter-attack saw the Wellingtons and British break and run but not, according to Lance Corporal Hill, before Downing had distinguished himself in a bloody bayonet charge. The crest was lost and fighting continued on the downward slopes. Men dug trenches behind the original support line as it filled with dead and wounded; they hurled back Turkish grenades and even threw stones. For twelve hours the Wellingtons, reinforced by the Auckland Mounted Rifles, fought off Turkish attacks. By nightfall Downing was dead: witnesses stated that he was 'blown to pieces'.

Chunuk Bair proved the last resting place of another All Black, Henry 'Norkey' Dewar, a machine-gun sergeant with the Wellington Mounted Rifles, who had played alongside Downing and George Sellars against the Wallabies in 1913. But it was another ridge, Belgian Messines, in June 1917, that was to claim four more men of the black shirt and silver fern among New Zealand's 3,660 casualties. On the opening day of an attack heralded by nineteen massive mines exploding along the ridge, the youngest, Private Jim Baird of the 'Unlucky Otagos', died of multiple shrapnel wounds, aged 23. On the same day George Sellars, a double try-scorer in America, was killed carrying a wounded comrade to safety. The next day was the last for Southland farmer Jim McNeece, another Otago private, who had packed down behind Downing in that last Sydney Test, as the first contingent of British soldiers crossed the Channel to face Germany. From Taranaki, the Wellingtons' Lance Corporal Reg Taylor, a try-scoring back-rower on his 1913 debut against Australia, survived only two more weeks.

By now the big offensives were numbered: it was time for Third Ypres. Another Māori All Black, Charles Rangiwawahia Sciascia, seventh son of an Italian lighthouse keeper and Māori mother, left New Zealand in 1914 as a private with the Main Force. He rose to the rank of sergeant, fighting for five months at Gallipoli before being sent to the Western Front, where he was awarded the Military Medal, the gallantry decoration for other ranks. His eldest brother, Corporal Jack Sciascia, who played alongside him in the red-and-black of the Māori[18] had been wounded and gassed at Messines in 1916. Just a few miles away, at La Basse Ville on the River Lys, on the last day of July 1917, the 25-year-old Charles went into action with his Wellington Regiment in the unseasonal but torrential summer rain that started that day and carried on like a New Zealand winter.

Four days earlier, 1st NZ Infantry Brigade had attacked the village, which had been heavily shelled by artillery. Under cover of a new barrage they secured the village, but the small garrison left in occupation was soon driven out by a strong counter-attack. A second attack was launched at 0350 hours on the closing day of the month: the concerted roar of artillery along the fifteen-mile front began the Third Battle of Ypres, with Passchendaele ridge as its first objective. Strong resistance in La Basse Ville was overcome, and this time counter-attacks were repulsed. Charles was reported missing, his body never found; five months after his death, a nephew he would never see, born on 23 December, was named Frank La Basse, after his uncle's last known resting place.

Charles was not the only rugby man to fall that day. It is no coincidence that Official Histories picked out sportsmen of all ranks and communities of the New Zealand population:

> La Basse Ville claimed many athletes. Never more would Gordon Kinvig, that sterling athlete, take his place on Wellington football or cricket fields. Here Wellington-West Coast Company lost Sergt. C. Sciascia, M.M., a well known Horowhenua Māori footballer, and a gallant soldier, while a few days later, that doyen of Māori footballers, Lieut. A.P. Kaipara (Pioneers), was killed in the same locality.[19]

'Kinny' Kinvig was a five-eighth and utility back for the Oriental Club and gained representative honours in both rugby and cricket for Wellington in the same year. Autini Kaipara played for Poverty Bay for seven years and captained two Ranfurly Shield challenges against Auckland as well as playing for North Island and the touring Māori in 1910 and 1913; the *Sydney Bulletin* called him 'as sharp as a needle and as slippery as an eel', and he was also nicknamed 'India Rubber Man' or the 'Wizard'. Decades after his death, he was revered as 'one of the greatest five-eighths New Zealand has produced'. Invalided home from Gallipoli, he spent a few months recuperating in Rotorua, then rejoined the 1st Māori and was posted to D Company (of course), New Zealand Pioneer Battalion. Whilst wiring posts in front of La Basse Ville on 3 August, he was killed by a shell fragment: like George Sellars at Messines, he was carrying a wounded man, his batman Te Tui, to safety. Sergeant C.W. Tepene,[20] another Māori, who toured the Americas in 1910 and would play again in Britain, was more fortunate in his bravery, winning the Military Medal 'for conspicuous gallantry and devotion to duty'. The citation for this rare 'lucky Otago' stated:

> On 29 September 1918, at Bon Avis Ridge [near Cambrai] he led his platoon with great dash and skill against the enemy machine

gun positions putting several of these out of action and capturing many prisoners. Later, when consolidating in an exposed position though himself wounded, he risked his life in rescuing a wounded comrade under heavy rifle fire and machine gun fire. He was an example of what a platoon commander should be and inspired everyone with whom he comes in contact.[21]

The fighting spirit of the New Zealand Division, and the bond with their distant land and family, was sustained in no small part by the game they loved at home. In 1917 Lieutenant Colonel Arthur Plugge was appointed as divisional sports coordinator. Like the Australians, NZ units played each other at rugby whenever there was a lull in the fighting, and strings were pulled to get the best players. Māori Tom French – the first player sent off at Eden Park, for fighting an opponent who fancied his girlfriend – was transferred from his Māori battalion to the 1st Auckland, allegedly through the influence of Gallaher, who had coached him at home and wanted him in his trench teams. Extra spice was added by 'international' challenges, although they were sometimes less than evenly matched. Australian Tom Richards, watching a game at Laventie, south of Ypres, pitied the frail Welshmen facing the magnificent Māori:

> The Maoris were in the field waiting quite a long time for the Welshmen. While they were waiting the Colonials looked physical giants compared to the lean and wiry Welsh. There were other features in the appearance of the two teams that bothered me quite a while – the great self-possession and confidence of the Maoris, also their straight built bodies and big limbs; while their opponents seemed stage frightened and their awkwardly put together forms bent with hard work and cramped by confinement at the workshop benches.[22]

The NZ Division even met a French military XV in a wartime 'Test', played for a '*Coupe de Somme*' in 1917. The 40–0 rout was the more embarrassing for the French as it was supposedly witnessed by a crowd of 60,000.[23] But, relishing the opportunity to pit themselves against senior rugby nations, the French took heart in an improved performance the following April, played in a carnival atmosphere after America's entry into the war. At the Olympic velodrome, Bois de Vincennes, the close margin of defeat 3–5 was no dishonour. Bordeaux forward Jean-Jacques Conilh de Beyssac, briefly of Rosslyn Park while studying philosophy in London, and capped five times for France before the deluge, played both matches. As a tank commander he would die two months later when his Schneider, nicknamed 'Ace of Spades' – the death card – took three direct hits; the wounded lieutenant died in an ambulance on the way to hospital at Compiègne, a name of echoing significance in November.

Taranaki sapper Charlie Brown was one of a handful to play for the All Blacks either side of the war and was even invited, as a *pakeha*,[24] to represent the Māori against Australia in a 1913 benefit. He played both French games for the NZ Division side and was scrum half in the NZ Services side which played in Britain and South Africa in 1919. War over, he picked up the oval where he had left off, resuming his All Black career in 1920. Flanker Sergeant Arthur Wilson, another pre-war All Black, also played at Vincennes; although an exceptional player, his unexceptional name did not stand out in this game, but that would change a year later.

Such was the English appetite to see the men in black that in early 1917, it was announced in London papers that 'the authorities have permitted a number of New Zealanders to leave the front and play a brief series of games in this country for the benefit of the Red Cross'.[25] *The Times* reported that ticket applications were already being taken.[26] But with the annual spring offensive in mind, the generals were loath to lose crack colonial fighting troops and the tour was quietly cancelled. Men returning to England for rehab or unable to fight again did play, however. A team selected from troops convalescing at Hornchurch hospital played sixteen matches in 1916 and lost only two.

Some had only temporary respite, before returning to France. One damaged officer, Lieutenant Harvey Chrystall of the Royal Naval Division, mentioned in despatches at Gallipoli, was glad of the opportunity to play rugby again: 'I shall very much miss the pleasant Saturday afternoon recreation; the games have got me thoroughly fit in wind and limb, after being a physical wreck through shell-shock and given up by the doctors.'[27] These players were not always well-equipped: it was hard enough to get uniforms that fitted, let alone sports kit, and most rugby at the front was played in what they stood up in. Journalists watched 'teams of convalescents . . . some of them playing without boots', but the contests were immensely popular, attracting crowds of seven or eight thousand.

The magnetism of the New Zealand reputation made their military teams the biggest wartime draw, with all manner of units providing sides for charity and services games. In October 1918 at Torquay, the small print in the 'BARBARIANS v NEW ZEALAND' programme reveals this is 'Devonport Barbarians' against the 'NZ Discharge Depot'. The seven in the pack were listed en bloc but that enduring curiosity, the 'wing-forward', Rifleman Curtis, got special billing. Two parallel rugby squads were maintained either side of the Channel: a 'United Kingdom' HQ XV in England and the Divisional Trench Team in France; they would later unite to become the NZ Services team. Another side of Māori Pioneers, including Parekura Tureia of Ngāti Porou, defeated the crack Welsh Guards team and the Royal Naval Division; Tureia was included in the Services side in 1919 but would later find himself shamefully excluded from that team on the way home.

New Zealanders left many indelible marks of their time in Britain. One you can still see – if you can access Bulford Camp – is a kiwi bird carved by soldiers into the chalk hillside at what used to be Sling Plantation, one of many colonial camps on Salisbury Plain. But the most profound mark is not visible: it is etched since 1905 into the collective psyche of rugby players and supporters around Britain by that first Originals tour. Whenever the All Blacks come back to these shores, they bring that same sharp-edged ruthlessness and a century-old tremor of excitement. They rarely leave empty-handed.

In 1919 their soldiers left as battlefield victors. More than any team, the All Blacks are acutely conscious of their heritage and the weight of expectation from an entire nation. In 2015, the descendants of those 1905 founding fathers of New Zealand's national identity return as reigning world champions, seemingly invincible and certainly intimidating. And everyone will want to beat them.

Canada

Our home and native land
True patriot love in all thy sons command.

Canada is more than a vast country: the 'Great White North' is the frosted crown of a whole continent. Its land mass measures 9,093,507 square kilometres and there's an extra 10 per cent or more of permanent ice. The land alone would hold over a billion rugby pitches, although not all of them would take a stud too well and a few trees might need to be cleared. In 1914 that would have meant 135 pitches for each of some 8 million Canadians.[1] The two factors of unforgiving climate and almost inconceivable size help explain the early development of rugby in Canada. A first game was played by artillerymen in Montreal in 1864. A Canadian Rugby Football Union (CRFU) was founded in 1884, but a national team was a financial and geographical impossibility: only the following year was the Canadian Pacific transcontinental railway completed.

A confusion of Unions did not help. The first North American cross-border game was played in 1874 between Montreal's McGill and Boston's Harvard University.[2] Ontario and Quebec formed their own Rugby Unions on the same January day in 1883, possibly stung into action by the founding twelve days previously of the Ontario Football Union, precursor to the gridiron Canadian Football League (CFL). The Canadian Interprovincial Rugby Football Union was formed in 1907 by the 'big four' of Hamilton Tigers, Toronto Argonauts, Ottawa Rough Riders and Montreal Foot-Ball; in its first game, Montreal defeated Toronto. But these eastern province club names betrayed the influence of the American football code that, with so many other cultural influences from the noisy neighbours to the south, crept irresistibly over the world's longest international frontier.

In the vast expanses of the western and central provinces, even where a club took root, fixtures were hard to come by: Calgary City RFC, founded in March 1906, only played their first game nineteen months later in October 1907, defeating Strathcona RFC 15–0 at Calgary. The taste for victory took them to Edmonton and its Exhibition Grounds in November to defeat Edmonton RFC 26–5 in their first game. Manitoba, Saskatchewan & Alberta Unions jointly formed the Western Canada RFU in 1911. A new Rugby Union of Canada was later formed in 1929 and the CRFU finally went over to the dark side in 1931 when it permitted the forward pass. The Grey Cup, originally donated in 1909 by Governor-General Earl Grey for the 'Canadian Dominion Rugby Football Champions', is now the modern CFL Championship title game and trophy. Rugby players rarely get excited about a Cup of Earl Grey.

Resistance to gridiron encroachment continued until wartime: in 1913, Londoner Cecil Crossley 'was instrumental in introducing and organising Rugby rules for the University football matches' at McGill, as well as being Canadian middleweight boxing champion. With the Royal Irish Fusiliers at Gallipoli in 1915, he would take a fatal punch from a Turkish grenade, the impact described by the plain-spoken Lance Corporal Hardman: 'His head was nearly destroyed by a bomb and death was immediate.'

As its name indicates, British Columbia's strong links to the Mother Country, *fons et origo* of the game, ensured that rugby thrived in this provincial pocket of strength. From the 1870s, local men played Royal Navy sailors stationed at Esquimalt; clubs formed at Vancouver, Chemainus, Comox, Nanaimo, New Westminster, Cowichan and Victoria, mingling the British and the 'Columbian', provided regular opposition for each other. The BC Rugby Union formed in 1889 'to unite in one organization all lovers and players of Rugby Football in British Columbia'. Its teams competed for the McKechnie Cup from 1895 and BC remains a stronghold of rugby in Canada to this day, but rugby's reliance on immigrant British players meant that clubs would suffer heavy losses when the time came to fight.

Canada's eastern provinces are closer to Britain than they are to BC. A pioneering but ramshackle tour of Britain in the winter of 1902–03, funded by private interests in Montreal, included only five BC players. The team played on Christmas Day, lost thirteen of twenty-four matches, but claimed notable scalps at Bristol and Ulster. BC instead looked westwards and south for its rugby challenges: as early as 1894, BC played rugby at the Midwinter Fair in San Francisco. Exchanges between Victoria, Vancouver and the two Californian universities at Stanford and Berkeley took place annually from 1906 for the Cooper Keith Trophy. British Columbia as a province welcomed international teams: the Anglo-Welsh in 1908 and Australia in 1909 and 1912.[3] The

New Zealand All Blacks on their 1906 North America visit twice played a 'sturdy aggregation from Vancouver'[4] (actually a BC Province team) in San Francisco, and in 1913 All Black tourists played a representative side at Brockton Oval, Vancouver.

As with Aviron Bayonnais in France, rugby was the winter game of oarsmen at Vancouver Rowing Club (VRC). Dating back to 1886, the year of Vancouver's incorporation as a city hewn out of frontier forest with just 1,000 citizens, VRC is its oldest sports club. In 1908, Reggie Woodward encouraged VRC rowers playing rugby at other clubs to form their own XV: dual participation lasted until the 1950s. For 'wet-bobs' with a floating clubhouse, their initial steps on dry land were shaky: over the two seasons 1908 and 1909, they lost all but one game in the City Senior League. But a triumphant 1910 saw 'Rowers' win all ten games and the city's Miller Cup, with 186 points scored and just 5 conceded. The secret, said skipper Theo Byrne, was 'relentless training. A good man who refused to train was dropped for a less skilful player who was keen.' He added, in memory of his Edinburgh school, 'as for the slow lobbing pass, anyone guilty of committing this sin was given one hundred lines of Greek verse' – a penalty sadly under-employed today.

By the outbreak of war, Vancouver's population had grown to over 130,000 and supported two Militia infantry regiments, the Seaforth High-landers and the Duke of Connaught's. Ninety of the 115 VRC members eligible for military service volunteered immediately. Their last summer regatta was a subdued affair: 'very few left at the Club, all gone to the front'. Another forty-nine, under-age in 1914, would enlist, making a total of 164 volunteers from an active membership of 200.[5] Sporting activity ground to a halt, as it did at clubs worldwide; rugby was discontinued and the Vancouver Rugby Union did not reform until 1919. At the 1917 AGM, life members were asked to donate $5 or more towards the club's upkeep, 'owing to the fact so many members were on active service and to the difficulty of getting new ones while the war lasts'. All soldiers were 'kept on the membership roll during their period of service', but by 1918 the active roster numbered only thirty-five, not one of whom was a single man fit for service; forty-two never returned.

The Seaforth Highlanders went to war as the 72nd Battalion, 7th British Columbia Regiment, Canadian Expeditionary Force (CEF). The regiment was raised in 1910 by Scots-born local magnate, Henry Bell-Irving. His six sons, all 'splendid specimens of manhood', were all sent away to Loretto for schooling and to Europe for fighting (with two sisters for nursing). Malcolm, who had faced the All Blacks, was the first native-born Canadian to join the RFC in December 1914. He arrived in St-Omer in March 1915 to make his first operational flight; wounded twice flying sorties over enemy territory, he was awarded the MC.

On 20 June 1916, while flying a Morane scout plane between Lille and Ypres with an observer named Scott, Bell-Irving was attacked by three German aircraft. He shot one down in flames – the first Canadian RFC 'kill' – and drove off the others. He evaded three more attackers but was severely wounded in the head by 'Archie' – anti-aircraft fire. Half-blinded by blood, he turned for the nearest airfield, but feeling he could not last, landed behind Allied lines to save Scott's life. After giving orders for the safe delivery of his photos, he collapsed. His exploits won him the DSO – another first for Canada in the RFC. He was transferred to Lady Ridley's Hospital in London, – sister Isabel was nursing there – and remained semi-conscious for three months. He had been wounded three times and ended the war with the rank of major.

Sibling rivalry reached new heights with the Bell-Irving boys: four brothers collected nine bravery decorations between them. Duncan, also in the RFC added an MC and Bar to his seven kills, was twice wounded and thrice shot down; the French threw in a Croix de Guerre for good measure. Henry earned the DSC with the Dover Patrol for shooting down two German seaplanes. Roderick's DSO was posthumous: he was commanding the 16th Battalion, CEF (Canadian Scottish), when he was killed near Cambrai on 1 October 1918, six weeks short of the Armistice.[6]

When Britain declared war on Germany in August 1914, Canada also found itself at war as part of the Empire. Yet its army numbered only 3,000 regulars and 74,000 part-time militiamen. This tiny peacetime force grew tenfold almost overnight: in September, 32,665 volunteers arrived by special trains at the new camp at Valcartier, the assembly point for the CEF, north of Quebec City on the St Lawrence. By the Armistice, 619,636 Canadians, including over 3,000 nurses, would be in uniform – a huge proportion of the country's population.

Built in just two weeks, the purpose-built Valcartier, with the world's largest firing range of 15,000 targets, was a soft launch into the nasty business of war. Latter-day Toronto has been described as 'New York run by the Swiss' but Valcartier could have run it close:

> . . . electrically lighted, with purified water and baths for every
> unit, with broad roads and board walks, with post-office and
> hospitals, a network of telephones, a bank and YMCA tent, with

canteens for soft drinks, goodies and smokes. The camp was scrupulously clean: metal incinerators like burning-ghats lined the streets; left-over food was hourly consumed while nightly carts removed all refuse. On either side the main road, ditches carried away the dirty water.[7]

These early days were documented in September 1915 by the Canadian Field Comforts Commission, after the contingent had seen action, gas and death at Ypres. It aimed to 'raise funds for the purchase of many extra comforts, which are welcomed by the officers and appreciated by the men'. Creature comforts at Valcartier featured a menagerie of pets, some not purchased but 'requisitioned' on the journey east:

> Plenty of mascots: a cinnamon bear from the west, a cross little black one from New Brunswick, a calf kidnapped near Winnipeg when a troop train stopped for water, a monkey for the artillery and dogs beyond mentioning . . . two doves of the Royal Canadian Engineers, bill by nose with the horses, they used to eat their oats – poor little emblems of vanished Peace.

The volunteers described as 'only the fittest, the Dominion's finest and best' also brought with them their sporting enthusiasms: 'In spite of the constant drilling, riding, marching and practising with rifles and artillery, the men were still keen for football.'

Nearly 70 per cent of this first volunteer contingent was made up of young men born in the British Isles. Many British immigrants had come searching for riches (or simple subsistence) in minerals, engineering or ranching. 1914 Canada was in the grip of economic depression: unemployment had risen since 1912, credit was squeezed, and farmers had abandoned their land to look for work in the cities. Disappointed, many returned to fight with British regiments or joined this First Canadian Contingent. As with the working-class 'Pals' in Britain, the martial imperative was as much basic survival as patriotism: they needed to eat and the daily rations were good. But for the Canadian press they were,

> Our own giving heed to the Motherland's call,
> Our own steeled to face whate'er may befall!

After the Elysium of Valcartier, they 'sailed away on thirty-one great grey transports guarded by seven cruisers, down the big river so many would never see again'. General Sir Sam Hughes, Minister of Militia and Defence, bade them farewell in an address of which

Churchill (or Maximus Decimus Meridius for that matter) would
be proud:

> What reck you whether your resting place be decked with the
> golden lilies of France, or be amidst the vine-clad hills of the
> Rhine; the principles for which you fought are eternal.

His optimism that the war might reach German soil is, with hindsight,
bittersweet; the inadvertent pessimism of his past tense 'fought'
is inescapable.

On arrival in October, the Canadians' first taste of Western Front
conditions, even before reaching 'somewhere in France', came on
Salisbury Plain. Spread over its 300 square and bleak kilometres in camps
at Bustard, Larkhill and Sling Plantation, they endured the 'rainiest,
most flooded winter England has known in years'. It rained on 89 of
the 123 days they were there, making them oddly nostalgic for the icy
Canadian climate: 'in the heart-sickening, never-ending fall of rain, how
preferable would have been ground-hardening frost and good deep snow,
to keep out the cold'. Reports reached the home press:

> Salisbury today bears a slight resemblance to Venice. The two
> main streets are streams, and rowboats have been put into use by
> enterprising citizens who charge 'thruppence' for a ride chiefly
> from Canadians, who don't mind paying for a novel experience.
> The fact that the city is flooded in such a way gives one an idea
> of what the officers and men must endure on the Plain . . . it
> amounts to active service conditions without the 'excitement.'
> A wounded soldier who fought for several weeks in France said
> that the living conditions were worse here than at the front. In
> Belgium or France a soldier fought an enemy he could in most
> cases see, but here it was the unseen enemy – sickness – which
> must be encountered. No man will be satisfied until he goes to
> France. The constant waiting under such conditions has caused
> considerable discontent. Having had about five months of
> training, the men think it is quite enough.[8]

They were nonetheless fascinated by ancient Stonehenge, where they held
church parade and speculated that the fallen cross-slabs provided 'a place
for the druids to sit and keep their feet out of the mud'. An anonymous
soldier-poet complained of the effect on Sam Hughes's boots:

Our soldiers like to stroll
In the mud,
And the horses love to roll
In the mud;
Our good Canadian shoe
It goes quickly through and through
Peels the sole and melts the glue –
In the mud.[9]

Battle-hardened and decorated for bravery by late 1915, one officer still grumbled, 'We think there should be a special clasp for Salisbury Plain.' Another wrote with feeling: 'Things over here are not pretty wet, they are most blighted soaking.' It was a far cry from Valcartier. The doggerel poetess of the *Daily Mail*, Jessie Pope (to whom Wilfred Owen sarcastically dedicated his first draft of 'Dulce et Decorum Est') wrote a tribute to the 'Lads of the Maple Leaf':

Ripe for any adventure, sturdy, loyal and game
Quick to the call of the Mother, the young Canadians came
Eager to show their mettle, ready to shed their blood
They bowed their neck to the collar and trained in Wiltshire mud.

Even King George, who inspected the Contingent on 4 February, sent an apologetic 'gracious message to be read to all units on board ship after embarkation for France':

I am well aware of the discomforts that you have experienced from the inclement weather and abnormal rain. I am confident that you will emulate the example of your fellow-countrymen in the South African War and thus help to secure the triumph of our arms.

The cannier of the 'sturdy, loyal and game' realised that exhibitions of rugby to assist recruitment might release them from the sodden Plain. When the First Canadian Contingent challenged Sid Smart and his 5th Gloucestershire Regiment to a game, Colonel Collett of the Gloucesters secured the prestigious Queen's Club ground. The Canadians were the first colonial troops to arrive in Britain (the ANZACs being delayed by the small matter of Gallipoli) and curiosity made them a major attraction around the sports fields of Britain, even if their rugby prowess was in its adolescence. On 12 December, 'In spite of depressing weather [again] and a somewhat one-sided game, for the Canadians had no opportunities of playing together, it was an exhilarating afternoon . . . there was some really fine football and the atmosphere, as of a rollicking military festival, permeated the crowd.'[10]

Discipline was good. Civil offences committed by the troops were few; more than half of military offences were for absence without leave, which usually meant overstaying a pass, a crime classified as minor, 'for determination was needed to forsake the bright lights of London or the kindly warmth of home and friends, when the alternative was a tent on a wind-swept waste where darkness lasted fourteen hours a day and all was wetness, mud, and misery'.[11] Inevitably, not every red-blooded Canadian soldier used his London leisure time profitably. Two from the Royal Montreal Regiment, incarcerated at Christmas in the Tower of London for disorderly conduct, broke their window bars, escaped and returned to camp. These first escapes in a century from the Tower were saluted by the newspapers: 'Stone Walls do not a Prison make for Canadians'.

At Richmond, the contingent next played the Public Schools & Universities (UPS) Brigade, to benefit two Belgian charities. Recruiters were present, adorned with badges of red, white and blue, 'ready to enrol any that offered themselves' for the Regular or Territorial Armies, or the grandly titled 'Central Association Volunteer Training Corps for Home Defence (Veteran Athletes Battalion)'. The programme warned that 'men of enlistable age will not be accepted for this Battalion, unless they can show good and sufficient cause'. The Canadians took the field in light blue and brown. Support was one-sided: 'in the matter of noise the Englishmen had certainly an unfair advantage, for those who might have been shouting for the Canadians were on Salisbury Plain'.

> The ring seats along the touchlines presented the appearance of being almost solidly military – rows of khaki caps and of khaki figures leaning forward with hands on knees, rows of canes waving in time to the tunes or war cries that rose and fell. There was one splendidly fierce hoarse voice that rang out every now and then with 'Come on Canada', and was unquenchable.[12]

The UPS team featured former Wales winger Hopkin Maddock,[13] whose 170 tries for London Welsh still stand as a club record, and G.G. Ziegler of Cambridge, Barbarians and Richmond. The game was 'very fast and very hard fought-out in the friendliest spirit' and the home side ran out narrow victors 13–11. On New Year's Day 1915, a crowd of 20,000 watched the Canadians at Leicester's Welford Road.

Five days later the first troops from Canada went into the front line, although they were the least 'Canadian': Princess Patricia's Canadian Light Infantry, or the 'Pats' – named for the glamorous daughter of the Duke of Connaught, the king's uncle and Canada's Governor-General – were mainly British-born, often Boer War veterans, but also included students. Montreal industrialist Hamilton Gault put up $100,000 to raise the 'Pats' privately, but insisted he fight with the regiment his money had bought. They were led by British officers and their CO was an ex-Guards colonel called Farquhar (probably not to his face). They kept their distance from Hughes's CEF, refused to train at Valcartier, sailed earlier and were integrated with the British 27th Division. Not until Christmas 1915 did they join the 3rd Canadian Division.

The Pats earned battle honours at Frezenberg, Mount Sorrel, Vimy and Passchendaele and, through losses and replacements, became more Canadian – if not completely so. Hugh Huckett, a British missionary's son born in Madagascar and games master at St George's, Harpenden, had moved to Canada in 1912, swapping a rugby ball for the American pigskin. He joined the Pats from his university company to replace the gas casualties of Ypres. He was wounded at Mount Sorrel, his right hand 'terribly lacerated by gun shot during an attack which his regiment was ordered to hold at all costs', and was 'Struck off Strength' (SOS) nine days later. This ended his rugby career, but meant he survived the war and lived to be 99. Both his less fortunate brothers were killed: Arnold[14] at Gallipoli and Oliver at the second Battle of the Somme in 1918. Inspecting her regiment in London in February 1919, Princess Patricia saw only forty-four 'Originals' from the thousand militiamen she had first reviewed in 1914 when presenting their Colours in Ottawa. One was Gault, his leg amputated and left behind at Mount Sorrel in June 1916.

The time came for the CEF to join the fight; they marched to Amesbury in February to entrain for Bristol and the crossing to St-Nazaire. As proof that they had absorbed both Britain's moisture and its sardonic sense of humour, they sang: 'Are we downhearted? NO. Are we wet? YES.' An officer observed: 'The men are so light-hearted and cheerful – full of life and ginger. Somebody is going to be badly hurt when these boys are let loose.' These boys first saw action at Neuve-Chapelle in March, but were unable to let loose as their Canadian Ross rifles jammed as easily as Sam Hughes's shoddy boots fell apart. Many seized the more effective Lee-Enfields from dead British troops.

On 22 April 1915, the Germans used chlorine gas at Ypres for the first time in the history of warfare. It was a terrible baptism for the Canadians, who were targeted where their line joined the French Algerians – the Germans considered both as 'unreliable colonials'. It was, wrote an officer,

> a low-down trick, most extraordinary stuff, a sort of bluish-green mist was blown over the trenches; it felt cold to breathe, and one felt it in one's lungs and began to cough and gasp for breath. It knocked the men out like ninepins and several have died of it.[15]

One was Private Owen Sawers, aged 31, a Miller Cup winner with 'Rowers', ever present with brother Norman in team photographs from 1908 to 1914, and old enough to have played the All Blacks in 1906. An insurance agent, he had volunteered exactly seven months before, joining the 10th Battalion. After the Algerians fled the choking gas, the 10th's counter-attack at Langemarck stopped the enemy advance but at terrible cost. Owen was never found; his name is commemorated on the Menin Gate. Both his brothers were wounded but survived; inaugural club skipper Captain Norman Sawers, MC, returned to coach rugby at VRC.

The Canadians suffered 5,975 casualties at Ypres, 3,058 on 24 April alone; in forty-eight hours, one in three was lost from Canada's small force. It was a grim introduction to mechanised and chemical slaughter. Another Canadian, Field Artillery Major John McCrae, a field doctor and Scots Presbyterian from Ontario in his second war, wrote from Ypres to his mother after 'seventeen days of Hades' spent in his aid post dug into the bank of the Yser Canal:

> The general impression in my mind is of a nightmare. We have been in the most bitter of fights. For seventeen days and seventeen nights none of us have had our clothes off, nor our boots even, except occasionally. In all that time while I was awake, gunfire and rifle fire never ceased for sixty seconds. And behind it all was the constant background of the sights of the dead, the wounded, the maimed, and a terrible anxiety lest the line should give way.[16]

His poem, written the day after he had read the funeral service of a close friend, Lieutenant Alexis Helmer, buried in a makeshift grave with a simple wooden cross,[17] gave the dead a voice:

We are the Dead. Short days ago
We lived, felt dawn, saw sunset glow,
Loved, and were loved, and now we lie
In Flanders Fields.

Spring poppies were blooming in the disturbed earth. The poem that began 'In Flanders Fields, the poppies grow / Between the crosses row on row' was published in *Punch* in December and widely reprinted. Not only was it popular in the trenches, but it was used to advertise the sale of the first Victory Loan Bonds in Canada in 1917; the campaign 'to take up our quarrel with the foe' raised $400 million, almost three times its target. It was influential too in the United States, where a 'response' by R.W. Lillard ('Fear not that you have died for naught / The torch ye threw to us we caught') added heft to arguments in favour of joining the war. A disillusioned McCrae would not survive, dying of pneumonia brought on by exhaustion in January 1918. More enduringly the poppy remains today a vivid and abiding symbol of Remembrance.

It was at Ypres that the Canadians' reputation as a formidable fighting force was forged. An officer wrote home on the day after the gas attack, as the desperate attempt to stabilise the line continued. His letter reminds us that this was indeed a first global war, with Canada now performing with distinction on a world stage:

There were English, Canadians, Algerians, French, Senegalese, Arabs, Belgians and Indian troops . . . The sun has risen on many a dead Canadian this morning. It is very unlikely that braver troops can be found; they have behaved splendidly. Canada can expect a startler on the casualties, but she can be sure she has good fighting material.[18]

Historian (and rugby fanatic) Basil Liddell Hart, himself wounded and gassed at the Somme, would later call them 'matchless attacking troops'.

Allied offensives followed at Festubert and Givenchy: frontal assaults against enemy positions defended by machine guns. The Canadians achieved their objectives, but gains were negligible, and the cost in lives extremely high. One life lost was that of Ralph Farrar Markham, originally from New Brunswick on Canada's Atlantic coast and an advertising agent whose father was a noted newspaperman. A military college graduate and Boer War cavalry veteran, he made a fresh start in Vancouver in 1910, joining the rugby club, and was a Miller Cup-winning forward. He volunteered with the Seaforths, but was made a signals captain in the Manitoba Regiment; he was killed at Ypres in August 1915 at the age of 38.

Despite the losses, patriotic enthusiasm prevailed at home and a Second Canadian Contingent sailed for Europe in the spring of 1915. By the end of the year, the 2nd Canadian Division and some units of the 3rd had reached the front to form a Canadian Corps of 38,000, kept together to build morale and unity, rather than scattered amongst British units. 1916 saw more local offensives in the southern Ypres Salient. In their first engagement, the 2nd Division suffered 1,373 casualties in twelve days of confused attacks and counter-attacks on a battlefield of water-filled craters and shell-holes at St-Eloi.

Amongst the rugby 'Rowers' to die here was Scottish internationalist forward Andrew Ross. Originally from Edinburgh, and educated at its Royal High School, he played his first Inter-City match in 1899 (helping to break a ten-year Glasgow winning streak). His second in 1904 led to his Scotland debut against Wales in 1905; he won four more caps. Against England that year, he played on with one rib broken and two cracked. The Scots' 8–0 victory sent the English home from Richmond 'tae think again' before Ross caught the night mail train of pain to Edinburgh, arriving home white-faced and in agony. An adventurous seafaring career had already sent him to sea at 16, sailing to Iquique and Tokyo; he nearly died of yellow fever in Rio, and played the bagpipes to an awed assembly of sugar plantation workers in Cuba. His move to Vancouver in 1909 had much to do with VRC's Miller Cup success the following season. In November 1914 he had rushed south from his work in the Arctic Circle to start military training, joining the 29th (Vancouver) Battalion, known as 'Tobin's Tigers'. He noted:

> Most of the men are splendid shots . . . the work in camp is hard, but we all like it, as we have to get into good condition for the British Army. A man feels that it's worth giving up his life to save millions of homes, such as ours, from the fate of poor old Belgium. We don't want to stay too long in England drilling, so it is with a jolly good will we go into our drills here.[19]

At 34, his ardent enthusiasm was hardly youthful, and his ideals were widely shared.

In England, he represented his new country of Canada in the regimental sports at Stamford Bridge in August 1915, before sailing for

France. Barely a year after enlisting, his appetite for the fight sharpened, he wrote gleefully from Ypres to team-mate Nelles Stacey:

> We lit a fire in the trench and put plenty wet wood on it. That made a big smoke. Then two men made all the row they could, shouting at each other and hitting an empty biscuit tin with sticks. Fritz easily located the row by the column of smoke, and all the Fritzes within hearing peeped round their sandbags to have a look . . . it was the last look for most of them.[20]

Sewell refrains from quoting another letter describing Ross's first bayonet charge, presumably in bloodthirsty detail. He was first wounded, then killed, aged 36, on 6 April 1916, while bandaging a wounded comrade under heavy artillery fire. 'Quite reckless as regarding his own life, he exposed it and gave it to save, as his quick attention undoubtedly did, the lives of a great number of our men.' His Miller Cup rugby cap is still displayed in the clubhouse at Stanley Park, Vancouver.

His Edinburgh classmate, Theo 'TED' Byrne, skipper of the all-conquering 1910 'Rowers', wrote from Salonika, where he was a lieutenant with 5th Royal Irish Rifles, having picked up some useful Irish phrases from the 'Fighting Fifth':

> Every time that I hear of further prowess of some VRC man the more proud (if possible) I become, when I remember I once had the honour to captain the championship team. How often have I tried to imagine that forward line with me in a go and the backs coming up like lightning in extended order ready to pass the bayonet through some *****. I want you to prepare a list of that football team . . . the unit to which the man belongs and any honours. Then I'll bet no football fifteen in the world can equal it.[21]

As for his own situation, after sixteen months' continual service at Gallipoli and in Macedonia, with 'only a few left of the original corps, only three officers now surviving', he shrugged off a recent commendation for a medal as 'what any one of our Vancouver chaps would have done'. But there was clearly more to it, and the street-fighter spoke with understated relish of close-quarter combat:

> The climate is hellish and as these Bulgars rather fancy themselves with the knife we are endeavouring to show them there are competitors at the game, and this makes a very untidy state of

> affairs after each engagement. So far my clothes are the only
> spoiled portion of me.[22]

In late August 1916, the Canadian divisions moved to the Somme front line facing Courcelette; on 15 September, they assaulted and captured the village. In the weeks that followed, repeated attacks gained only a few hundred metres over shell-pocked, corpse-strewn land. The Somme slaughter weighed heavily: the Allies suffered more than 620,000 casualties, 24,029 of whom were Canadian. More than 235,000 German soldiers were killed in what they called *Das Blutbat*. Canadian official historian Colonel Nicholson adjudged: 'we cannot close our eyes to the horror of the mass butchery'.

Four Canadians won the Victoria Cross on the Somme. Piper James Cleland Richardson of the 16th Battalion, another Vancouver Scot, earned a posthumous VC for piping his comrades 'over the top' at Regina Trench. His company, struggling through barbed wire, took heavy casualties; under intense fire, the 20-year-old strode about, playing his bagpipes, urging them on. The objective was taken. Having left his pipes behind, Richardson went back to find them and was not seen again. An army chaplain found the pipes in 1917, and took them back to Ardvreck School in Scotland. They stayed there for seventy years – a broken, muddied and bloodied remnant of an unidentified piper from the Great War – until a chance discovery saw them returned to British Columbia in 2006.

The Canadians had come to be valued as crack offensive troops. Their apotheosis was at Vimy Ridge in April 1917: superb planning and preparation, executed with bravery and flair by four divisions united for the first time in a Canadian Corps, supported by British infantry, engineers and artillery, achieved a victory with casualty levels far below the norm for this war of attrition. Intended as one element of the British Arras diversion for French General Nivelle's spring offensive (which failed), it was the only success of 1917 and quickly became a symbol of national unity and achievement for Canada.

From the west, open ground slopes gradually up to the Vimy escarpment that overlooks, then drops suddenly to the Douai plain, with its coal mines and industries then pressed into German service. Three defensive lines faced the Canadians, fortified since 1914 with a maze of trenches, concreted machine-gun emplacements hedged by barbed wire, and an underground network of deep dugouts and tunnels. Some vast chambers could shelter an entire battalion from Allied bombardment.

Canadian commanders had learned cruel lessons from past frontal assaults. They took time to train their troops, down to the smallest unit and individual soldier. Aerial reconnaissance identified German gun positions, as did new sound-ranging and flash-spotting techniques. Five kilometres of deep tunnels were dug through soft but stable chalk; troops and supplies could move safely to jumping-off points, wounded could be brought back under cover. Telephone cables were laid two metres deep to avoid shells cutting communications. To the rear, a full-scale replica of the battlefield enabled repeated rehearsals. Lieutenant General Julian Byng had picked up the pieces of the Gallipoli fiasco and now deployed his theatre learning; maps were issued to all units, and troops were fully briefed on their objectives and routes.

Continual trench raids in March gained vital knowledge but cost 1,400 casualties. The fittest and most aggressive were hand-picked for these raids and naturally included rugby men; Major Russel Johnston of the Seaforths, a 'Rower' from the outset in 1908, led one of the first raids and was killed, aged 33. Only two days later, VRC suffered another loss: 12978 Lance Corporal Thomas Percy Woodward, son of club founder Reggie, and a bank clerk who had enlisted at 20 with the same local regiment in September 1915. He had already seen action on the Somme and was killed raiding on 3 March. Tommy, 21, was posthumously awarded the Military Medal for his actions during the raid.[23]

After almost three weeks of artillery bombardment, a million shells passing overhead 'like water from a hose', at 0530 hours on Easter Monday 9 April,[24] the barrage crept towards the Germans – as did driving sleet and snow – shielding 20,000 Canadians of the first wave. Three of the four divisions captured their part of the Ridge by midday, bang on schedule. The 4th Division battled on to take Hill 145, the highest feature of the whole ridge, on the afternoon of 10 April. Two days later the enemy pulled back and by nightfall on 12 April Vimy Ridge was in Allied, mainly Canadian, hands. Four more Victoria Crosses were awarded. The Vimy action captured more ground, more prisoners and more guns than any previous offensive. Victory was swift and the cost of 3,598 dead out of 10,602 Canadian casualties relatively merciful; earlier struggles at Vimy from 1914 onwards had brought over 200,000 Allied casualties.

At home, the victory at Vimy, won by citizen-soldiers from every corner of the vast country, united Canadians in pride. Vancouver headlines lauded the 'GLORIOUS PART PLAYED BY THE MEN FROM DOMINION: Famous Vimy Ridge the Scene of Many Gory Battles Was Stormed and

Carried by Warriors from Canada'.[25] And now those warriors were led by one of their own: General Arthur Currie, a former real-estate agent from Victoria, BC, took command of the corps. This military coming-of-age inspired a new spirit of nationhood.

Four years of war would transform Canada from a colony into a nation, at a cost of nearly a quarter of a million casualties, one in four of them fatal. Canada's war record earned it a separate signature on the Versailles Peace Treaty and a seat at the League of Nations. For its fighting rugby players, 'combat without casualties' awaited them on hallowed English turf at Twickenham. As a salutary reminder of the sacrifice of so many sons, the Canadian government maintains the most moving memorials on the Western Front, staffed by young volunteers at the Newfoundland Memorial Park at Beaumont-Hamel on the Somme and at Vimy Ridge. Walter Allward's grieving monument was dedicated in 1936 by Edward VIII, practically his only official act, apart from the small matter of abdicating.

As Gallipoli is to Australia and New Zealand, and Delville Wood is to South Africa, Vimy Ridge has become the symbol of Canada in the Great War. This is as much due to the memorial as the battle itself. Canadians continued to lead as Allied shock troops at Passchendaele, Amiens and the Canal du Nord. They entered Mons on the last day of war, and a Canadian soldier from Saskatchewan was the last to die before the Armistice hour.

Today, Canadians prefer a military role as peacekeepers, standing between combatants to preserve peace. But the lofty ridge, soaring white pylons and solemn anniversary commemorations have seared Vimy Ridge into Canada's consciousness.

South Africa

Let us live and strive for freedom
In South Africa our land.

South Africans in their thousands fought and died in the war. In contrast to its sister dominions, however, South Africa's contribution as a nation was more diffused throughout the vast geography of the war and the infinite host of the Imperial forces. Over 146,000 men (20 per cent of its white male population) served in South African units during the war, fighting on three principal fronts. But there was no 'Main Force' that sailed as one like Australia's, or a corps with division-strength set-piece battles to cement national identity like Canada's. Their biggest unit in France was an infantry brigade. Of the 11,575 South Africans who lost their lives during the Great War, more than 3,000 served in Imperial units. If there was a signature moment of nationhood, then it was at Delville Wood in 1916; like the country itself, South Africa's Great War was complex.

This, after all, was a country whose Dutch farmers had been at war with Britain at the turn of the century, in between rugby tours given and received. Many of the British high command of the Great War, including Haig, cut their teeth in the Second Boer War; there is little evidence to show that this qualified them for twentieth-century industrialised European warfare. In fairness, however, man's inventive use of technology for mechanised murder was advancing faster than a British military mind made complacent by Victorian peace punctuated by colonial skirmishes. In the absence of any military competence or concerted success against Boer irregular guerrillas, Britain resorted to brutal tactics in its ruthless suppression of rebellion against Empire. It was Lords Roberts and Kitchener, not the Nazis, who invented the civilian concentration camp; over 26,000 women and children died in inhumane conditions on the high veldt. The memory was still raw; fighting for Britain's Empire in 1914 was not the immediate 'no-brainer' it was in other pink parts of the world map.

There was something rotten too in the state of its soldiery. Before the Boer War, the British Army had become a disreputable refuge for scoundrels: forget the pantomimic Flashman, but remember Thomas Hardy's Sergeant Troy. Lord Roberts and others, not least Lieutenant Colonel Guy du Maurier, returned from the Cape with unease about its fighting qualities, physical condition and 'right stuff' mentality. Roberts campaigned ceaselessly for military conscription in light of alarums from Germany that since the 1890s had filled popular fiction and newspapers, and even the new moving pictures. The British, however, have been suspicious of standing armies since Cromwell. After rugby's New Zealanders and South Africans came to Britain in the middle of the first decade and beat all comers – not narrowly but by wide margins – there were further rumblings of disquiet about the poor state of Edwardian manhood. The sensation of du Maurier's 1909 invasion drama *An Englishman's Home* did wonders for recruitment to the newly created Territorial Force. But the improvement of physical condition and nutrition in industrialised Britain took more than theatrical intervention.

In 1917, Australian Tom Richards found himself watching a wartime game behind the front at Laventie in foul weather. He mused upon the contrasting physiques of the outdoors nations and the indoors labourers of industry:

> The contrast was very marked indeed. The more notice I took of it the greater and greater was my love of the Colonial and my mind refreshed as to the difference in appearance of African and English athletes as they stood facing one another in both South Africa and in England. Also the Australians when they faced the Englishmen and Welshmen in 1908.[1]

Richards was at least qualified to judge having worked and played in most of the world's rugby countries, not least for the touring British against South Africa.

Diocesan College, known as 'Bishop's', in Rondebosch, Cape Colony, had introduced the Winchester game (football with some handling) in 1861 and the first Cape rugby club, Hamilton, was formed in 1875. Bishop's can therefore claim to be the cradle of South African rugby; it certainly chose its colour, when it lent its myrtle green jerseys for the first victory in the final Test against the British Isles 1896 Anglo-Irish tourists.[2] The Stellenbosch club was formed in the predominantly Boer farming district outside Cape Town in 1883. As Briton and Boer migrated to the interior, the game spread through the Eastern Cape and Natal, and along the gold and diamond routes to Kimberley and Johannesburg.

Rugby had become a common rallying point for the white races in the South African colonies since the missionary British tours of 1891 and 1896. After an inexplicable interlude where they shot at each other for three years – except for a truce offered by General Moritz at besieged O'kiep in order to play rugby – the British were back to play South Africa in Johannesburg only a year later in 1903 (and again in 1910). If we ignore (as the whites did, and far worse) the indigenous natives, the population was a complex mixture of English, Irish, French, German, Dutch and Afrikaners (oddly, the Scots names strewn over Canadian and New Zealand teams were not matched here). South African rugby teams reflected that and were also not above capping travelling mercenaries like Welshman 'Birdie' Partridge.

Both British soldiers in occupation and Boers in prison camps in Ceylon and St Helena after the *Tweede Vryheidsoorlog* ('Second Freedom War') had enthusiastically embraced rugby as warlike recreation. There is even rumour of a first confrontation between New Zealander and South African as soldiers met at Johannesburg, Dave Gallaher among them. Afrikaners as a linguistic and cultural group were increasingly independent: rugby rapidly became the ruling passion of the Afrikaans speaker, in rejection of the Anglophone imperialism of cricket. The religious fervour of rugby fanaticism would come later. South African officialdom also held attitudes on amateurism (and far more sinister ones on race) that put them to the right even of the righteous Scots. Being the 'right sort' got the Springboks invited to Britain twice before the war, while the troublesome All Blacks and Wallabies had to wait to be asked.

There had already been a stiffening of the Motherland's rugby backbone by Cape imports to national teams: for England, Reggie Hands before the war and Jannie Krige just after it, and Stephanus Steyn for Scotland. In exchange, England's Reggie Schwartz travelled in the opposite direction to play cricket for South Africa, and Cornish miner Maffer Davey captained Transvaal. The tradition continues with Catt, Stevens, Barritt, Abbott, Fourie and Botha, although the boat seemingly now sails only one way – but it does put in at France and Italy too. Hardly surprising then, that the same applied to the military in time of war. Many South Africans joined the British Army: 1912 Springbok captain Billy Millar was a Coldstream Guard; forward Toby Moll fought with the Leicestershires; Oxford's Walter Dickson with the Argylls at Loos. In wartime, it was still working both ways: Newport's Welsh 1909 Grand Slam winner, Lieutenant Philip

Waller, stayed in South Africa after touring as a proto-Lion in 1910, and captained the Johannesburg Wanderers for three seasons; he was killed at Beaumetz-lès-Cambrai in December 1917 when a stray shell struck his car. His companion, Major Percy Fitzpatrick, CO of his 71st (South African) Siege Battery, Royal Garrison Artillery, was killed instantly; Phil died shortly afterwards. Percy's father, Sir Percy Fitzpatrick, first proposed the two minutes' silence on Armistice Day and Remembrance Sunday.

Education more than family roots drew young Cape colonials to Britain, and Cecil Rhodes's eponymous scholarships helped sustain the traffic. Rosslyn Park has at least three from Cape Province on its memorial: Harold Broster, Gordon Bayly, briefly at Diocesan before coming to St Paul's, and Charles Aubrey Vintcent. Named after his father's Charterhouse school friend, one-time English cricket captain and future Hollywood actor C. Aubrey Smith, Vintcent came to study at Uppingham and Cambridge and won his rugby Blue. He joined the Rifle Brigade and was killed at Polygon Wood in April 1915. Jim Louwrens, the South African College scrum half of 1901, also appeared in Park and Middlesex colours. That only five Springboks are listed as fallen cannot be dismissed as a poor contribution; South Africans do not hold back, and the Western Province memorial carries 227 names. It is simply that its rugby players fought under many flags, with an estimated 3,000 in the RFC and its RAF successor alone. By the time the men of the South African Infantry Brigade arrived in April 1916 to join the 9th (Scottish) Division in France, some 7,500 of their countrymen were already serving in Imperial regiments.[3]

One of them, Stephanus 'Beak' Steyn, from Moorreesburg, Cape Province, was an (Edinburgh) Academical, a Bishop and an Oxford Blue, on a coveted Rhodes scholarship, and centre alongside Poulton-Palmer for Oxford. Capped twice for Scotland and attested to King Edward's Horse as early as 1910, he was embodied with them on 5 August 1914, before commissioning into the South African Field Artillery on 8 December. Typhoid laid him low in Salonika; on recovery he embarked for Egypt in August 1917 and went with 117th Brigade, RFA, to the Palestine front, where he was killed in action on the third anniversary of his commission, aged 25.

South Africa had been the first to deliver a rude awakening to British rugby. The 1903 British tour under Mark Morrison met the first series defeat inflicted by a supposedly cowed adversary emerging from a war that had only ended a few months before. The shock could not be concealed by an excuse that these tours were not yet officially sanctioned by all four Home Unions, and so were not fully representative. Official nonsense. Two Test draws allowed the final match, won 8–0 by the home side, again wearing the lucky green jerseys of Old Diocesans, to decide the series. It was a tight margin but this was a shift in power on the sports field that presaged much greater change in the Empire; South Africa would not lose a Test series until 1956 in New Zealand.

South Africans first travelled to Britain as Springboks in 1906, with the new badge on their green jerseys appearing on fields from Redruth to Pittodrie. Worried that the 'witty London press' might invent a nickname (like the 'Myrtles', from the distinctive green of their shirts) they chose the emblem of the small antelope typical of Africa; the press swallowed the bait, although they could not digest the correct Afrikaans plural of *Springbokken*. After the All Blacks indomitable 2–3–2 scrum and wing-forward of the previous year, British forwards now had to cope with the Boks playing a power game up front in 3–4–1. Led by forward Paul Roos, and starring centre Japie Krige, prolific try-scoring winger Bob Loubser and the place-kicking of Dougie Morkel, they stormed the country over a twenty-nine-match series, playing every three or four days. In the days before air travel, the boat home took eighteen days – enough time to have played another five games.

They only lost to Louis Greig's Scotland and Cardiff (who were down to fourteen men for the second half) and drew 3–3 with England. On fourteen occasions, they blanked opponents including several county and regional sides, and most surprisingly, Wales, whose highly rated side was one of their best, enjoying a golden era of Triple Crown success. Even the South Africans were surprised at the ease of their 11–0 win over the Welsh, who had beaten the All Blacks, but simply did not show up on the field at Swansea. Reuters reported that:

> The victory created immense enthusiasm throughout South Africa. Crowds thronged outside the newspaper offices in all the towns and villages awaiting the progress of the game. The result was greeted with extraordinary gratification and surprise. Cheering crowds marched through the streets for hours afterwards.

Captain Paul Roos, with his trademark 'black ribbon round his forehead and over his ears' instead of a scrum-cap, was carried shoulder-high from the field at Cardiff, considering it to be 'the greatest honour of his life to be borne triumphant from the ground by supporters of his beaten opponents'. He had been elected as captain by his team-mates, had spoken at church meetings on tour, with his deep voice and 'pronounced Dutch accent'[4] and was apparently much admired wherever he went:

> A man of strong character, with high principles, he combines with the natural powers of command, a fine presence, a splendid knowledge of the game, and ready tact, thus gaining the respect alike of his own men and that of his opponents. It is these qualities which have gained him a place in the football world that no man outside England has ever attained, not even Gallagher [*sic*]. His control over his men, both on and off the field, his ability to say and do the right thing at the right moment, has rendered him exceedingly popular in England, and has conduced to the better understanding of the Afrikander [*sic*] character, and to increase the respect for the Afrikander nation as a whole.[5]

What the panegyrist does not mention is the Devon game of 17 October. With 18,000 watching at the Plymouth County Ground, the visitors refused to take the field: they had belatedly noticed half back Jimmy Peters. The local club favourite had twice been capped for England earlier that year,[6] partnering the great Adrian Stoop and scoring his first international try against France. The problem for the Springboks was that he was black, born in Salford to a West Indian father; they refused to play if he was on the pitch. They were forced to relent by their own High Commissioner and Plymouth's mayor, who feared a riot if the match were cancelled.

The world had indeed gained a 'better understanding of the Afrikander character', but would do little about it, both in 1906 and again in 1919, as we shall see. Roos's own 1931 account whitewashed the incident:

> How pleasantly the Tour passed over from first to last. What hospitality we enjoyed, even in private homes. Never could a team wish for better treatment, both from governing bodies and from spectators, than was accorded to us. Coming as it did just after the Anglo-Boer War, the 1906 team probably played no small part in healing the breach and restoring pleasant relations.[7]

As captain that day, he must carry some stain on his 'strong character, with high principles' and, unlike Gallaher, martyred in war, is largely unremembered outside his own country.

Although Oxford University made the Springboks feel more at home with six of the dark blue scholars hailing from South Africa, Roos was injured during that match. Against Gloucester they faced the ubiquitous Tom Richards: on form alone for the Mines and Transvaal, he had been certain to make the tour party but was ruled ineligible because he had not been in South Africa long enough to qualify as a resident. For dessert, they polished off France 55–6 in an unrecognised game at Parc des Princes. The tourists had racked up 608 points in total with only 85 against.

One ill-fated Springbok tourist was Adam Francis Burdett of Bishop's, the Villagers club and Western Province. He was described by tour chronicler E.J.L. Plateneur as 'a hard working forward, who is seen to most advantage in the open, where his very clever footwork and pace render him always prominent. He is a good tackler, like most of the Diocesan College forwards.' His tour selection came as a surprise, but 'in England he has justified his place, playing some really good games, particularly in the [two] Internationals in which he took part'.[8] Burdett joined up on the outbreak of war and served in Tanganyika with the South African Service Corps, supplying the long campaign against the cunning German commander Lettow-Vorbeck. In disease-ridden East Africa, it was malaria not a bullet that felled him and so many others: he was shipped home to recuperate, but died just seven days before the war ended. Perhaps the saddest footnote to his life is that when his tour colleagues Billy Millar and Paddy Carolin furnished Sewell with information for his Honour Roll, they overlooked Burdett.

In 1910 King George V took the throne. On 31 May, the Union of South Africa brought its four colonies under one British flag, with General Louis Botha, former Boer commander, as its first prime minister. It failed to unite the people: blacks were excluded from any constitutional decision-making; Afrikaner discontent continued to simmer. The British rugby players returned under Dr Tom Smyth in the same year that Captain Scott set off for the Antarctic; they were plagued by injury problems, and lost the series but, unlike Scott, they returned home. Yet again, the roving Tom Richards proved that if there was a rugby party in the world, he would be at it, joining the British team as a replacement, under the banner of Bristol. Cherry Pillman was the dominant player for the tourists, revolutionising South African ideas of wing-forward play, taking the place-kicks and even inspiring unexpected victory in the second Test from the number 10 slot. A new system was introduced, honed by Adrian Stoop at Harlequins and for England, whereby the previous left and right half backs now played with one closer in as 'scrum half' and the other standing off a little, hence the name. In those days, however, and even now, there were few stand-offs who stood 6ft 3in like Pillman.

Douglas Morkel again proved himself prodigious with the boot: 'he wore red stockings, and a penalty might produce the uncanny spectacle of Douglas sniping at our posts from his own twenty-five yard line'. The series decider in Cape Town saw the British well-beaten; it also saw the arrival of yet another Morkel, William Herman – known as 'Boy', to distinguish him from William Somerset, 'Sommie', who had been a Boer PoW and toured in 1906. To the British press, Boy was a 'Prince of Forwards'. For South Africa he was a player with a bright future that many others would not have, surviving the war to captain the Springboks in 1921. One touring British forward, Harry Jarman of Wales and Newport, would die a hero, not in wartime but in peaceful 1928, when he threw himself in front of a runaway coal truck heading towards a group of playing children.

The 1912 tour of Britain by the Springboks saw Billy Millar return, this time as skipper, although he was the last player selected and not a popular captain, either with their hosts or his own team, being thought too fiery. Not only was Millar fortunate in being favoured with two tours, but he was lucky to be playing at all:

> He was badly wounded during the [Boer] war, and, on returning to Capetown convalescent, his great recreations were walking, mountain-climbing and shooting. It was in these exercises that he acquired the stamina, and gained the bodily strength which stood him in good stead at Rugby football.[9]

He would have his fill of war, fighting with the Coldstream Guards in this second conflict, until he was taken prisoner – his right arm broken – during the Battle of Hazebrouck in April 1918, as the German Spring Offensives pushed to end the war. He was sent to a camp at Stralsund on the Baltic; of seven battalion officers captured on that unlucky 13 April, he was the only one to be repatriated before the Armistice. It is not known if he did this by escaping, or by Red Cross intervention.

Other familiar names returned, including scrum half Fred 'Uncle' Dobbin and forward Dougie Morkel. In the manner of a poker game, the 1906 tour had bid three Morkels; the 1912 Boks raised it to four Morkels and also saw three Luyts. White South Africa was a tight-knit society, with family clans running production lines of great rugby players over generations: in 1914 there were no fewer than twenty-two Morkels playing first-team rugby. Seven were in an all-conquering Somerset West team, which supplied thirteen players to Western Province, including all seven Morkels.[10] Somerset West was such a rugby town that, in the days of slow trains and no telephones, its team was despatched to away games with carrier pigeons to bring back the result, which was posted in the town's hotel lounge.

When war broke out Sir Abe Bailey, diamond tycoon and financier, was planning a single-family Morkel rugby tour of England, with a twenty-third – the 12-year-old Denis, a future South African cricketing star – as team mascot; the Kaiser's little game fatally interfered with Bailey's plans. But the family name up in English lights in 1912 would be (ahem) Luyt: for the first time, three brothers – Richard, John and Fred – would play together in an international. The sheer volume of Springboks called Morkel, Luyt, de Villiers or du Toit over a century and more should not blind us to some of the finest individual rugby names. Who cannot love Long George Devenish? Or Spanner Forbes, Saturday Knight (a 1912 tourist) and the immortal Ebbo Bastard – the only mystery here being what his enemies called him.

The 1912 Springboks followed the pattern set by their predecessors: twenty-seven matches over fourteen weeks, losing only to Newport, Swansea and a London XV. Swansea also played the name game, with four Williamses and two Morgans, but they were not (close) family. A crowd of 35,000 turned out on Boxing Day at a sodden St Helen's to see captain Billy Trew mastermind a 'Whites' victory, despite being down to fourteen men for twenty minutes after an injury. South Africa played a London XV in front of 20,000 at the 'National Ground' for the first time as, according to a young Basil Liddell-Hart, a teenage *Daily Telegraph* rugby correspondent without by-line, 'everyone was agreed that Twickenham is the only place in England for big matches'. That Welsh rugby fervour could, however, double the size of crowds says much about both Wales and Twickenham.

The Londoners were largely drawn from Harlequins (Adrian Stoop's brother, Tim and Ronald Poulton-Palmer in centre harness) and Blackheath (both Pillmans), the two aristocrats of capital rugby. They also included two Guy's Hospital doctors, one from the Bank of England club and naval cadet W.J.A. 'Dave' Davies, a future England star at stand-off. Outlying Twickenham was still unable to host a dinner, so the visitors received the hospitality of the Blackheath pack, both on the pitch (losing 8–6) and at dinner afterwards. Nevertheless, they pulled off a first Grand Slam of Test victories by a touring side: grievous Dublin damage was done to the Irish by 38–0 at Lansdowne Road, and Poulton-Palmer's try in the finale at Twickenham was the only Test score against them: lock Arnold 'Saturday' Knight presumably lived up to his name in the celebrations.

The Morkel who made his name on this Springbok expedition was Jan Willem Hurter, known as 'Jackie', a 'very quiet, unassuming fellow, a man of few words',[11] who let his rugby do the talking. The outside centre played all five Tests, scoring four tries, including a brace against the Irish. Against Llanelli at Stradey Park, he chipped over the three-quarters, caught the ball on the full and repeated the trick on the full back, scoring under the posts to win the game by a single point. Brother Gerhard was behind him as a faultless full back, with cousins 'Boy' and Douglas up front. Jackie and Dougie shared all the points in the 9–3 victory over England.

During the war, Jackie served as a mounted trooper in Van Deventer's Scouts. Like Burdett, he succumbed to illness, this time dysentery, in the East African campaign, and died on 15 May 1916. Politics were never far away in any discussion of South African rugby, then as now. Sewell, in his admiring 1919 obituary of Jackie Morkel, could not resist a backhanded slap at the Boers when he wrote:

> He has upheld in the worthiest possible manner the teachings of the Rugby game, which cannot, unfortunately, be written of all British subjects of Dutch descent, and his case will stand for all time as a shining example to his countrymen.[12]

Jackie Morkel is buried in Dar-es-Salaam War Cemetery, just yards away from Gerald 'Tommy' Thompson, his great friend and Western Province and 1912 Springbok team-mate, who had 'played like one possessed and as though the Irish XV were like a lot of unpractised schoolboys' in Dublin, but was killed by a bullet at Katanga. Neither lost a Test; both lost a young life. As for 'British subjects', Sewell was already behind the curve of a world in transformation.

In a final fling on the way home, the Springboks' steamer called at Bordeaux, where they beat France at Le Bouscat, 38–5. In this unofficial game, Douglas Morkel dropped a goal from his own ten-yard line; a Frenchman ran from the crowd and kissed him. French crowds of the day rarely showed such cordial hospitality. It was the last game of a long tour; claret was liberally taken at dinner on the Route du Médoc. In January 1913, they could not know this was the last international for *Afrique du Sud* for many years. For Septimus 'Sep' Ledger, who elbowed his way onto the score-sheet amongst the Morkels and Luyts, this was his last ever, as claret would again flow in France, in a fatal attack by his South African Infantry regiment on the village of Roeux in April 1917.

In August 1914 President Louis Botha and Defence Minister Jan Smuts, another former Boer military leader, took the Union of South Africa into war in support of Britain with a Defence Force founded only two years beforehand. Their troops seized the German protectorate of South-West Africa by July 1915. Many Afrikaners opposed war: Germany had aided them during their Freedom War (and secretly agitated ever since). An attempted coup in September 1914 failed when Christiaan Beyer – an Afrikaner hero from the Boer War – was killed by police, and a later armed uprising in the Orange Free State and Transvaal was also suppressed. Continued resistance was finally quashed by mid-1915, although Botha's National Party only narrowly held on to power at a general election.

In the meantime the South African Infantry Brigade was assembled for overseas service. Comprising four regiments – 1st Regiment from Cape Province, 2nd from Natal and Orange Free State, 3rd Transvaal and Rhodesia and 4th the South African Scottish (wearing the Atholl Murray tartan) – it mustered 160 officers and 5,468 other ranks when it docked in England in November 1915. Supporting units of artillery and medics, without which infantry cannot fight, were added to the strength. Frank Mellish joined the artillery with Reggie Hands, 'a charming, rather dreamy fellow who gave the impression that he had been caught up in the war, but was not particularly interested in it'. Reggie's brother 'Pam' was 'more of the swashbuckling type; it was no surprise when he was transferred to the British Army, and won a DSO and Bar'. Dr Alex Frew, capped three times for Scotland while an Edinburgh student and South African captain in the first 1903 Test against Britain, was in the Medical Corps. For the many rugby players in the brigade's ranks, they were surrounded by familiar symbols: their cap badge was a springbok head, with the motto 'Union is Strength – Eendracht Maakt Macht'. The Scottish even took with them a springbok mascot, called Nancy.

Naturally, one of their first acts was to look for a rugby game: they found one as early as 6 November 1915 against the Welsh Division in Aldershot, and South Africa's medics played the RAMC two days later. On the 20th they played the Barbarians, billed as an 'International Services XV' and skippered by Harold 'Dreadnought' Harrison (who would command Hands and Mellish's Heavy Artillery), at Richmond, 'in aid of the Comforts Fund for Colonial Troops'. This was the first Barbarian outing since the April defeat of Wales (whose Clem Lewis and

Billy Jenkins now featured, along with Birdie Partridge, the Welshman with the South African cap), and the last in wartime, as so many were now in France. C.F.S. Nicholson, who would later write a history of South African rugby, played that day, but there were no pre-war stars, with the exception of a single Springbok, 'Sep' Ledger, the try-scorer in Bordeaux. Sergeant Ledger would cross to France with his 2nd Regiment on 25 July 1916, missing the carnage of Delville Wood. He would survive until the Battle of Arras in April 1917, where they attacked over exposed ground at Fampoux. John Buchan recorded in his Official History:

> The result was a failure. A gallant few of the South Africans succeeded in reaching the station . . . where their bodies were recovered a month later when the position was captured . . . before the attack was brought to a standstill, the casualties of the 2nd Regiment, who went in 400 strong, amounted to 16 officers and 285 men.[13]

Sep Ledger was among them, but his body was never recovered, and his name is carved on the Arras Memorial. As are 35,000 more.

During their training at Bordon Camp, rugby was never far from their minds, and was closely followed in the press at home: almost every week a game was reported involving South African troops from varying units.[14] The South African Heavy Artillery (SAHA) was not a nickname for their pack, but a successful team who took on – and beat 21–5 – the Army Service Corps (Motor Transport) XV with its Northern Union stars. In March 1916, they also inflicted a first defeat in twelve games on the New Zealand HQ side at Queen's Club, drawing 5,000 spectators. The SAHA side included England internationalists Harrison and Hands. More games followed against the crack ASC team and the New Zealanders, but by autumn there were no unit representative teams as they had all gone 'overseas'. The continuing South African rugby contribution came from individuals: in Ireland, Dougie Morkel, he of the howitzer boot, played for the Curragh camp against Dublin Garrison; Billy Millar arrived to join the Coldstream, and led the Public Schools' Services XV, organised by Rosslyn Park, in victory over the Canadians, the Welsh Guards and a 58–0 thrashing of the RFC. In late 1917 and during 1918, there were enough reinforcement drafts and rehab cases to play matches against (among many) United Services and the Canadian Army Pay Corps, while Springboks stars like Millar and 'Bay' Wrentmore, or C.F. Krige, brother of Japie, made regular appearances for hospital or services sides.

Lieutenant Walter 'Wally' Mills of Western Province and the Welsh exile William 'Taffy' Townsend also saw action for them on the rugby field.

Although the brigade was trained for service on the Western Front, it was first sent to join Imperial forces in Egypt, engaging the Senussi and Ottomans. A crisis was averted after mascot Nancy walked off into the desert; a Scottish patrol was sent out to lure her back with the siren call of the pipes. Nancy reappeared, the campaign was successfully concluded (the Hague convention did not forbid cruel use of bagpipes against the Turk) and by 20 April 1916 the brigade had disembarked at Marseilles to enter the European theatre. The Battle of the Somme began in sunshine on 1 July 1916 and ended in November mud; as part of 9th (Scottish) Division, the South African Brigade moved into the front line on 2 July and on 4 July relieved the 89th Brigade at Glatz Redoubt, near Montauban. Four days later, elements of the brigade were in Bernafay Wood and supported British attacks on Trônes Wood. Its first week in hell cost the brigade 537 casualties. But the devil had much worse in store.

On 14 July the entire brigade of 3,153 men attacked Delville Wood, an important salient protruding into the enemy second line. For six days it was subjected to an onslaught of such ferocious violence that the wood itself vanished, smashed to splinters by high-explosive shelling from both sides, as British artillery rounds fell short. The infantry ran out of ammunition, and resorted to savage hand-to-hand combat with bayonet, rifle-butt and knobkerrie; only 142 souls emerged from the shattered stumps when they were relieved by the Suffolks and Berkshires on the 20th. Eventually 780 men regrouped to answer the roll call; South African Brigade casualties numbered 1,709 wounded and 763 dead (457 killed in action, 120 died of wounds and 186 missing, presumed dead). From its parent 9th (Scottish) Division, Lieutenant Eric 'Puss' Milroy of the Black Watch, Scottish captain in that terrific last Calcutta Cup at Inverleith in 1914, was also lost in the devastation. The 'Devil's Wood' had taken the foremost as well as the hindmost.

On the very day that his countrymen began this blood-soaked battle fighting as one brigade, Transvaaler Tobias Mortimer 'Toby' Moll, capped just once against the British in 1910, died of his wounds serving as a second lieutenant in the British 9th Leicestershires, just two kilometres to the west. He had left his bank job to serve in South-West Africa, and then came over to England. A former Cape rugby team-mate met Toby in a lull from fighting, but not safety from lethal shellfire:

> We were now out of that nightmare wood, in what was once the village of Bazentin-le-Petit . . . The village was a shambles and nothing remotely resembling a house was to be seen. Here I came across an old friend from Hamiltons, Toby Moll, who told me that Cyril Bam had been killed. No trace of him was to be found. Soon after this, Toby was hit by shrapnel when he was quite near me and I saw at once that there was no hope. It was hard to see Toby go – everything else was impersonal, almost unreal, but with Toby one was up against it.[15]

Moll was buried in a marked grave. Cyril Bam, who had come from Cape Town with Toby to join the Tigers, is one of those 72,000 bodiless names on Thiepval.

What was left of the South African Brigade remained at the Somme. In October it fought again at the Butte de Warlencourt, an ancient mound that formed a German stronghold. As reinforcement drafts arrived, 1917 saw further action on the Arras front and at Third Ypres. In March 1918, it was back on the Somme during the *Kaiserschlacht,* almost annihilated once more at Marrières and Gauche Woods. The tattered remnants of the brigade fought on at Messines, Wijtschaete and Mount Kemmel. Now down to battalion size, they helped capture Meteren in July, but then left the Division, to reform in England, rejoining the 66th (East Lancashire) Division in September 1918.

Given South African rugby fervour, it is not surprising to find that rugby was equally popular in Flanders, both behind their own lines (playing for the Lukin Cup donated by brigade commander, sport-loving Major General Henry Lukin) and for an unfortunate few (or fortunate, depending on your view) behind the enemy lines. Just as Boer prisoners of war had embraced the game, so did their equivalents at Schweidnitz, Freiburg and other camps. Andries Venter, the fabled 'Boer Giant' at heights variously reported as 6ft 7in to 7ft 2in, experienced both wars as a prisoner; his second internment came in 1914 when the outbreak found him working in a circus in Germany.[16] Sport in the prison camps reached a level of organisation that seems parodic, but provided a comforting reminder of home: Bishop's boy and 1913 Oxford Blue J. Moresby-White served as president of the 'Ruhleben Rugby Union' for two years.[17] Barracks teams named after Blackheath, Harlequins, Wasps, Nomads and Barbarians played in a daringly experimental league format. There were even 'international' sides, some necessarily composite, with

Moresby-White skippering the 'Scots–Colonials' against 'England', 'Ireland' and 'Wales'.

On 11 November 1918, the South African Infantry Brigade had the honour to be at the easternmost point gained by any troops of the British Army in France. The casualties of the brigade were close to 15,000, nearly 300 per cent of the original strength. Of these some 5,000 were dead.

Nancy the springbok died of pneumonia during the harsh winter of 1918. She was the only animal in military history to be accorded full military funeral honours and to be buried in an Allied war cemetery, at the South African shrine that is the Delville Wood Memorial. South African rugby, however, was very much alive.

United States of America

And the rockets' red glare, the bombs bursting in air,
Gave proof through the night that our flag was still there.

There was a moment in the early twentieth century when America was on the brink of becoming a rugby nation. That moment may have been 16 November 1912 at the University of California (UCal) at Berkeley; specifically the midpoint of the second half when the All-America team led 8–3 in the first ever Test between Australia and the USA. Rugby was vigorously contested between a cluster of universities in California, with the 'Big Game' between Stanford and Berkeley an annual highlight since 1906. The Australians were billed by the US press as 'world champions' in deference to their 1908 Olympic gold. The omens were good for an exciting game:

> The day was a marked contrast to that of a week before when Stanford and California met in a sea of mud. The sun shone bright and clear, and the ground had dried to such an extent that both teams were able to use their full quota of speed and accuracy. The crowd on the bleachers was in fine fettle, although there was no organised rooting. The thousands that thronged the field to see the international game witnessed some of the best Rugby ever played on this coast.
>
> From the start to the finish, the game was one of fast concerted action. Back and forth across the field the ball travelled in a series of quick rushes that threatened first one goal-line and then the other.[1]

Australia fielded a strong team against the students, including vice-captain Tom Richards, fellow Olympian Daniel Carroll, and the doomed trio of Harold George, George Pugh and Twit Tasker.

Billy Hill, a former NSW player accompanying the tour, had been invited to referee: 'His affable and responsible personality was such that both sides approved his appointment.' His brother Ralph had played most of the games against the Californian university sides, but he sat this one out; it is not known whether this was to avoid accusations of bias, or if he was simply nursing a huge hangover. One excuse given for the poor Australian performances (they had lost every game so far, apart from at Santa Clara, the weakest of the varsities, and would lose every game in Canada) was the prodigious hospitality of the college fraternity houses in which they roomed. Bob Adamson recalled: 'We were never in bed. That was the trouble. I've never had such a time in my life.' *Animal House* has a heritage.

On this occasion, the Australia team needed no official assistance, although they faced an uphill battle. After a first-half interception try by Phillip Harrigan (the first rugby points scored by the USA) and a penalty from 40 yards, the tide turned in the last twenty minutes to deliver a final score of 8–12:

> From this point on, the Australian goal seemed invincible, and the foreigners began their march to victory. Score followed score with lightning rapidity so that when the pistol shot announced the end the visitors stood 4 points to the advantage. Something seemed to snap in the American line-up, the defence weakened and the speedy backfield action of the previous half died away. Rush after rush swept the All-Stars from their feet and four tries were piled up against them.[2]

The crowd numbered under 10,000, although the previous week's Big Game had a much bigger pull at the 23,000 capacity California Field (despite a low-scoring 3–3 draw, anathema to American sports fans). This stands testament to America's unwavering enthusiasm for domestic rivalries over international contests – it still boasts its baseball play-offs of one American city against another as the 'World Series'. Was this, however, the Damascene conversion for America? The *San Francisco Chronicle* certainly thought so:

> America has arrived on the international map, and it will be looking down upon all the other nations in a few more years, ready to lend a hand as it does in all other forms of athletics.

Such modest and generosity in the same breath: what if they had actually won? A century later, there's just one small problem.

The first green shoots of American rugby had emerged on the East Coast at Yale in the 1870s, courtesy of an Old Rugbeian, D.S. Schaff. Harvard

and McGill of Montreal played their first match in 1875. But disputatious
Ivy League academics argued over the laws, with games sometimes played
to a different set in each half, and the gridiron code muscled its way to pre-
eminence. Real impetus behind rugby only came as a result of a crisis over
the innate violence of American football. The 1894 Harvard–Yale match,
known as the 'Hampden Park Blood Bath', crippled four players. Add the
death of fifty players since 1900, fifteen in 1905 alone, from 'unnecessary
roughness' including the 'flying wedge' formation, and sharp practice by
college coaches, and it became a matter of national debate as the 'Football
Crisis of 1905–6'. After the death of Harold Moore of Union College,
kicked in the head in a tackle, a newspaper cartoon showed the Grim
Reaper perched on goal posts.

Even that vigorous advocate of outdoor life President Roosevelt
intervened against the increase of 'foul play and intentional brutality'.[3]
Columbia, Duke and Northwestern dropped football and the presidents
of the two leading West Coast schools, Stanford and Berkeley, opted
for change: in 1906, the Big Game rivals since 1892 dropped football in
favour of rugby. The states of America were disunited: President Wheeler
of Berkeley foresaw a Pan-Pacific Union of rugby and predicted that 'the
West's football future would be with rugby-playing countries rather than
with American universities'.[4]

As in Canada, the seat of power was firmly in the east and geographically
distant; the danger for universities in western states was marginalisation
from America's national winter sport. However, this unilateral declaration
of independence by the Californian enclave of rugby-minded varsities
attracted Canadians and New Zealanders. The 1905 All Blacks, with
their innovative scrum and roving wing forward, were too successful
in England to be popular with the RFU; they contented themselves by
battering Australia repeatedly, and looked further afield. By way of smart
reconnaissance, the Blacks had steamed westwards after their British
marathon, playing two exhibitions in February 1906 against British
Columbia teams in Berkeley and San Francisco, via an unofficial match
in Brooklyn. The hardened veterans of the silver fern thundered on to
the field and put the hapless Canadians to casual slaughter, scoring an
aggregate 108 points to 12. It would be tempting, if not seismically sound,
to blame them for the earthquake two months later.

The local press, previously lukewarm, were delighted at the first game
– which was fast and open and without the 'clash of beef, the steaming,
straining of two highly organized machines'[5] found in gridiron. The

Daily Palo Alto agreed that from the 'spectacular point of view Rugby was far superior to the American game'.[6] The second game only increased their fervour: 'The superiority of Rugby to our own amended game was demonstrated even more forcibly.'[7] It was widely observed that Americans relied upon bulk, strength and tackling, whilst other teams emphasised speed and skilful ball handling. Rugby was preferable because it was a pastime not professional commerce; it was less brutal and could be played by smaller men, not just giants, and at class as well as varsity level; and it was free of coaches and the 'immoralities' of the American game.

The rugby heresy spread further through student intellectuals venturing outside the confines of North America. An 'All-America' side, selected exclusively from the two California schools, including future 'Captain America' of 1912, Laird Monterey Morris, and dressed in suitable 'winged-shield' jerseys, travelled 16,000 miles to tour New Zealand and Australia in 1910. They lost most matches but acquitted themselves honourably, salvaging a draw against Auckland. That same year, Princeton's Donald 'Heff' Herring, gridiron footballer, wrestling champion, hammer-thrower and Rhodes Scholar 'Yank at Oxford', became the first American to win a rugger Blue. Stanford medico H.R. 'Bert' Stolz, also at Oxford, would not get his Blue, but later played for the USA against New Zealand. Bert was another adventurous academic: in a gap year from Stanford he almost sank Jack London's yacht *The Snark* off Honolulu by opening the seacock. Later he wrote the 1951 educational classic *Somatic Development of Adolescent Boys*; he had joined Rosslyn Park in 1910, but there is no connection between those two last facts, allegedly. He served as a captain in the Army Medical Corps in the war and would skipper the USA rugby XV in 1919.

Heff Herring caused a stir at home by writing to *The Princetonian* from his dreaming spire at Merton, Oxford, after another rash of serious gridiron injuries. He urged that 'in light of the fate of football being sealed unless radical changes in the rules are made, so that men may take part in the game without the great liability of injury', that 'the English game of rugby be taken into serious consideration with a view to either substituting it for American football or improving the American game with the best features of the English game'.[8] He further advised that, 'The English game subjected the players to less danger and was at the same time more interesting both to the players and the spectator than the American game.' If this all sounds dangerously un-American, he redeemed himself in the war as a lieutenant in the 94th Aero Squadron, alongside America's top ace Eddie Rickenbacker, flying French-made Spad fighters over enemy lines. Sadly, he also abandoned his rugby prophecy in the wilderness of war – America was by then not listening anyhow.

One extra benefit to America of the 1912 Wallabies tour was that they left a joey behind: Daniel Brendan Carroll was born in Melbourne, and scored two tries in winning his Olympic gold medal in London. He was an elusive ball-carrier, blessed with great acceleration. First capped against Wales on that 1908 tour when he was the baby on the team,[9] he won his second in California. He decided to stay on in the sunshine to study geology at Stanford – and naturally to play rugby. As America did not enter the war until 1917, this had the added advantage of extending not only his playing career, but quite probably his life.

Carroll won his third international cap on 15 November 1913 against New Zealand, this time playing for his adopted country of the USA. The pitch at Berkeley's California Field was familiar, as was the referee, Billy Hill. The All Blacks had warmed up at home by eating Australia for breakfast, 30–5; they left the second string to finish off the meal (they made a mess of the dessert) and took a strong team, skippered by Alec McDonald, the last of the class of '05, to California. They held daily *haka* practices aboard ship. In America, they dined royally on the local sides, racking up 457 points in twelve matches and conceding only one try. Stanford and UCal were despatched twice each, without ceremony and almost without points – the solitary score from UCal prop Jack Abrams. The inevitable happened in the Test: New Zealand ran in thirteen tries for a 51–3 win, the result of 'even more than usual excellence of the New Zealanders and the lack of team-work of the Americans'. In a sad postscript, a trio of All Black forwards would die in the forthcoming war: Dewar, Downing and Sellars.

As tours go, this was flat-track bullying: little wonder then that they did not return to the USA until 1980. The previously exultant San Francisco press was crestfallen:

> The Californian players are the best we have developed in seven years of intercollegiate rugby – the very best. And the score against them was 51 to 3. The only conclusion is that we have not yet learned how to play rugby. It is still a foreign game.[10]

The US sporting almanac *Spalding's Guide* (whose L.A. Wolff had accompanied the All-Americans down under in 1910 and even appeared in the team photo) was no cheerier in its admiring review:

> The visit of the New Zealand 'All Blacks' ... was easily the feature of the season of 1913, and the indelible impression of their whirlwind tactics will remain in the history of California football for years to come ... They came at a period when the development of Rugby in California appeared to have reached successful stages, at a time when the effects of Australia's competition was about to materialize in wonderful strides on the part of local efforts.

American rugby was truly demoralised by the men in black: 'the overwhelming defeat of the All-American fifteen left us with little appreciation of the extended effort on the part of our selected team. The rumblings are not just giving vent to a wounded pride. We have not mastered the rudiments of rugby.' The West Coast began to feel isolated from America's national game of Football. UCal threw in the towel and returned to the pigskin in 1915, with Stanford following two years later; by post-war 1919, the Big Game was again played on the gridiron, as it has been ever since.

With great power comes responsibility to the game.[11] There is a deep echo in Chicago a full century and another dozen tries later in October 2014. If one of the undisputed joys of modern rugby is that the sporting world order is turned on its head by a Pacific nation of 4.5 million as its established superpower, there is equal pleasure in the occasional French *bouleversement,* Bokke mugging or Aussie dancing lesson meted out to the All Blacks – let alone a rare England win. They may have sold out 61,500 seats at Chicago's Soldier Field, and even more replica shirts, but will a ruthless, basketball-score 74–6 trouncing of the USA Eagles really be 'inspiring Americans to fall in love with rugby', as the match programme claimed? Or will it send rugby's development in this proud but brittle sporting nation into reverse, and renew a splendid isolation in games that no one else plays? Let's hope it's not '*déjà vu* all over again', to quote New York Yankee, Yogi Berra.

The 1913 All Blacks did do some work to spread the rugby gospel. As they sailed west for home across the wide Pacific, they could not resist stopping off at Suva, Fiji, to stretch their legs in a pick-up game 'against a side of countrymen, working on the building of the Grand Pacific Hotel. This match – deemed "not of first class status" – was won 67 to 3.'[12] This was real missionary work, playing labourers on an island where rugby was otherwise the exclusive preserve of colonial administrators and constabulary against crews from visiting warships. Hallelujah.

Back in the States, Aussie import Danny Carroll proved resilient in every way, both in rugby defeat and fighting prowess. He resumed his rugby at Stanford until its final season of 1917 when he joined the US Army, as America threw its industrial might and manpower behind the Allied effort on 6 April. But it was not until 1918 that the USA could muster troops in sufficient numbers to bolster the beleaguered Allies. Carroll won the Distinguished Service Cross (DSC) for extraordinary heroism in action while serving with 364th Infantry Regiment, in the 91st Division, American Expeditionary Force (AEF) – the unit numbers alone show the vast size of this army and explain the series of desperate German onslaughts from March onwards, intended to end the war before it could reach the front.

His rugby captain on that November day in 1913 was Stanford's Frank 'Deke' Gard, who had also been skipper when Carroll played for the opposing Australians the year before. Born in Ohio, but a Los Angeleno since 1908 when his family moved west to grow oranges, he graduated in chemistry the year after playing the All Blacks. When war arrived, Gard enlisted at Glendora, California, in June 1917; he received honourable mention for his rapid progress in training at the Presidio, San Francisco, and made lieutenant in the 362nd Infantry Regiment, in the same division as Carroll. Recruited from eight western states, it was nicknamed the 'Wild West Division'. Appropriately enough, Lieutenant Gard was a real straight-shooter: he hit ten bulls-eyes in eighty seconds, all the more impressive for reloading between each shot.

The 362nd sailed from New York to Liverpool aboard the *Empress of Russia* on 6 July 1918 in the largest convoy to cross the Atlantic. The inexperienced doughboys trained for several more weeks in France and then marched to the front; Deke and Danny were once again battling side by side, this time against German opposition. Also initially in their division, with the 342nd was Lieutenant Ralph Noble, the Stanford and USA back, who had joined up in May 1917 and was posted overseas on Boxing Day 1917. From the infantry, the flying winger transferred to be an aerial observer with a French squadron; he was shot down in May 1918, dying of his injuries in a Red Cross hospital behind German lines. The grateful French awarded him a posthumous Croix de Guerre, citing him as an 'Officer remarkable for his skill, initiative and devotion in the performance of his duties, humbly demonstrating the superb qualities of his race'.

News of America's impact in the war travelled behind German lines and reached some unusual rugby touchlines. On 30 July, Frank Vans Agnew noted in his diary at Heidelberg, where he was a prisoner:

Rugby in evening from 4.15 to 6pm, acted as touch judge. War news really most inspiring. Germans on the retreat from Marne, for second time, after three years fruitless fighting. Americans doing quite splendidly.[13]

When Frank travelled from America in 1914 to enlist, he was 46 – which may explain why he was touch judging. A former veterinary surgeon, farrier in Roosevelt's Roughriders, mines assayer in Canada and Kazakhstan, and orange grower in Florida, he was posted to the front in May 1915. By 1917 he had transferred to the Tank Corps, winning an MC at Messines. He was wounded and captured in November. South African Frank Mellish was less impressed by the 'American invasion': 'We tired veterans adopted a sullen attitude at their every success. We felt we had borne the brunt of the show and deserved the spoils of victory – were there to be any.'

On 26 September 1918, General Pershing's First Army took the place of the French Second Army and began a series of attacks on the Germans dug into the wide valley of the River Meuse. The Battle of the Argonne Forest was the largest so far fought by the US Army, involving 1.2 million soldiers. The key objective was the Sedan–Mezières railway, the principal supply line for the German forces. The 91st Division went into bivouac in the Forêt de Hesse, with orders to attack on 26 September at 0230 hours. As the artillery barrage lifted, the infantry rushed ahead and took the deserted enemy front-line trenches at Bois-de-Cheppy. When the first waves penetrated the shattered wood, through wire entanglements and over shell-scarred ground, Lieutenant Carroll was wounded in the arm.

The next day when his regiment moved towards Gesnes, as there was no aerial reconnaissance, Deke Gard was tasked with identifying enemy gunnery positions. Heavy fire was encountered but eventually silenced, and the Americans advanced steadily. Carroll led his platoon through the Bois under torrid shelling and machine-gun fire. Leading an attack near La Neuve Grange farm on the 28th he was wounded a second time, earning the Purple Heart. Gard was killed the next day by a sniper's bullet. The village of Véry was captured after strong resistance; headquarters were established but there was only brief respite from the fighting to bury Deke Gard eight days later.[14] He now rests at Meuse-Argonne Cemetery, its 14,246 graves the largest number of American military dead in Europe.

The offensive continued until the Armistice and took 117,000 US casualties, 40 per cent of their wartime total. On 11 November Danny Carroll's war was over, but not his rugby: there would be yet more twists to his international playing career. Despite living in America since 1912 and serving with the US Army, he was co-opted by the land of his Australian birth into the AIF rugby team to play for the King's Cup in England in 1919, of which more later.

The American forces staged their own sports tournament in France and invited their allies in typically expansive and energetic style; they 'hit upon the idea of holding a big victory athletic festival and of giving some practical demonstration of their friendship for France'. Or in Henri Garcia's words, '*une garden-party monstre*'. Australian Lieutenant Goddard quipped, 'the American reputation for "hustle" was considerably enhanced'. When French contractors downed tools on an 'immense stadium of ferro-concrete', US Army engineers stepped into the breach and completed the new 25,000-seater Pershing Stadium at Joinville-le-Pont near Paris. The Inter-Allied Games was partly a useful distraction for two million American troops in Europe, part prototype sporting 'Marshall Plan' to cheer up an exhausted France – complete with 'free ice cream and other dainties' – and part demonstration of a new sporting imperialism. A victory party for the heroic 'winners' of the Great War:

> The Yankee, more than any other man, loves to best someone at something, and he puts into his game the same fighting spirit, the same unconquerable zeal that he displayed at Belleau woods, at St Mihiel, in the Argonne and along the Meuse.[15]

Eighteen combatant nations took part in this 'military Olympics', although eleven sent their apologies as they were keen to be off home, or their troops were still busy fighting; Britain probably felt it was not quite gentlemanly and pleaded a prior engagement for most of its sportsmen. As it was America's ball, they could decide what games would be played: they chose to stage sports they had a good chance of winning and – surprise – they did. But they were magnanimous in victory:

> America's notable success in winning first and second places in so many varied events was due of course in no small degree to the preponderance of entries and to the consistent preliminary training. It is no mean tribute to the sportsmanlike spirit of the competing nations that they fared gaily into the competitions against this handicap.[16]

The 554-page committee report covers everything from catering to advertising and its prose is endearing proof that America just does not do irony:

> ... there was nothing about the Games to suggest the *champs de bataille*. The Sports were the standard events usually held in great meets and in no way reflected the gigantic contests fought on the battlefields of the Western Front. The only exceptions were the rifle and pistol competitions and the hand-grenade-throwing contest . . .

Nothing of the battlefield there, then. That well-known 'standard event' of bayoneting was only rejected as 'there could be no satisfactory manner of judging such a competition'; the committee deliberations must have been grisly. In the end, the only world record set in the games was indeed in the grenade-toss (pity the officials who measured this event) by the American Thompson, who threw 245ft 11in. The doughboys may have been late to arrive, but with them on our side it's no wonder we won the war.

Rugby was included as an event, although perhaps because they were still smarting at the memory of pre-war Berkeley, the Americans made it low profile, with just three games played, not at the Pershing Stadium but at Colombes. (For the baseball, by contrast, 58,963 balls and 12,646 bats were imported). France, Romania and the USA team assembled by Captain Bert Stolz competed at rugby for (bizarrely) the Lou Tsung Tsing silver cup, donated by China. The Romanians were thrashed by both France and USA in the space of four days.

In the decider on 29 June in front of 5,000 spectators, 'against the science and experience of the French, the Americans pitted their youth, perfect physical condition and an extreme eagerness to win'. Some of the gridiron-style 'eagerness' resulted in violence on both sides, 'probably the best anyone could do without a knife or a revolver', according to the Philadelphia-born French rugby internationalist and Federation president, Allan Muhr (a wartime volunteer ambulance driver like Hemingway).[17] France won 8–3, proving again that age and cunning beats youth and fitness every time. The French sports writers 'paid tribute to the athletic prowess and enthusiasm of the Americans which enabled them, with but a short period of intensive training, to match more experienced opponents'.

Danny Carroll was not yet done. His war game over, he returned to Stanford and more rugby, finally graduating in 1920 at a mature 32. He was then asked to return to a war-torn Belgium to coach (and play for) the USA rugby squad at the 1920 Antwerp Olympic Games. His pedigree and experience were vital, as American rugby had all but ceased in wartime and many players were new to the game. On his team were former Lieutenant George Winthrop Fish (another ambulance driver), Corporal

James Fitzpatrick and Private John O'Neill, now all demobbed, who had all played in the Inter-Allied Games in Paris. The German-American Randolph 'Rudi' Scholz had not made it to the fight – thankfully, for his parents were from Bavarian Burgstadt – although he would get a second chance against different opposition at Okinawa in 1945. Rudi made his rugby debut at 17 for Santa Clara in 1913, faced the All Blacks six weeks after first picking up a rugby ball, and played his last game in 1979 for the Bald Eagles Rugby Club of San Francisco against the Belfast side Instonians, at the age of 83.[18]

At Antwerp on 5 September 1920, the Inter-Allied defeat of 1919 was avenged and USA ran out surprise 8–0 winners over France. Weather was a factor in upsetting the form, as it often can in rugby, infamously at Murrayfield. Scholz later recalled:

> At a council of war we decided that because the ground was wet and slippery and the ball likewise, we would make it a forward game. The French tried a backfield game, and they lost although they were fast. Our forwards outweighed the French easily . . . we dribbled to their five yard line and when the French first five fumbled, Hunter picked it up and fell over the line. Converted. Final score 8–0.[19]

Carroll had his second Olympic gold medal. He was the only Australian to carry away gold from Antwerp, this time under a star-spangled banner.

The victors then did their lap of honour through France in September and played four matches, carrying all before them until their return to Paris. In Lyons, they defeated a side selected from the French southeast, 26–0; a southern team was defeated 14–3 in Toulouse, and a southwest team 6–3 at Bordeaux. Carroll's fourth and final Test was in October, in a return fixture with the France national side at Colombes. This again proved a luckier ground for the French who triumphed 14–5 – small consolation for their silver second in Antwerp's Olympic Stadium. It is unlikely that diplomacy played a part in this defeat.

USA, with Carroll as coach and Scholz playing, returned to Paris to repeat their winning feat in the 1924 Olympics. It did not start well. At Boulogne, immigration officials refused them entry and the players had to force their way off the ship onto dry land. The French had made the game a matter of national pride, and the Parisian press whipped up fierce anti-American sentiment, branding them 'streetfighters and saloon brawlers'. When Paris authorities cancelled previously arranged warm-ups against local clubs and restricted training to scrubland near their hotel, the American players scaled the fences at the Stade de Colombes. 'They were looking for a punching bag . . . we were told to go to Paris and take our beatings like gentlemen,' wrote one. This, however, is not the American way, and a squad dominated by gridiron giants drafted in for the purpose, were bone-juddering and uncompromising. Having again crushed poor Romania 37–0, they unexpectedly upset the odds (5–1 against from the local bookies) to vanquish the hot home favourites 17–3, with six players getting onto the score-sheet.

Not for the first (or last) time, French spectators let their side down in the final. A partisan crowd of 40,000 at Colombes booed and hissed the Americans after the star French winger, Adolphe Jauréguy, had been flattened by a tackle and taken bleeding from the field; they then rained abuse, bottles and rocks onto the players throughout the rest of the match. A riotous mob (a popular Paris tradition since long before 1789) forced the Americans to escape the field under the protection of the opposition players and armed police; Gideon Nelson, one of the reserves, was pole-axed by the crowd on the touchline. In one last act of sacrilege, the US national anthem was jeered during the medal presentation.

Rugby as an Olympic sport was then cancelled due to a lack of interest from its prime exponents, other than the French, whose unseemly crowd behaviour sounded the death knell for the event. This left the USA – to the confounding of many a pub-quizzer – as unlikely reigning Olympic champions at rugby, at least until Rio 2016. Will the sleeping giant reawaken? That will be another story.

9

England

The love that asks no question, the love that stands the test
That lays upon the altar the dearest and the best

Exactly a year and a day after Grand Slam Saturday at Colombes, another rugby match took place in France, on 14 April 1915. By now the old pre-war world had vanished, never to return; so too had hundreds of thousands of men who had died since August 1914, including 57,253 Empire soldiers. On that Wednesday, the French Army, strung along a wide front with their homeland at stake, made progress at Berry-au-Bac on the Aisne north of Reims, but failed in their desperate attacks at Maizeray 160 kilometres away, to the east of infamous Verdun; the British, meanwhile, played rugby. The game was played behind the lines at Pont de Nieppe, near song-famed Armentières on the Franco-Belgian border. This was in the relatively short but infinitely bloody sector of the 730-kilometre Western Front held by the British, around the Ypres Salient and to the south.

Two British divisions played that day: the 4th Division of Regulars against the 48th (South Midland) Division of Territorials. The 4th had originally been kept back from the Expeditionary Force to defend against the invasion threat, betraying Kitchener's low confidence in the Territorial Force, specifically created for home defence. No invasion materialised and the division was now taking the fight to the Germans in Flanders fields. Out of deference to the exhausted men who had just come out of the front-line trenches, they played a shortened match of twenty-five minutes each way. The scratch XVs had to depart from their nocturnal routine of hates and bombardment, punctuated by the stand-to at dawn and dusk, and return to what passed as normality in wartime: the night-fighters now played games in daylight. Rugby helped as a reminder of past years of sanity; its full-on physicality was an absorbing distraction for the frayed nerves of men under fire for days on end.

It is claimed that twenty-seven rugby internationalists served with the 4th during the war, but not all could be assembled on this day; the men from the trenches still managed to muster some considerable rugby talent from three nations, including two future presidents of the Irish Rugby Union. At full back, Lieutenant William Hinton, of Wesleyan College, had sixteen caps for Ireland and seven games for the Barbarians. Ulsterman Captain William Tyrrell, with nine caps in the green jersey, had toured South Africa with the British in 1910.[1] As Irish pack-leader in their last game of 1914, he had fought that notorious running battle with Welsh collier Percy Jones at Belfast. He was a medical officer who won the DSO and Bar, MC and Belgian Croix de Guerre. He joined the RAF after the war and ascended to the height of air vice-marshal; appointment as honorary surgeon to King George VI during the Second War earned him a knighthood in 1944. Tyrrell was also buried by an explosion not long after this game, an experience which allowed him to contribute personally to the findings of the Committee of Enquiry into 'Shell-Shock' in 1922. His conclusion was that shell-shock is caused by attempted repression of fear.

A second RAMC captain in the side, Harold James Storrs Morton, Blackheath prop and Cambridge Blue in 1908 and another Baa-Baa, was capped four times for England in 1910. Scots internationalist Lieutenant Rowland Fraser, a front-row forward from Edinburgh, won three light Blues, captaining Cambridge in 1910. He was later promoted to captain in the Rifle Brigade but was killed on the first day of the Somme; his name is carved on the Thiepval Memorial to those 72,194 killed in the chalk-lands, who could not be identified to give them their own resting place. J.N. Thompson of London Scottish and Ireland triallist J.G. Keppell made up the known rugby names, but nine more of the side have faded into anonymity.

English rugby and regiments were both organised on county lines, and there was close identification between club and battalion. The 48th Division team mainly comprised 'Soldiers of Gloster', with eleven players from the 1/5th Gloucestershires, who were serious about their rugby. In wartime, they had challenged the newly arrived Canadians and played for a company cup, won by D Company, before they crossed the Channel to Boulogne on 29 March 1915. Ten of the division's players had turned out for Gloucester Football Club, some over many seasons, others for only one; some were county champions with Gloucestershire in 1913 and several had also faced the Springboks.

Notable among them was hometown boy, Private Sid Smart, a back-row forward with 195 games for Gloucester in a thirteen-year career that would last until 1923, skippering the club in his final season. He also amassed twenty-six County caps and twelve for England, including both pre-war Grand Slam seasons, and led the recruitment charge on that August 1914 day at Shire Hall. Twice wounded in the war and eventually discharged from active service, he resumed rugby after the war for his club, a resurgent Gloucestershire[2] and his country, with a further three Test caps. A lifetime clubman, he died aged 81 in 1969 at his beloved Kingsholm, while serving as a steward in the grandstand during a game against Cambridge; when we consider what he lived through in his twenties, this has to count as a great result. Gloucester FC's memorial lists thirty players lost in the war; seventeen of them have no known grave.

Analysis of the 48th Division team throws up interesting comparisons with peacetime rugby and wartime casualty stats; of its fifteen men, three were killed and six wounded. Fourteen men are identified by name, with a guest appearance by the prodigious and ageless A.N. Other; records show that he has played for a prolific number of clubs in a remarkable career that still endures today, yet is still uncapped. Like Zorro, his real name is unknown (Andrew, Arthur, Algernon?) but his is a rugby biography that one day must be written. Eight players were privates: Smart, Sysum, Webb, Washbourne, Hamblin, Harris, and two Cooks (broth unspoilt), which gives the lie to any generalisation that rugby was exclusive to the officer class. Four officers played on this side: Gloucesters' Lieutenant Lionel Sumner, later MC, wounded and acting major; Royal Warwicks Captain Francis Deakin, skipper of Moseley and Midland Counties and a 1914 Barbarian; and two from the Royal Berkshires including Lieutenant Charles Cruttwell, an Oxford University triallist, who was also wounded. He later wrote a history of the Great War and engaged in a running feud with Evelyn Waugh. The fourth officer, who surpassed them all in talent if not rank, would die by a sniper's bullet three weeks after his final game, at Ploegsteert Wood on 5 May.

Two more Gloucesters in the 48th's side, Syd Millard and Sydney Sysum, would later be killed at the Somme on the same 23rd day of July 1916, a dark day for two battalions of the regiment and the rugby club. At 0630 the whistle blew along the trenches for a pincer movement on the fortified village of Pozières, the 48th attacking from the northwest and the 1st Australian Division from the southeast; they were mown down like summer corn by scything German machine guns. The pair can be found on the same pier and face of the Thiepval Memorial, still side by side (Syd by

Syd?). Another NCO on the team, half back Lance Corporal Alec Lewis, was wounded that day; his younger brothers, Tom and Melville, both rugby players, were listed missing and later joined the Gloucester roll on Lutyens's arched ziggurat. Alec was later commissioned and rose to become Captain Lewis, MC and Bar, giving another lie to the stereotype of the public-school officer class. The fifteenth man remains unheralded: for a man so extensively documented in his playing career, the wartime service of A.N. Other remains a mystery. It is commonly acknowledged that some military records were later destroyed by Luftwaffe firebombs; his must surely be amongst them.

The referee was Ireland's genius Captain Basil Maclear, of the Royal Dublin Fusiliers. He too was killed a few weeks later in May. The match was reported in the first April edition of *The Fifth Gloucester Gazette*, one of the first trench newspapers produced at the front.

> The Fourth kicked off with the wind and immediately began to press, their forwards doing splendid work. Then Sysum broke away and scored after a bout of passing . . . The Fourth returned to the attack and almost scored, but after some loose play our forwards broke away and 'got over.' Hamblin converted. Soon after, Washbourne intercepted and a combined movement with Hamblin resulted in the ball being taken over the line by J. Harris. The score at half-time was 11 points to nil. The South Midlands continued to keep the upper hand and Harris again scored. Five minutes before time Washbourne scored a brilliant try, leaving us victors by 17 points.

'Despite the difference in the scoring' wrote this soldier-scribe, 'the game was most interesting and was thoroughly enjoyed by all the spectators, especially the Welshmen who had turned out to see a football match after many months in the trenches.'

The man we have to thank for such a complete team-list for the 48th, unusual for these scratch games of teams thrown together at the front, is touch judge Lieutenant Colonel Gilbert Collett, DSO, of Gloucester County, a Cambridge Blue of 1898 and a 1903 British Lion. His reason for preserving his list is our fourth officer and South Midlands captain, whose name was famed throughout the rugby world: Lieutenant Ronald Poulton-Palmer, 1/4th Royal Berkshires, Harlequins, Liverpool FC and England Grand Slam hero. Originally Poulton, the addition of Palmer to his name came as a condition of a legacy from the biscuit family.

Collett supplied the list to Ronald's father when he was killed three weeks after this final game. Ronnie had written to his father about the Nieppe game: 'The match was quite amusing. We won 14–0 [actually 17–0], and there were millions of Generals there.' He added more detail in his journal entry for the day before turning in, adding a hefty swipe at the 'red-tabs' of Divisional Staff, comfortable away from the trenches:

> After breakfast, drove into Nieppe in a motor lorry to see an exhibition of bomb throwing. After that we drove in a motor ambulance to Armentieres to have lunch and to shop. This town seems none the worse and there is plenty of business, though everything is expensive. After lunch we moved to Nieppe and I played rugger for the South Midland Division against the 4th Division. It was an amusing game.
>
> Several of the Liverpool Scottish from Ypres came over including Dum Cunningham and Dick Lloyd. It was splendid to see so many rugger players about. I changed in the room of the Captain of the 4th Divisional Staff. They lived in great style, quite unnecessary I thought. In fact they rather bored me. They ought to do a turn in the trenches with us all. Back to bed.[3]

It was Ronnie's magnetic attraction that allowed the opposing 48th to enjoy the services of two ringers from the Liverpool Scottish, former team-mates at Liverpool FC, who had heard there was a game on and Ronnie was playing.

'Dick Lloyd' was Richard Averill 'Dickie' Lloyd, a rugby and cricketing star at Portora Royal School 'the greatest school side in the history of the game',[4] which beat adult sides like North Ireland and Lansdowne, and annihilated school rivals by cricket scores to nil. He made his Ireland debut in 1910 while at Dublin University, playing half back with his opening partner at bat, H.M. Read. Either side of the war, Lloyd won nineteen caps, eleven as captain, and held a kicking record of 69 points that lasted until the 1960s and Tom Kiernan. On New Year's Day 1914, Lloyd had played on French soil under happier circumstances, and behind William Tyrrell's pack, when Ireland beat France 8–6 at Parc des Princes; Tyrrell added his try to Joseph Quinn's first, but the winning difference was the conversion by captain Dickie. He was described by one writer as 'a genius, one of the superlative half-backs':

> He was the completely equipped player, but excelled as a kick. Opposing captains might tell off their wing forwards to suppress

him, but he would circumvent them. Other men have kicked as quickly; no player of modern times has been more accurate . . . usually he was the man of his side and the man of the match.[5]

Lloyd's Liverpool season netted him 183 points, including 114 with the boot. In August he commissioned into the local 10th King's Liverpool Regiment (KLR), known as the Liverpool Scottish, and was in France by February 1915. An erroneous report of his death in April 1915 confused him with club colleague and near namesake R.A. (Robert Arthur) Lloyd, killed with the 4th Battalion. Former Dulwich XV schoolboy Paul Jones was half right when he mourned his lost rugby idols:

> Do you realise what a fine part amateur sportsmen are playing in this war? I really doubt if there will be any great athletes left if things go on as they are doing. On the same day I read that Poulton Palmer and R.A. Lloyd are gone. Only last year, I remember seeing these two as Captain of England and Ireland respectively, shaking hands with each other and with the King at Twickenham.[6]

Dickie's companion, Robert 'Dum' Cunningham, was an old Rugby School chum of Ronnie's, as was fellow school XV centre Rupert Brooke who would die on Skyros nine days later, on St George's Day, of septicaemia from an insect bite on the way to Gallipoli. Dum was another Liverpool FC player who took his place with Poulton-Palmer and Lloyd in a poignant photograph from the final season of peace: six of the sitters perished. Dum was a pre-war volunteer in the first draft of the Scottish aboard the *Maidan* when it crossed to France in November 1914. Despite his best efforts, being wounded three times, he achieved his majority and survived the war, winning the MC at Rivière for remaining under fire while severely wounded to get another wounded man to safety.[7]

That photograph of the Liverpool Football Club team in 1914 taken outside Birkenhead Park's pavilion, with six doomed players in red, black and blue hoops, captures a vanished moment for Liverpool, for rugby and for imperial Britain. The year marks a pinnacle in the economic fortunes of a city that considered itself, with good reason, the 'second city of Empire'. Its growing confidence built on global maritime trade in 'commodities' especially with America – once slaves, now cotton and insurance – would be crowned by the completion in 1916 of the waterside trio of magnificent buildings at Pierhead, known as the Three Graces, including the Royal Liver Building. Liverpool FC was the oldest open rugby club in the world, formed in 1857, when a group of Rugbeians challenged local boys to a football game under their school rules. In 1871, the club provided four of the England team that played Scotland in the first rugby international.

The 1895 schism that created the breakaway Northern Union almost did for first-class rugby union in the region. The *Liverpool Mercury* warned in 1897 that 'The Rugby code in Liverpool and district will in a few years be as extinct as a dodo.'[8] The writer, nervous of being branded a heretic, tentatively suggested a 'Manchester and Liverpool District Rugby Union League', observing that the success of leagues in Association and Northern Union is 'a sufficient object-lesson of the utility of such a system in vastly increasing the interest not only of the general public, but also of the players'. The proposal was ignored, as its author almost certainly expected. But as the city's thriving economy attracted an influx of businessmen and professionals, so amateur rugby union prospered, although it hardly spoke with a pronounced Scouse accent.

In 1914, as if to prove the city's stature, the club's first XV was graced by its own trinity of international captains: Poulton-Palmer of England, Ireland's Dickie Lloyd and Frederick Turner of Scotland. It is a unique honour for a club to claim in a decade, let alone a season; between them they amassed an impressive (for the era) fifty-one caps. The reputations of these three men alone would merit the team's label as 'one of the best sides ever', but there was strength in depth. Alex Angus, capped fourteen times for Scotland from 1909, did not make the team photo but was another great star in the pre-war firmament; he shone again with four more caps and a try against Ireland in 1920. He started the war as a private in the 9th Royal Scots, was mentioned in Haig's despatches, and ended it with a DSO as CO of the 5th Cameron Highlanders.

Not that the internationalists were alone in their glory: Tracey Fowler, at wing forward, won a Cambridge Blue and was an England triallist; George Davey was a regular county selection at scrum half for many years and Tommy Williams Lloyd and Robert Raimes Jackson, a Barbarian, were widely regarded as one of the swiftest pairs of wingers in the business. Seven of the side represented Lancashire – it would have been more had the rules not forbidden those with Irish or Scots caps from playing for English counties. The season's haul was 191 tries with Jackson (39) narrowly pipping T.W. Lloyd (34) for the title of top try-scorer in this *annus mirabilis*.

With Turner and Dickie landing goals from all angles, they were defeated just four times in thirty-one outings: a shock defeat at Carlisle was ascribed to the absence of key players and to 'the fact that Turner played in the centre, leaving us without a hooker'. Let that be a warning to today's hookers who loiter with intent in the backs. Carlisle supporters, disgruntled that some stars had not turned up, behaved in a very French fashion and pelted them with mud. That season they scored a club record 838 points and conceded only 239. According to forward Henry Royle, interviewed for the *Liverpool Post* in 1964, the winning formula was simple:

> Our pattern of play seldom varied; Turner would hook, the forwards shoved and kept our legs out of the way, and as soon as Davey had the ball we had no further trouble. As a comparatively light pack we worked very hard in the scrum. I have a pair of thick ears as a memento – but it was well worth it.[9]

To his thick ears, Royle would add serious shrapnel wounds to thigh and groin at Second Ypres, and a gassing at Third Ypres: he was invalided for home duty in March 1918, but rejoined his 2/6th KLR battalion in France, happily seven days after the Armistice.

The Great War sparked many changes in Britain and would signal the start of a long fall from grace for the city of Liverpool; the club's title would be usurped by a football team in red, and the game of rugby union would lose premier status in the northwest city, overwhelmed by a rising tide of Association success. It was the city's blue side, Everton, who would finish the controversial 1914–15 season in April as League champions; they would hold the title for another five years, as football finally gave reluctant way to the demands of war. By the time soccer was suspended on 23 April 1915, Liverpool's rugby club from the last pre-war season had already lost two of its finest, and would suffer the loss of four more. When the final reckoning came, the club counted a sad toll of fifty-seven members killed. The original LFC added a white hoop to its colours in the 1986 merger that created Liverpool St Helens – the true Football Club is still alive on Merseyside.

As in Gloucester, when war arrived, most Liver-birds of a rugby feather flocked together as one battalion, in this case the 10th King's Liverpool Regiment (Liverpool Scottish). In November 1914, the *Liverpool Echo* reported several new commissions in the Scottish, including rugby players George 'Pinkie' Cowan, Dickie Lloyd and his cricketing brother William, and the Turner brothers, Frederick and William. During the war, this single battalion would include in its ranks an extraordinary seven rugby internationalists. Such was their stellar reputation that men like Lawrence

Blencowe of Oxford, Headingley, Yorkshire, Harlequins and Barbarians – a mere England triallist – rarely get mentioned in the 10th KLR tributes, but he too fell at Ypres in 1917.

Frederick Harding Turner, the Liverpool captain of captains, who sits flanked by his two stellar lieutenants, Poulton-Palmer and Lloyd, was capped fifteen times by his country and led the Scottish team in 1914. He was Liverpudlian by birth, in Sefton Park in 1888, but Scottish through his parents, such that he occasionally turned out for the London Exiles when moonlighting from university in the Big Smoke. His schooling was amidst the Howgill Fells at Cumberland's rugby nursery of Sedbergh and then Trinity, Oxford. He won three Blues 1908–10 and first played alongside the wizard Poulton-Palmer, who later recalled his 'cheery and infectious laugh' and practical joking. Their Varsity Match photo of 1910 is sobering: Oxford skipper Turner sits with Poulton-Palmer again on his right hand, Billy Geen (Wales), Ronnie Lagden (England) and David Bain (Scotland). Hindsight turns the formal gravity of young men in such photographs into the look of the grave.

On leaving university, Freddy joined his father's printing firm and was ever present in three seasons for Scotland from 1911 to 1913, winning his final honours in 1914 against Ireland and in the England game at Inverleith. Eleven players competing that March day for the Calcutta Cup of melted-down rupees already walked in the valley of the shadow of death. Yet they feared no evil, as they were too busy playing the most exciting and closest fought game of the championship, with tries from Huggan and Will prompting a second-half comeback to a narrow, single-point defeat. It was not a vintage era for the Scots with only four of Freddy's caps bringing victory. The origins of his 'Tanky' nickname are not as obvious as they seem, as Ernest Swinton's armoured landship would not be invented until after his death, but he was undeniably physically robust. The versatile Turner played flanker for his country, which goes some way to explain his switch from hooker to centre for his club when the need arose.

Turner prepared early for war, as so many rugby players did: he had enlisted with the Territorial 10th as a private and was gazetted second lieutenant in May 1912. Turner went to war on 1 November with (in its full Order of Battle) the 1/10th (Liverpool Scottish) Battalion, The King's (Liverpool) Regiment, 166th (South Lancashire) Brigade, 55th (West Lancashire) Division. He wrote from France:

> We are not yet the finest battalion in the British Army, nor have
> we absolutely annihilated the Prussian Guard; all we have really

done is to take our share in the discomforts and in some of the dangers of the campaign without grousing.

His admiration for the Regular Army 'Old Contemptibles', who had borne the brunt of the German onslaught from Mons onwards, knew no bounds:

> Don't believe all the yarns you see in the Liverpool papers about us. True we have had some hardships and not a little discomfort, but it has been a picnic by comparison with what the Regulars went through. They are a magnificent lot and one admires them more and more every day.[10]

His own service overseas lasted ten short weeks. On 10 January 1915 in trenches near Kemmel, he was shot by a sniper while supervising a wiring party:

> After breakfast on 10 January 1915, he went down to the trench to look at the barbed wire he had put out in front the night before. On the way he looked up twice for a second and each time he was shot at but both shots missed. He then got to a place where the parapet was rather low and was talking to a sergeant when a bullet went between their heads. Lieutenant Turner said, 'by Jove, that has deafened my right ear'. The sergeant remarked, 'and my left one too, sir'. Turner went a shade lower down and had a look at the wire and was shot clean through the middle of the forehead, killing him instantly.[11]

He was 26 years and 226 days old. His body was retrieved and buried by RAMC medic and double VC winner, Noel Chavasse, Surgeon-Captain to the battalion.[12] Noel and his brother were both Liverpool players; Christopher, future Bishop of Rochester, played amateur rugby league for St Helens when a young curate and was barred from Union for life – both his God and the RFU move in mysterious ways. Turner's was a mournful burial in pouring rain in the local Kemmel churchyard, but Chavasse and his detail did their best for Freddy:

> The grave, though baled out in the evening, was 18 inches deep in water. However it is quite the best cared-for grave in the churchyard and looks very pretty, with a nice cross put up by one of the other regiments in the brigade, and also a nice wreath.

Poulton-Palmer, who had only four months left of life himself, wrote a fond encomium in tribute to his friend, fell-walking companion, team-mate, captain and adversary on the international field, and one of the many natural leaders who emerged from the rugby ranks:

> Those who saw last year's England v Scotland match could realize what an anxiety to his opponents his peculiarly infectious power of leading was. His play, like his tackle, was hard and straight, and never have I seen him the slightest bit perturbed or excited; and in this fact lay the secret of his great power and control. His kicking ability is well-known, and his tenacious determination to stick it was well shown in the Varsity match of 1909, when he returned to help his scrum when in great pain, with one knee useless owing to a displaced cartilage.[13]

Freddy's older brother, Lieutenant William Stewart Turner, also with the Scottish, was killed in action five months later at Hooge, a few miles away in the small but horribly formed Ypres Salient, on 16 June; he left no trace of an earthly or watery grave and is commemorated on the Menin Gate Memorial. Although Freddy was buried with care in his 'pretty grave', the site was destroyed by later fighting around the church: his white CWGC stone, set apart from the main war graves section in the West Flanders churchyard, does not mark his grave but is a Special Memorial. But this does allow him the small consolation – and remarkable rugby coincidence – of being next to another local rival and internationalist, Percy Dale 'Toggie' Kendall, of Birkenhead Park and England.

The glamour boys of Liverpool FC were not the only show in town: there was rugby across the Mersey too. Toggie Kendall, an Englishman with the Scottish, read law at Cambridge but did not get his Blue. While qualifying as a solicitor in London, he made his mark playing for Blackheath and the Barbarians before returning to his home club, Birkenhead Park. He was England's scrum half in the early years of the new century, making his debut against Scotland in 1901 at the familiar Rectory Field. It was a wooden spoon game for England; with Oughtred, his half-back partner, he was 'slow in getting the ball and uncertain in passing, they never really gave their three-quarters a chance'.[14]

Kendall skippered England in the same fixture two years later (a rare honour in only his third Test) in front of 25,000 at Richmond, to no greater effect, as the land of the thistle was then going through one of its purple patches. This time, however, the match was hard-fought, with the 6–10 result (and another spoon for England) only settled late on. His English side on both occasions featured Bert 'Octopus' Gamlin, not at number eight as you might expect, but at full back, where he was once reputed to have tackled two men, one with either hand, to earn his nickname. Percy's only other cap – against Wales – was also a defeat. As the Wirral was in Cheshire, he represented that county on forty-five occasions, captaining the side against the All Black Originals at his home ground; as for most English sides in 1905, it was a crushing defeat but Percy was 'energetic and extremely useful'.[15] By 1914, the 35-year-old veteran was still turning out for the 3rd XV, helping them to 500 points in an unbeaten season, and coaching youngsters at Park.

In the pre-war years of mounting military tension, Kendall had served as colour sergeant with the Liverpool Scottish Territorials. Despite his age and being father of two children, he did not hesitate to re-enlist within twelve hours of the outbreak of war. He was commissioned in October and went over with Cunningham and Turner in the first contingent on the *Maidan*. The manner of his death on 25 January, a fortnight after Freddy Turner, was singularly unlucky. Noel Chavasse described it in a letter to his father, the Bishop of Liverpool: 'He was in a safe part of a trench giving orders to a Corporal, when a bullet struck the branch of a tree above the trench and glanced down upon him. Three minutes later he was dead.'

Although high-explosive shells obliterated their graves and churned their bones into Brooke's 'richer earth', Tanky and Toggie have some dignity in Kemmèl Churchyard cemetery: their twin memorials acknowledge their last resting place – which is more than was accorded to many soldiers of the Great War. Shoulder to shoulder, they both carry the legend, 'Known to be Buried in this Cemetery', and – touchingly for two renowned sportsmen from the same field – 'THEIR GLORY SHALL NOT BE BLOTTED OUT',[16] the standard phrase for destroyed graves proposed by Rudyard Kipling from one of his raids on the Apocrypha.

Liverpool's class of 1914 still had more men to bury and to honour. Scrum half Captain George Davey, MC, also with the Scottish, was one of only three 1st XV players to resume rugby after the war. Full back Eric Hamilton Cowan, a lieutenant in the Royal Garrison Artillery, died in February 1916, after an operation in Canterbury. He was buried in Toxteth Park Cemetery with full military honours; his brother George or 'Pinkie' survived until 1985. Charles Hill mobilised with 9th KLR in August 1914, and won both an MC and Bar in 1918, first leading a trench raid, later taking company command when his superior was killed and 'consolidating the captured position under very heavy fire'.[17]

The prolific try-scoring winger Captain Robert Jackson, MC, initially of 4th KLR, later with the Royal Artillery, was also prolifically wounded, with three wound stripes on his sleeve, before dying from his fourth in November 1917. He lies in Dozinghem Military Cemetery, one of three with mock-Flemish names (with Bandaghem and Mendinghem) that serviced the massive hospitals near Poperinghe. His wing partner Tommy Lloyd, also of 4th KLR, was wounded in France, and could not return to front-line fighting. This did not stop him having a busy war: he helped evacuate the Serbian Army from Albania to Salonika, served in transport in Mesopotamia and Italy and was awarded the DSO (as well as the order of St Sava from the grateful Serbs). He would be Intelligence Officer for the 'Dambusters' 617 Squadron in the next war, and was killed in a flying accident in 1944. Captain John Edgar Ross, also 4th KLR, a Barbarian and Scotland reserve, was killed in April 1916 and is buried at Bethune. Tracey Fowler served as Sub-Lieutenant, RNVR, and Lieutenant James Clegg, transferred from 13th KLR to the King's African Rifles in East Africa; both survived. James Gibson Grant battled enteritis and influenza before resigning his commission in 1917 due to persistent ill-health.

No club in Liverpool was immune from the ravages of war. Aliens RFC (precursor to today's Sefton RUFC) was founded in 1907; not by extra-terrestrials, who would not fathom the Laws of Rugby, however advanced their technology, but by a group of schoolteachers who all came from outside the city. One player who sounded suspiciously alien at the time was Hubert von Mengershausen: this threequarter and Manchester University medical student actually came from Natal, South Africa, whither his German father had emigrated after fighting in the Franco-Prussian War. A house doctor at Manchester's Ancoats Hospital, when war broke out his application for an RAMC commission was refused because of his German surname. Curiously, Swedish doctor Rudi von Braun of Barts' and Rosslyn Park encountered no such problem and served in Gallipoli and France. The Aliens' minute book records the names of sixteen members killed and missing, noting: 'It is a singular fact that every one of our fallen playing members had occupied the full back position.' It still is one of the most dangerous places on the pitch.

England rugby and the Liverpool Scottish would suffer again – a double blow on a single day in 1916 on the Somme, though not on the notorious 1 July or the terrible 15 September, but almost exactly midway, on 9 August at Guillemont. On that day English rugby had two locks broken in battle: Noel Slocock of Liverpool and Lancashire, and John

Abbott 'Jack' King of Headingley and Yorkshire. The men of the White Rose and the Red would both be dead 'where poppies blow, between the crosses, row on row'.

Christmas-born Slocock was christened Noel by his reverend father. A growing reputation for line-out work at Liverpool FC, while working in the city's cotton trade, brought the call for his England debut against the touring South Africans at Crystal Palace in December 1906. Farcically, in a clerical error, the letter went not to Slocock, but to Guy's Hospital medical student, Arnold Alcock – a right 'cock-up' by the RFU, not a conspiracy. Noel had the consolation of facing the Springboks for Lancashire the following week; Arnold was never heard of again.

On 5 January 1907 Slocock made his 'second debut' against France at Richmond, taking the precaution of getting his name on the score-sheet, for any RFU blazers able to read. He was ever-present in the 1907 and 1908 Test side, although it was not a successful English era. He signed off his international career against Scotland in March 1908 with a personal flourish: captain for the day and a try, but not the team win he would have perhaps preferred. Liverpool kept him busy as Club Secretary and the siren call of King Cotton became more insistent. He took his family to Savannah, Georgia; it was from America that Noel returned to fight in France with his home-town Liverpool Scottish.

Jack King, a most unlikely lock and number eight at 5ft 5in, made his England debut at Swansea in 1911 and won ten more caps. In France, he wearied of the patrols and police work of his Yorkshire cavalry unit and longed 'to be more of a soldier'. A chance meeting with old rugby mates in the Liverpool Scottish, including the 'famous old English forward Slocock' saw him transfer to 'X' Company, willingly swapping his dry saddle for waterlogged knee-deep mud in the Poor Bloody Infantry. He refused to apply for a commission, preferring to stay in the thick of the scrum. His last letter to Bob Oakes, his Headingley mate, was relentlessly cheery: 'I am absolutely A1 in every way – but one can never tell and so long as I don't disgrace the old Rugby game, I don't think I mind.'[18]

The initial Big Push at the Somme had famously failed; a series of summer battles now saw battalion offensives designed to 'bite and hold' small chunks of enemy territory. These also failed. On 9 August, three assaults were made by the Scottish on the village of Guillemont and two of its England men were killed: Second Lieutenant Noel Slocock, leading his men into action, and Lance Corporal Jack King, two years to the day after he had stood an inch taller in front of the recruiting sergeant and taken the King's Shilling. In the same action, Edgar Mobbs was wounded with his 7th Northants; they were just three of more than 82,000 casualties in this phase of the Somme campaign, sacrificed for a thousand-yard gain.

Edgar Mobbs, promoted to major in March 1916, had taken over command of the 7th Northants in April. Having helped to raise the battalion and risen from the ranks, it was the job he was born to do: formal promotion to lieutenant colonel swiftly followed. At Guillemont, where King and Slocock were killed, both he and his sidekick Grierson were wounded by shrapnel. Their recuperation in Blighty afforded another welcome interlude of rugby:

> Then we went to the Somme, and just before we went over the bags Edgar got hit. I took a bit of the same shell in the Headmaster's area, so we came home together. When better we went to the Old Deer Park at Richmond to see the A.S.C. [Army Service Corps] Grove Park XV perform. I was much struck with Wagstaff, the NU [Northern Union] centre who was the best player I ever saw in this position. He had everything – pace, hand-off, swerve, lovely kick etc, but Mobbs wasn't keen, for he thought the lot should be in France. I believe he told [Major] R.V. Stanley so, and I don't think the latter had much to say in defence of his charges.[19]

After two mentions in despatches, Mobbs was awarded the DSO in December. His battalion suffered severe casualties at Arras in April 1917. Mobbs was again wounded, this time in the neck, at Messines on 7 June, but returned to the battalion nineteen days later. As Grierson said, 'Edgar didn't stay in England until he was fit – he wasn't the kind of fellow who would – but went back to his battalion as soon as the doctors would let him.'

The battle that would be called Passchendaele opened on 31 July 1917. Walking wounded arriving at his headquarters near Zillebeke, in Canada Street tunnels, told of officers killed; Mobbs decided to lead from the front, and moved to Shrewsbury Forest. There he bumped into Lieutenant Norman Spencer, also from Bedford; in the heat of battle, the pair reminisced about rugby and mutual friends. Spencer witnessed Mobbs's heroic effort to bomb a machine gun:

> In the tornado of hostile shelling he got ahead and seeing a number of his men cut down by an undiscovered machine-gun strong-point, he charged to bomb it, certain death under such a terrific hail of shell.[20]

Before he died, Mobbs scrawled a last note of gunnery instructions and sent it back with his runner. The battalion history states, 'The fact that his body could not be recovered and buried, as all ranks would have wished, was perhaps a good thing, as it helped keep alive his memory in the battalion, and inspired in everyone the resolve to avenge his death and to end the war that had already caused so much misery and suffering'. He is commemorated on the Menin Gate Memorial.

Mobbs, said Grierson, was 'one of the finest fellows his generation will see. As a footballer he had of course his limitations, but as a man he had practically none. He was big, in every sense of the word.' He revealed Mobbs's intentions to emigrate to Canada; Grierson believed that he would have 'made his mark there in much the same way and as quickly as Mr. S.M. Bruce, the old Cambridge Rowing Blue has done in Australia'.[21] He recounted one final story:

> Lt Colonel Mobbs had been asked to send in a return in *red ink*. We were in the trenches at the time, so the return was typed in black, which we thought good enough. Back it came in due course, signed by some Subaltern 'for Major General', drawing Edgar's attention to the fact that it should be in red ink and requesting him to comply. Edgar replied at the foot of the letter. 'Reference the above. We are in the front line trenches and have no red ink. There is however plenty of red blood here, so if you would like that instead, please instruct me to use it.' He heard no more. He died as he lived – a sportsman and a gentleman.

No less heroic was the later death, in the same prolonged, mud-logged battle, of another 'big sportsman', Northampton bootmaker Private Tom Collins. This powerful Saints forward, heavyweight boxing champ of his division, had played against the Springboks in the same Midlands side as the lauded Mobbs and Poulton-Palmer. On 7 October, at Zonnebeke, Collins and eight men went out as a stretcher party to bring in the wounded; a single shell wounded five and killed three, including Poor Tom. It was, said the *Northampton Independent*, a 'painful shock to all followers of Rugby Football'. He met his death in a 'chivalrous, courageous way characteristic of him'.

Colonel Davidson of the Liverpool Scottish sent his sympathies to Corporal Jack King's sisters at the farm in Wharfedale, paying tribute to their brother and indeed to all rugby players:

When I saw him, absolutely cool and collected under a murderous machine-gun fire, with shells falling all round, one thanked God for such men to set such a priceless example. He was absolutely lionhearted, and had he come through, I should have promoted him on the field and recommended him for the D.C.M. [Distinguished Conduct Medal].

It was a sad day for football. We can ill spare men like these, but if another game of football is never played in Britain, the game has done well, for after two years' command in the field, I am convinced that the Rugby footballer makes the finest soldier in the world.[22]

Ireland

Together standing tall
Shoulder to shoulder
We'll answer Ireland's call[1]

In England, there was no Rugby Battalion: the rugby boat had already sailed, with its players rushing to enlist or taking up commissions in August and September. The closest was D Company, 7th Northants, raised at a rugby ground by Edgar Mobbs, whose own story, as he rose inexorably from enlisted man to commanding officer, annealed the bright armour of his 'Own' company, or even 'Corps' – the nickname burnished with the myth.

Across the Irish Sea, another D Company, 7th Battalion, would be raised from volunteers at a rugby ground, under the banner of the Irish Rugby Union, and would suffer the same bullets and bombs of outrageous fortune as Mobbs's men. Nine Irish internationalists lost their lives in the war. But it was a single company of ordinary men, many of them from one Dublin club, who stood tall and fell the hardest.

Ireland was then part of Britain, but by no means happily so. It would take more than this chapter (and already has taken many books) to unravel the entanglements of Irish politics. The country was divided on sectarian lines with a minority of mainly Protestant loyalists concentrated in northern Ulster, amidst a Catholic majority that was lobbying from Dublin for Home Rule. The Unionists feared for their future and clung on resolutely to their status within the United Kingdom. This simplifies the complex web of loyalties far beyond its tortuous reality, but a solution seemed close before war intervened.

The Government of Ireland Bill, passed three times by the Westminster Commons in 1912, 1913 and 1914, was repeatedly rejected by the Lords. As the Parliament Act stipulated, it then automatically became law, receiving Royal Assent on 15 September 1914. But the declaration of war with Germany six weeks before, and fear of civil war at Britain's back door postponed its implementation. King George's presence at

Twickenham for the England game against Ireland had carried a clear political message. Rugby provided a shining light of unison which rose above the sectarian divide and marked it out from the inevitably Nationalist sports of Gaelic football and hurling. In rugby, players from north and south, Catholic and Protestant, stood shoulder to shoulder in a 'Combined Irish' team, a remarkable display of rugby's ability to put aside political tensions in vigorous common pursuit by all 'four provinces' of an oval ball. While Association still cleaves the Emerald isle in two, rugby holds it together.

The August declaration of war signalled an extraordinary outburst of patriotism by Empire loyalists and Nationalists alike. More decisively than C.J.B. Marriott in England, and as swiftly as the SFU, Frank Henry Browning, President of the Irish Rugby Football Union (IRFU) since 1912, issued a circular to the clubs in the Dublin district, urging members to place themselves at the disposal of the country in war, in response to Irish-born Lord Kitchener's first appeal for one hundred thousand men. Dublin-born in 1868, Browning (nicknamed 'Chicken') had been a cricketer for Marlborough and MCC, captaining Ireland thirteen times.[2] He played his rugby at half back – as befitted 'a short and stockily-built man with powerful forearms' – for Trinity College and the Wanderers club, narrowly missing out on a double cap. The response to his call was immediate: Browning inaugurated the 'Irish Rugby Football Union Volunteer Corps', headquartered at the Lansdowne Road ground. He extended membership beyond rugby to all sporting clubs and engaged several drill sergeants, including one Sergeant Major Guest: in a few weeks, he had over 300 recruits under military instruction, drawn from the commercial and professional classes of the city. Browning and Guest stand proudly in front of their men in a photograph; in September 1914, Guest is the only one who is in uniform.

Browning contacted an old friend, Lieutenant Colonel Geoffrey Dowling, CO of the newly formed 7th (Service) Battalion of the Royal Dublin Fusiliers (RDF), who had been a renowned rugby footballer as captain of Monkstown. Dowling agreed to keep open a special company for 'Pals' from the IRFU Volunteer Corps and advertised in the press:

> *To the Irish Rugby Football Union Volunteers*
> I am keeping my Battalion open for you to join. Come in your platoons (fifty men). Mess, drill and work together, and I hope, fight the common enemy together. I am waiting for YOU, but I cannot keep open long. Come at once TO-DAY.

Like 'Mobbs' Own' this sub-unit was denominated 'D' Company.

Dowling's Monkstown had a long association with the military, with many officers playing in its ranks. It had already lost one Irish cap, Pierce O'Brien-Butler, in the Boer War; during this new conflict it would lose internationalists Ernest Cotton Deane and Basil Maclear. Deane was killed in action, serving as a captain with the RAMC attached to the Leicestershire Regiment, near Laventie on 25 September 1915. A month earlier, he had won an MC when,

> a patrol in front of the line was bombed by the enemy. Captain Deane, without any knowledge of the enemy's strength, at once got over the parapet and ran by himself to the spot under rifle and machine gun fire. Finding four wounded men, he returned for stretchers and got them back into safety. This was not the first time that Captain Deane's gallantry under fire had been brought to notice.[3]

It would however be the last.

On 16 September, those who had enlisted at Lansdowne Road – barristers and solicitors, doctors, stockbrokers, barbers, students of medicine, engineering and art, commercials, civil servants and insurance salesmen – marched off to Kingsbridge station en route to the Curragh Camp for training, cheered by a warm ovation as they went. Training involved drilling, musketry, trench-digging and gruelling route marches. This was no ordinary company of soldiers. In December, they took a break from training, as guests of Lieutenant Cochrane at Bray, south of Dublin. The subaltern was also Sir Stanley Cochrane, Baronet, whose father had made a fortune by inventing ginger ale; Stanley spent some of it on building a cricket field and railway station at his Woodbrook estate, where he hosted the national XIs of Australia, South Africa and India. Fortified by a weekend of ginger ale and mineral waters from Cantrell & Cochrane Ltd (other famed Irish beverages almost certainly available), D Company marched in full battle gear from Bray to the Curragh: by road that is 40 miles, or less by the direct but mountainous Wicklow scenic route. As ever, less is more.

D Company trained at the Curragh for seven months. One newspaper correspondent watched the volunteers at their 'labour of love and loyalty':

> I was particularly interested in 'D' Company, the 'Footballers', as they were known when they were first drafted to the Curragh. The title is steadily drifting into abeyance. They were footballers

when they went to the Curragh. They are soldiers of the King now; and proud to be nothing else; and, above all, proud to be serving in the 'Old Toughs'.

I watched them at their drill . . . and they went through their movements with splendid precision and confidence. It was difficult to believe that the majority of the men were civilians like the rest of us only a month ago. They marched and countermarched, and formed fours; and wheeled and counter-wheeled, and deployed and performed all the other evolutions of the parade ground with, so far as I could judge, the smartness and certainty of veterans. The Prussian drill-sergeant is supposed to be the last word in efficiency production. No cursing, swearing, jack-booted, bullying Prussian non-commissioned officer could have his men in better shape or fit.[4]

The 'Old Toughs' was the nickname for the 2nd Battalion, Dublin Fusiliers; predictably (and justifiably in many cases), D Company became known as 'the Toffs among the Toughs'. When the battalion embarked for mainland Britain in May 1915, their progress through Dublin's streets was again reported in fond detail, as proof 'that the city pulses with ardent enthusiasm for the cause of the Allies':

Led by the band of the 12th Lancers and the pipers of the Trinity College Officer Training Corps, they marched off from the Royal Barracks. Along the Liffey quays, crowds on the pavements and spectators in the windows cheered and waved. Outside the Four Courts, a large group of barristers, solicitors, officials and judges shouted good-bye to their friends. Little boys strutted alongside the marching column, chanting their street songs:

Left, right; left right; here's the way we go,
Marching with fixed bayonets, the terror of every foe,
A credit to the nation, a thousand buccaneers,
A terror to creation, are the Dublin Fusiliers.

Not for them the direct route along the Liffey quays to the ships. Diverting across Essex Bridge, they marched through the commercial centre of Dame Street, then College Green, passing the Bank of Ireland and Trinity College where many of the Battalion had been students and one a Professor. Spectators became dense as the marching column crossed O'Connell Bridge and right wheeled onto the quays skirting the statue of O'Connell the liberator. Emotion rose when well dressed ladies from the fashionable Georgian and Regency squares of south Dublin mingled with their poorer sisters in shawls from the Liberties and lesser squares of north Dublin. Together they joined their husbands and sweethearts in the ranks to keep step with them the last few hundred yards.[5]

The professor was Ernest Julian, Reid Professor of Criminal Law at TCD when he enlisted.[6] Many from the TCD contingent did not take commissions, although it is unclear whether this was out of a desire for equality or, as is more likely, a hunger to get to the front without tiresome and lengthy officer training. Another lawyer, Henry Hanna, KC, lived next to the rugby ground, was secretary of the Pals committee, and wrote a remarkably fresh and vivid chronicle of D Company which was published in wartime, and stands as tribute to the Irish rugby men who marched away.

They were not all Toffs: Private John Boyd played rugby for Clontarf and worked as a clerk; Harry Boyd worked with his father in a well-known pharmacy William Boyd (no relation) was a travelling salesman from Bective Rangers RFC. Charles Ball, Assistant Keeper in the Botanic Gardens and editor of *Irish Gardening*, added a cultivated touch to the company. Douglas Gunning, 19 years old, working in a Sligo bank, cycled 50 miles to join up with his elder brother, Cecil; they kept a joint diary throughout. Private Hugh Pollock, of Wanderers, an assistant manager on a tea plantation, travelled from Sumatra, Dutch East Indies, to enlist. Wanderers, whose clubhouse was tucked away in a corner of the Lansdowne Road ground, already boasted two Victoria Cross recipients from the Boer War in Tommy Crean and Robert Johnston. A third would be awarded in this war to its Fred Harvey, a record unmatched by many regiments, let alone a single rugby club. Its war memorial lists thirty-three names.

As they crossed the Irish Sea, one Dublin Fusilier and rugby hero of Ireland already lay dead in Flanders. Basil Maclear was always destined to be a star: his Ulster-born grandfather Sir Thomas Maclear, Astronomer Royal at Cape Town Observatory, has a crater on the moon named after him, as well as a beacon on Table Mountain. Born in Portsmouth and rocked in the rugby cradle of Bedford School, Basil played for Blackheath, Monkstown, Cork County, Munster and the Barbarians. Fellow Bedfordian, Henry Grierson, described him admiringly:

Six feet tall, weighed well over fourteen stone, and could do the hundred in ten and three-fifths – good time for so big a man. In his clothes he looked a trifle on the heavy side but stripped he was a picture, and possessed those delightful abdominal muscles lying in ripples, which are rarely encountered today, but which are familiar to the students of ancient statuary. No wonder the ladies of Dublin called him the broth of a bhoy.[7]

On the field he was 'a forceful rather than subtle player, he was dangerous in attack and formidable in defence, running straight and hard, and handing off with a force which was only equalled by the tremendous vigour of his tackling'.[8] Even the fearsome 'Darkie' Sivright was once knocked almost unconscious by Maclear's hand-off. However, it can be said that he handled his opponents literally with kid gloves – he played on the wing wearing a trademark pair of white leather mittens, as well as a khaki puttee wrapped round his waist, for reasons no one ever discovered. Despite these quirky trappings of a sporting genius, Maclear was also a 'Tough': he won the Sword of Honour as top cadet at Sandhurst, was gazetted as second lieutenant to the 2nd Royal Dublin Fusiliers and at 18 years old served in the Boer War, being wounded at Spion Kop and mentioned in despatches. In 1905, he took full command of the Lagos Battalion, West Africa Frontier Force. On his return to Britain, rugby took centre stage.

Unaccountably passed over by England's selectors, after being watched in a game in which he scored four tries and converted twelve, he repaid their myopia by choosing to play for his father's country, beating England three times, and appearing eleven times overall in the green jersey. He captained Munster in one of his four games against the 1905 All Blacks, on 28 November at Limerick (a 33–0 hiding but not unusual on that tour). But his moment of glory came a year later against the Springboks at the Balmoral Showgrounds in Belfast. Grierson wrote:

E.H.D. Sewell told me that Basil's try for Ireland against the South Africans in 1907 was the finest he had seen and he had observed a good number. Maclear playing 'dead' centre, received the ball on his own 25 line and with characteristic dash burst clear through [opposite wing Loubser] and when clear, swung to the left. Little Joubert was playing full-back and when the time came, he attempted the tackle at the right-angle, only to be handed-off in the face. He made a second effort when he recovered with similar result, but nothing daunted had another gallant go and was put down for good.

The Globe reinforced the significance of the score and its timing:

> Basil Maclear's run will go down to posterity. It is not at all likely to be forgotten by those who were fortunate enough to be present. It was altogether out of the common in an international match for a man to score after running from his own '25' and the incident gathered particular force from the fact that Ireland then were apparently in a hopeless position. Maclear's try gave Ireland a new lease of life.

The try and two more from Harold Sugars ran the South Africans close in the 12–15 final score.

Basil's last match in March 1907 was a less glorious 29–0 pasting from Wales in Cardiff in front of 30,000 Welshmen, and an unimpressed Irish ladies hockey team. The match may be more remembered for the debut of Fred Harvey, an 18-year-old schoolboy at Portora, Enniskillen. Half-back Fred, part of the Wanderers XV that won the 1906 Leinster Cup, followed in the footsteps of his brothers, both capped for Ireland. His debut must have been traumatic, and perhaps, like Ireland, 'thoroughly demoralised and upset . . . stupefied by the brilliance of their opponents', he emigrated to Canada. His second cap on his return came as fourth-choice full back in 1911 against France; despite the 25–5 victory, a poor display (his error let in the French try) ended his Irish career.

Back in Canada, Fred married and joined the Mounted Rifles, transferring into Lord Strathcona's Horse in 1916. Cavalry regiments were under-employed in the Western Front conditions, but Harvey proved the value of the horse in March 1917 at Guyencourt on the Somme. Seeing a previously invisible strand of wire protecting the machine-gun post they were attacking, he 'jumped the wire, shot the machine-gunner and captured the gun'. According to his Victoria Cross citation, 'his most courageous act undoubtedly had a decisive effect on the success of the operations'. A year later, Fred repeated his heroism, when he was awarded the MC in the same action that earned fellow Canadian Gordon Flowerdew the VC.

By 1912 Basil Maclear was Inspector of Physical Training at Sandhurst. He rejoined 2nd RDF as a captain in February 1915 and went to France as second-in-command, in time for the heavy fighting at Ypres during April and May. In a brief respite, Basil refereed the game on 14 April at

Nieppe, where Poulton-Palmer threw his last pass and Ireland's Dickie Lloyd, sixteen-cap Billy Hinton and William Tyrrell played for the 4th Division. On returning to his unit, for four days from 8 May he was in company command. Every day, in brief intervals snatched from the fighting, he wrote to his mother, his last letter dated 23 May. The next morning he was killed at the age of 34. Seven months later his mention in despatches cited:

> Captain Basil Maclear, who showed great coolness in handling the Reserve Company of the Battalion, which he was able to bring up almost intact under very heavy fire; and also the great power of command which he showed himself to possess when suddenly called upon to command the Battalion for four days during a trying situation.

He was the youngest of five sons who all served in the First World War; brothers Percy and Harry, both lieutenant colonels, were killed in action. Of the thirty caps won by Irish internationalists who died in the war, he collected over a third.

The 7th RDF joined the 10th (Irish) Division near Basingstoke for three months of more warlike training, including bayonet practice. After inspections by King George V and Lord Kitchener, the division received orders in June 1915 to sail for Gallipoli. D Company's strength was 239 men; of those, 160 would be killed, wounded or taken prisoner and only seventy-nine would return intact. The Lansdowne club itself would lose thirty-nine of its members over the war, most of them with D Company. They embarked at Devonport in July. Salt-water baths, sea air and morning runs around the deck had them 'in the pink'. The voyage was one of exotic discovery, with ice cold oranges from the refrigerator and stops at Gibraltar and Malta as they sailed to Alexandria. The 'Dubs' took their leave of Egypt with a rousing rendition of 'Tipperary'. Their mood would soon change.

The British, ANZAC and French forces sent to Gallipoli were not only comprehensively outwitted by the Turks, but betrayed by an ill-conceived plan (of Churchill's making) and the incompetence of their own leadership. The New Zealand commander of Irish parentage, General Alexander Godley, wrote to his cousin in Cavan, Lord Kilbracken, 'I do not suppose in history, that anything so utterly mismanaged by the British Government will ever be recorded.' The general himself was not above critical comment from those who served there: Wilfred Jesson of Rosslyn Park and the 5th Wiltshires, wounded and shell-shocked at Gallipoli, recounted of one silent night operation with bayonet only, no weapons fired:

> The password and countersign were to be 'Godley' and 'Success'. Of the four days operations which followed, perhaps 'ungodly failure' would be more appropriate.[9]

The 'Dubs' disembarked at Suvla Bay on 7 August, as dawn broke just before five o'clock, to the north of the tangled knot of hills and crests where the ANZAC divisions were still enmeshed. The morning of the landing was beautifully fine. Henry Hanna described the scene:

> The naval guns were vigorously shelling the ridges round the Bay. The shells exploded with bright red flame edged with a black fringe of smoke, just like a tulip with the red leaves tipped with black. The noise was terrifying . . . as the light became stronger nothing was visible to the naked eye on the shore save the stretcher-bearers carrying wounded down the slopes of a hill.[10]

They arrived without maps or clear orders. They had no gunnery support as the division's artillery had been sent to France instead. Water was in very short supply. The horrors of war soon hit the Pals: stretchers passed with blood-soaked burdens. In lowering the parapet of their trench they found it crammed with Turkish bodies, their stench overpowering as the heat rose; one was a young girl sniper, around her neck fourteen identity tags taken as trophies from dead Munster Fusiliers. Twenty-two of the Dubs died on the first day of the landing. Lieutenant Ernest Julian, shot in the back, was one of them. Another Lansdowne FC player, Lieutenant Ernest Weatherill, brought in five wounded men under fire.

Vital high ground at Scimitar Hill had been taken by England centre Jimmy Dingle and his 6th East Yorks, but his unit was ordered to vacate it to attack another height. The Turks retook it and enfiladed the Dubs with machine-gun fire, as well as the 6th Border Regiment of Jimmy's Durham rugby friend, Nowell Oxland, who was killed.[11] As the scrub on the hill burned and left 'little mounds of scorched khaki', Captain Richard 'Paddy' Tobin of Lansdowne FC wrote his last letter home:

> I was out from 6am to 9pm. I got up into the firing line in a hail of bullets and dumped along the ammunition, but not without losing six more of the company. We had to dig ourselves in as the enemy were stronger than we thought.

A terrible battle was later fought over two days from 15 August at Kiretch Tepe, the ridge to the north of Suvla, where the beauty of the sea view ironically reminded the Dubliners of Killiney Bay. As the Turks sheltered behind a knife-edge ridge crest, hurling grenades, the Gunnings' diary recorded:

> Some of our fellows throwing back the bombs which the Turks threw over and which had not exploded. One fellow caught them like catching a cricket ball. Wounded and dead lying everywhere. The sun streaming down and not a drop of water to be had. Neither had we bombs to reply to the Turks and drive them out.[12]

One Private Wilkin caught and returned four bombs, but was blown to pieces by the fifth; the heroism was not recorded at the time as almost all the officers were killed, but Captain Kelly, 7th RDF, wrote of it in 1931.

D Company was told that the only chance they had of keeping the hill was to charge the bombers. They fixed bayonets and 'with a terrific shout rushed off to the top of the crest', led by Captain Hickman, who was instantly killed. Machine-gun fire from the right flank killed or wounded almost everyone in the charge: only four were able to crawl back over the ridge to cover. Lieutenant Weatherill, hero of the first day and 'a fearless leader and good friend to us all', was killed on the ridge. Sergeant Charles Sawyer who was with him on the first day of the landing said 'I can truly say that a more brave and cool officer never took men into action in that awful peninsula.' Paddy Tobin was also killed, as was Lance Corporal Arnold Moss, 19, another rugby man, who had been recommended for the DCM for helping comrades under fire. Colonel Downing was wounded.

Under fire, the sectarian divide at home was forgotten as Father Murphy, 48, and Canon McLean, Church of Ireland and 60 years of age, held services together. One grateful Pal wrote, 'Catholic and Protestant are hand in hand, all brought about by the gentleness and undaunted courage displayed by these two splendid soldiers of Christ.' By 16 August Lieutenant Hamilton, a TCD medical student, was the only D Company officer left; when he was hospitalised the next day with a foot wound, Company Sergeant Major Kee took command for six weeks. Hamilton had seen too much: he became a chronic alcoholic, was court-martialled and dismissed. He returned to Ireland but never continued his medical studies; he never worked again and did nothing with his life. Ten of the thirty-nine Lansdowne men named on the club's memorial died at Gallipoli. 250 current and former members in 1914 joined the fight; seventy-two did not come back.

The Dubs were withdrawn on 30 September with the 10th Division and reorganised at Salonika, where the stalwart Regimental Sergeant Major Guest received his commission. The Gallipoli remnants were hastily reinforced with raw recruits shipped out from Britain and Egypt but they were short of equipment, supplies and winter clothing: 7th RDF still wore shorts and pith helmets. The weather and local Greek population at Salonika were equally cold and hostile. November found the division in Serbia, holding the front between Kosturino and Lake Doiran, awaiting an assault by the Bulgarians. In a repeat of Gallipoli, the front line was in hill-top country broken by deep gullies, barren rock and scree, with scant cover from grass, scrub and stunted oak. When a raging Balkan blizzard struck, the exposed infantrymen, their health already weakened on the peninsula, collapsed; hundreds suffered frostbite, disease and exposure. Sergeant Richard Sealy Swan, a prominent Lansdowne player, was one of those to die.

Another man who, like Hamilton, saw too much of war for his own good was Jasper Thomas Brett. The trainee solicitor was a flying centre threequarter with Monkstown, who won his only cap on the wing for Ireland against Wales in the 'battle of Belfast' in 1914 (he also travelled to Paris as an unused reserve). It was Ireland's last game of the championship, and at such a tender age he was surely to be capped again. War had other ideas. Brett enlisted in D Company, became a machine-gunner and as officers fell considerably faster than the resilient flies of Gallipoli, was commissioned in the field in September. Salonika was the final straw that broke the mind of this 19-year-old lieutenant. He was hospitalised with 'shell-shock' in June 1916 at the Latchmere Hospital in Richmond, Surrey. On his release in January 1917, he returned to the family home in Kingstown (now Dun Laoghaire). On 4 February, he found a dark railway tunnel that matched his state of mind and lay down on the rails; the 10.10 p.m. from Dalkey to Bray severed his head from his body. War had claimed another casualty, acknowledged by the Commonwealth War Graves Commission in 2011.

There were men too who died from across an Irish border yet to be created, like Irish cap Major Albert Stewart of North of Ireland FC, who died with Chavasse at Broodseinde in 1917. The 36th (Ulster) Division broke the rules and took their objectives on the first day of the Somme (the anniversary of the Battle of the Boyne) before being forced to withdraw with grievous losses. Belfast's Captain William Victor Edwards of Malone RFC, twice capped by Ireland, joined the 6th East Belfast Battalion of the Ulster Volunteer Force in 1914. He took command of ill-fated D Company, 7th RDF, on Boxing Day 1917, but was killed three days later at Deir Ibzia, Palestine.

The man who first called out the Lansdowne Road recruits would also die, this time on his own doorstep. While the young and fit went away on active service, the older members formed a 'Dad's Army' home guard under the direct command of Frank Browning, now 47 years of age. They became part of the Irish Auxiliary Volunteer Training Corps (IAVTC), 'an organisation for gentlemen of above military age', known in Dublin as the 'Gorgeous Wrecks' because of the initials GR (*Georgius Rex*) on their armbands. They wore a motley array of uniform and civilian clothes and carried dummy rifles.

On Easter Monday 1916, news reached them on a march of a rising in the city. As they returned to Beggar's Bush Barracks and crossed the Mount Street Bridge, they were mistaken for real soldiers and came under fire from Irish Volunteers on Northumberland Street. The rebels ceased fire when they realised that, although carrying rifles, the VTC men had no ammunition, but not before Browning and three others were fatally wounded. News of this attack on elderly unarmed men did little for the popularity of the Rising in Dublin, which was ruthlessly put down. Inevitably, there were rugby men on both sides and Kevin Barry, of University College Dublin Rugby Club, died in the cause of Irish independence.

Frank Browning died two days later. On his gravestone, erected by the IRFU in Dublin's Dean's Grange cemetery, not far from Jasper Brett's, the inscription reads: 'He will live in the memory of all as an honourable comrade and distinguished sportsman.'

Wales

Ei gwrol ryfelwyr, gwladgarwyr tra mad,
Dros ryddid collasant eu gwaed.

Its valiant warriors so gallant and brave
For freedom their life's blood they gave.

R ugby in Wales was always a different ball game. The earliest green
shoots may have sprung from the same social roots as England,
Scotland and Ireland: schools like Llandovery and Cowbridge Grammar
followed the English public-school model and the professional classes led
the founding of clubs along the southern coast at Neath, Cardiff, Swansea
and Newport in the 1870s. But black gold in green valleys drew a massive
influx of workers to the pits and collieries as coal production boomed in the
following decades. Working class they were, but these immigrants from
England's south-west and rural Ireland did not come from traditional
association football hinterlands. With no shadow from soccer falling over
its fields, the sapling rugby grew strong; its physical grunt matched the
tough and often brutal life of the miner.

The popularity of rugby amongst the hardworking-class also fostered a
pragmatic approach to amateurism. If the pits worked six days a week and
Sunday was sacred for chapel, then broken-time payments and expenses
for Saturday and midweek games were necessary to sustain players and
their families. Although the amateur principle was staunchly upheld by
the Welsh Football Union (WFU, as it then was), an official enquiry in
1907 admitted that some clubs 'were in the habit of paying and receiving
hotel or travelling expenses in excess of the sum actually disbursed'. The
WFU itself tried to buy a house for its greatest player, Arthur Gould; when
the Scots and English objected, Wales withdrew from the International
Board and fixtures rather than accede to pressure.

Rugby's devotees also faced religious opposition. The Welsh Revival of
1904 led by minister Evan Roberts railed against violence and drunkenness
in sport: 'even an ape would not disgrace itself by seeking pleasures
in kicking a football'. Tens of thousands were converted to his cause;
Senghenydd RFC was forced to disband, for want of players. But rugby

soon developed its own brand of religious fervour as its followers flocked to worship of an afternoon, and it became the pastime of the people. The Senghenydd club re-formed and was sanctified by tragedy when five of its players were among 439 dead in Britain's worst-ever pit disaster in October 1913. The South Wales mining community led hard lives and they could be forgiven for playing hard too. It did, however, gain them a reputation, as Henry Grierson remarked of the Welsh:

> A wonderful race and they have the love of the game in the blood, and though in the past their play has sometimes left something to be desired in the matter of cleanliness, I am convinced that they are improving yearly in this respect, as is also the sportsmanship of their crowds.

It was not all gnarled pit props and hard centres, as the professional and commercial classes were also caught up in a common passion. Welsh rugby had its share of Varsity Blues like Clem and Bryn Lewis of Cardiff, and Oswald Jenkins and Horace Thomas of Swansea. Thomas Jones, secretary to Lloyd George, proclaimed 'a game democratic and amateur is a rare thing – a unique thing to be cherished'. The sportsmanship and passion of their crowds was unique: huge numbers squeezed into Welsh grounds. At Cardiff 47,000 watched the All Blacks and 45,000 saw the Springboks at St Helen's; Twickenham, even in Wavell Wakefield's mid-twenties pomp for England, only drew 35,000. Only Londoners ogling New Zealand's unshrinkable underpants at Crystal Palace in 1905 matched Welsh rugby congregations.

There was too a fierce national identity regularly asserted in rugby against the English rulers and rival Celts; from 1900, Wales won six of twelve Triple Crowns in its first 'Golden Era'. Pride was redoubled when Wales offered almost the only isolated pockets of resistance to defy the colonial invaders: famously against the All Blacks in 1905; Cardiff against the 1906 Springboks; Wales again, Llanelli, Cardiff and Swansea against the 1908 Australians; Newport and defiant Swansea once more against the 1912 Boks. The 0–11 Welsh defeat by the earlier South African team was taken heavily and many international careers ended that day at St Helen's. Tom Richards, musing on the upright Māori against the Welsh Guards at the front in May 1916, seemed to have forgotten his Wallaby touring experiences of 1908: 'The Englishman, though, always stands up better and finer than the Welshman, but the Colonial is vastly superior to any of them.'

Not on your watch, Tom. Fuelled by *hwyl*, Welsh clubs triumphed where national sides had failed: a distinctive ethnic Welsh culture rolled *calon*, colliery, chapel and choir into one powerful ball, melded with ancient mythology. It was at rugby Tests in 1905 that *'Hen wlad fy nhadau'* ('Old land of my fathers') was first sung and became an unofficial Welsh anthem, first alongside 'God save the Prince of Wales' and, since 1975, proudly sung alone.

Five Cardiff men heard referee Gil Evan's whistle in all three games against the best teams in the Southern Hemisphere. One was John Lewis Williams: 'Johnnie' was a flying winger, 'a universal favourite with the crowd' according to the *South Wales Daily News*, and a man that opponents like Tom Richards would seek out at the front in wartime. He scored seventeen tries in as many matches for Wales, and was leading try-scorer with 1908's Anglo-Welsh side that failed to impress Richards. After four seasons with Newport, he switched to his home-town Cardiff club, forming with Wales centre Rhys Gabe a sparkling partnership, 'the very acme of polished cleverness in all they did', and playing 199 games. In 1905, he scored thirty-five tries in Cardiff's blue-and-black jerseys and twice faced the fearsome All Blacks (for his club and Glamorgan), although the Welsh wing berth went to match-winner Teddy Morgan. Johnnie made his international debut a year later at St Helen's against the Springboks, playing outside Gabe; the 11–0 defeat wasn't a great start, but it was one of only two Wales Tests he would lose. Welsh honour was salvaged from the mud by Cardiff three weeks later: Boks' full back Arthur Marsberg graciously shook Johnnie's hand after he was left for dead by his try in the momentous 17–0 victory.

Johnnie was prolific in 1907: he scored a hat-trick for Wales against Ireland, a feat he would repeat in 1910 and also ran in five tries for Cardiff against the Barbarians. The following year he did the same to Blackheath, in front of Lloyd George, who declared rugby 'an extraordinary game . . . more exciting than politics' (but then so is drying paint). He then scored the final Welsh try of a triumphant season in which the red shirts won a fifth Triple Crown and carried off a first-ever Grand Slam (if you count France, which officials then did not). After such heroics, the 1908 Anglo-Welsh tour down under is largely (and best) forgotten, although Johnnie notched a dozen tries. This was the year when anti-British articles by the Kaiser, published in the *Telegraph,* amplified distant rumblings in Europe.

Williams also faced the First Wallabies in 1908, in a 9–6 Wales win at Cardiff on the day that Paddy Moran, Tom Richards and Danny Carroll all made their international debuts. The reffing hat-trick for Gil Evans came at a stunning victory by 24–8 over the Wallabies at the Arms Park, with Johnnie bagging a brace. No wonder Tom Richards remembered him so well in Flanders; and no wonder Cardiff RFC had the historic whistle engraved for Evans. A wintry Wales, Cardiff Arms Park in particular, did not suit the Wallabies: they lost three and drew one in a punishing sequence of seven games between 12 and 28 December – the entire tour only saw two other losses, to Mobbs's Midlands and Llanelli. They must have been glad to see in the New Year in England and a return to winning ways at Blackheath. Wales and Williams meanwhile went on to a second successive Triple Crown and Grand Slam.

Johnnie's final season in red brought yet another Triple Crown. His last try was against France in Paris and he was given the captaincy (his coal-exporting business meant he was fluent in French and could decipher their calls) and the match ball from the 13–0 victory. His farewell in 1911 – the decider against Ireland – was played in front of a record 50,000 crammed into a besieged Arms Park: as fans scaled the walls and rushed the gates, mounted police were called in. There was no try-scoring flourish for Johnnie, but the 16–0 result crowned Wales' Golden Era with a third Slam, this time officially recognised with the admission of France. The next would take another thirty-nine years. Johnnie played rugby once more at Cardiff in November 1913, with Wales' Dai Westacott and Dick Thomas, in aid of the Senghenydd Disaster Fund; it was there also that he would enlist in the 20th Royal Fusiliers, seven weeks after war was declared. He soon transferred to the 21st Battalion, where his platoon boasted a full international back line with Welshmen 'Hop' Maddock, Willie Watts and English winger, Alan Roberts.

In March 1914, the WFU declined an invitation from the German Rugby Union to play in Hamburg; in August, the choice to face Germany or not was taken out of their hands. The familiar letter had been circulated to clubs by the WFU, its own version full of Welsh pride and somewhat long of wind:

> We are sure some of the more patriotic spirits amongst our leading players have already joined the Army, but we are equally well sure of the fact that a far larger proportion has not yet done so. Considering that our players comprise probably the very pick of men eligible for service in the Army, and considering that Welshmen have a reputation for not being deficient either in patriotism or pluck, we feel sure we shall not appeal in vain.

> If only every man on every First XV in Wales were to enlist, what a magnificent body there would be at the service of our country, and even then there would still be plenty of players left to enable the game to be played as usual.

In South Wales, war provoked the same contrasting response from rugby and football as elsewhere in Britain; only here rugby was in a majority not only moral but sporting. Eleven survivors from mourning Senghenydd RFC volunteered as soon as war broke out. When Cardiff City went ahead with its football fixtures, a letter to the *Western Mail* protested: 'how much nobler if the 22 players, fine specimens of manhood, had rifles on their shoulders, marching to the battlefield instead of playing with a leather-encased bladder'. In January 1915, the 16th (Service) Battalion (Cardiff City), The Welsh Regiment, was finally raised after eight weeks' hard pushing by the city's mayor, but its name had nothing to do with the football club. Recruiting outside Ninian Park had been as unsuccessful as it was at Chelsea and Arsenal.

The Cardiff City Battalion was now Johnnie's military home with his new subaltern's commission; war inverted rugby's pecking order as he discovered his club vice-captain, the older Major Fred Smith, was now his company commander. Cardiff RFC donated a full rugby strip and boots to the 16th, which numbered internationalists Clem Lewis, Bert Winfield and Dick Thomas, as well as a host of club players. Lewis, Johnnie's Cardiff team-mate in 1909–10, was:

> one of the best outside-half backs of his time, a very neat and elusive player, nice looking and popular. He served the club well in the seasons 1909–10 to 1923–24 [as captain], won eleven Welsh caps, was a Cambridge Blue [twice] and a Barbarian [once, in wartime, against the South Africans] and held, probably the unique distinction of having played for his club, his varsity and his country prior to and after the War.[1]

We will meet him again. Clem, Bert and Johnnie soon played rugby for the Welsh Regiment against 11th South Wales Borderers (SWB), but 1915 was spent in Colwyn Bay and Wiltshire in a different sort of training. Their unit's last public parade before going overseas in December was held in Cardiff, where else but at the Arms Park; seven months later, half of its thousand men would be killed, wounded or missing.

If Lewis and Williams were the backs of legendary Welsh flair, then E.J.R. 'Dick' Thomas was the grunt up front. Sewell put him amongst the 'hefty and tough men in the [Welsh] pack. Burly and hard bitten sons of the hills, caring little or nothing for physical hurt whether to self or opponent, and one of the toughest and fairest was Dick Thomas.' The miner began his rugby career with Rhondda junior clubs Ferndale and Penygraig and, briefly, Cardiff; when he joined the Glamorgan Police, duty postings made the calls on his team loyalties, to Mountain Ash, Glamorgan Police and County. Strong showings for the last against the overseas tourists commended him for his first cap against the 1906 South Africans; it was appendicitis, not poor performance, that delayed his next cap until 1908 and the first Welsh encounter with France. He starred in the Grand Slam win against Ireland, but a regrettable incident against the Wallabies for Glamorgan – Grierson's 'clean play' jibe comes to mind – may have cost him another cap for Wales against Australia.

Dick's international career ended against Scotland in 1909, but he had years of club rugby left. He won only four caps but his presence in Welsh rugby seemed greater. On his next police posting in 1911 he joined Bridgend, where he became captain. On the outbreak of war, he already had years of service to his community behind him before he joined the City Battalion to serve his country with friend, colleague and team-mate Fred Smith, and Johnnie Williams. He was natural NCO material and was rapidly promoted to company sergeant major before crossing to France.

Rugby continued behind the lines between British units, with guest appearances by any former Wallaby captain who happened to pass: for six months the battalion was in a quiet, if rain-soaked, sector – routine conditions for Welsh rugby. The *South Wales Argus* launched an appeal to send footballs 'both rugby and association' to the troops at the front. Captain Herbert Butler of the 2nd Battalion, Monmouthshire Regiment, wrote: 'I beg to acknowledge receipt of the Rugby Football you so kindly sent us. I can assure you it will be a great source of amusement to the men of this battalion.' In May 1915 Private George Noyes of the Welsh Regiment wrote from prison camp in Altdamm, with news of Welsh victories over the Yorkshire Light Infantry and the Rest of Camp: 'There are sixteen Cardiff men here and we would very much like a rugby ball sent out, or anything else to banish the monotony. PS it may interest Cardiffians to know that Wales still leads in sport.' Williams had his treasured ball from the 1911 Paris match sent out for an inter-platoon competition in February 1916. In June they moved south to the Somme, in preparation for their first action in the Big Push. For many it was their last.

Their 38th (Welsh) Division was spared the first-day slaughter but moved into the front line facing Mametz Wood on 5 July, when the awful mismatch of 'bare chests against machine-guns' (Churchill's phrase) was already plain to see on the interminable casualty lists. The City Battalion was joined by 11th SWB, their rugby sparring partners of 1915. Like Noel Hodgson's doomed Devonshires before action at Mansell Copse a week earlier, their planned morning attack looked suicidal: down a slope, across 'Death Valley', then up into the wood, with their flank enfiladed from the right by machine guns dug in at nearby copses, all in broad daylight. A request to attack before dawn was denied; at 0830 the first wave set off.

In a familiar Somme story, the artillery bombardment had failed to take out the enemy wire and emplacements. The verbatim battalion War Diary account, scrawled in pencil under unimaginable pressure, makes for stark, unpunctuated reading:

> 8.30am Bn. under orders drawn up on their own side of slope facing MAMETZ WOOD in lines of platoons with a 2 platoon frontage. 11/SWB in support 10/SWB in reserve. Our artillery ceased firing at wood at 8.30am + first lines of Bn. proceeded over the crest of the slope but came instantly under heavy machine gun frontal fire from MAMETZ WOOD, enfilade fire from FLATIRON COPSE + SABOT COPSE + the German Second System, which now between MAMETZ WOOD + BAZENTIN LE PETIT WOOD, Bn. suffered heavily + has to withdraw to their own side of crest. Bn. made two more attacks but position was much too exposed for any hope or success + orders were received to cease operation. 11/SWB attempted to approach the wood through a gulley running between CATERPILLAR WOOD, slope mentioned above but machine gun fire drove them back. Our losses:- 6 offs. killed, 6 wounded, 268 OR's killed, missing or wounded. Weather very wet, this adding greatly to exhaustion of troops Bn. received orders to return to their Bivouac. Moved off 10.30pm Arrived 4.am 8/7/16.[2]

One of those 'Offs', Captain Johnnie Williams, led his company into the maelstrom of machine-gun bullets. Shrapnel shattered his left leg and his famous 'side step and inward swerve' would be seen no more. Infection followed amputation, and by the time his last letter of good spirits reached his wife, he was dead; he was one of 140 killed in 300 battalion casualties that day.

One OR (Other Rank) died instantly. Survivor William Davies of the 11th SWB told the BBC seventy-one years later how he hid all day from the bullets behind the body of the 'old rugby international, Dick Thomas from Mountain Ash . . . a big, huge man . . . killed just like that, just in front of me'. Sewell had said of Thomas that he 'could always take a knock without moving a hair; this served him well in the police force as on the football field'. On the battlefield, his hulking body soaked up leaden punishment for twelve hours and saved another man's life. In 1987, William Davies was humbly grateful to Dick for 'laying his body on the line'.

That huge body was lost. WFU official, T.D. Schofield of Bridgend, paying tribute in 1917 to Thomas as one in the 'large army of heroic Welsh Rugby players who have laid down their lives on the altar of sacrifice in this worldwide war for righteousness, liberty and justice', recalled one Monmouth player 'who would sooner face any man than Dick Thomas the fiery chariot'. Another Thomas from Bridgend, captain of Wales and the Lions, Gareth, would visit the Mametz Wood site, now marked by an imposing scarlet dragon clawing at barbed wire. There he heard of the Welsh remains that still break the surface in the harrowing harvest time of Owen Sheers's verse:

> And even now the earth stands sentinel
> reaching back into itself for reminders of what happened
> like a wound working a foreign body to the surface of the skin.[3]

Dick Thomas now lies in name only on the Thiepval Memorial where his namesake Gareth would make the 'surreal, spine-tingling' discovery of his own great-uncle William's name, which 'made the concept of sacrifice more vivid and personal'.[4]

David Watts, the Welsh lock newly capped in four Tests in 1914, was also killed on the Somme two days after Johnnie Williams died of his wounds. His Shropshire Light Infantry battalion was in the same offensive to capture Bazentin Ridge that killed South African Toby Moll with the Leicesters. Watts, a Maesteg miner who played rugby for his home club, and whose body was never recovered, was in that ferocious 'Terrible Eight' with Percy Jones, led by the Reverend Jenkin Alban Davies, from Aberaeron. Davies served as a chaplain with the RFA; asked if his pious ears had ever been assailed by 'colourful language' on the rugby field, he said: 'I always wear a scrum cap.' He lived to be 90.

There was more carnage amongst Welsh internationalists in 1916. Sergeant Lou Phillips, a Newport half back, was in at the start of the

Golden Era with Wales' first Triple Crown in 1900. His rugby career was cut short after four caps by a knee injury originally suffered with Newport against Cork Con, but which broke down after ten minutes against Scotland in 1901. More sedately, the architect went on to win the Welsh amateur golf title in both 1907 and 1912. He served with 20th Royal Fusiliers, in which Johnnie Williams had begun his brief military career. Lou's was even shorter as he was killed in March. No set-piece battle for him, just the nightly piece-meal attrition of trench life in the 'quiet' La Bassée sector: he died in a wiring party surprised by German raiders, the only casualty in his unit that day.

Just a mile away lies Lieutenant Colonel Richard Davies Garnons-Williams, who also wore the black-and-amber of Newport. He had played in Wales' first international in 1881, a humiliating experience as England chalked up thirteen tries; he never played for Wales again. After Sandhurst he took a Regular commission in 1887, formally retired in 1892 but kept a voluntary Militia post until 1906, then was 'dug out' of retirement to serve again in his country's hour of need in 1914. Although he won just a singleton cap, Garnons-Williams is 'Father of the House' and one of the 'founding fathers' of Welsh international rugby: he was 59 when shot in the head at Loos in 1915, leading his 12th Royal Fusiliers battalion. One of his soldiers reported:

> He led his men on September 25th into trenches lately occupied by the Germans and on the 27th the battalion were in a support trench and the furthest they had captured. This trench became untenable and retirement had to be effected to straighten the line, the supports, both right and left having retired, so that their flanks were 'in the air'. As the colonel gave the necessary order to retire and instructions to the machine-gun section to fire over the trench to keep back the Germans, he was shot in the head from an adjoining house and did not move again.

Alongside in the line were the 7th Northants and Edgar Mobbs, who would meet the same fate at the head of his own battalion in 1917.

Men from Rodney Parade made up six of the thirteen Welsh caps to die, but the club lost many more. Newport had defeated the 1912 Springboks with 'Billy' Purdon Geen on the wing; he pulled off trebles of Oxford Blues and Welsh caps and played in the ill-fated backline with Dingle and Mobbs for the wartime Barbarians in 1915. He died at Ypres on 31 July 1915, aged 24, with 9th King's Royal Rifle Corps (KRRC), his last moments described by a Major Hope (little of that in 1915):

Geen fought gloriously and was last seen alive leading his platoon in a charge after being for hours subjected to liquid fire and every device the Germans could bring to bear to break through. Seventeen officers and 333 other ranks were killed in this engagement.[5]

Fruiterer Ben Uzzell played rugby for Newport and Pontypool and was Welsh 440 yards champion in 1912, later winning the English 220 yards hurdle title in 1913. He was killed in September 1918, serving with the New Zealand Army. Richard Brinley Stokes, known as 'a wonderfully fit man', was initially rejected by the army because of his flat feet. He eventually joined the Monmouthshire Regiment in 1917, but was killed with the Cheshires at Glencorse Wood during the Third Battle of Ypres. Newport's captain against South Africa, Walter Martin, was more fortunate. Paired with the Wales scrum half Tommy Vile, he formed an 'outstanding half-back combination'. He joined the Newport Athletic Club Platoon of the South Wales Borderers and reached the rank of company sergeant major. Martin was awarded the Distinguished Conduct Medal (DCM) for obtaining 'very valuable information at great personal risk', carrying a wounded man to safety under heavy shellfire.

Horace Wyndham Thomas from Bridgend, like Phillips and Clem Lewis a Monmouth Grammar boy, was killed in action with 16th Rifle Brigade at St Pierre Divion[6] in September 1916, aged 26. He had faced Billy Millar's Springboks on his Wales debut, almost winning the game with an attempted drop goal (four days after winning his Blue for Cambridge), and then England in January 1913. He would have won more caps if he had not been shipped off to a commercial position in Calcutta, where of course he captained the rugby club. In the congealed stagnation of the Somme, Horace's end came at a patch of pulverised red-brick dust that was once a village near Hamel: the front had not moved in a month. Horace Thomas was one of seven light Blues to die from the 1912 Varsity Match that fed thirteen young men into the mincing machine. From the Wales team photograph at the 1910 France game, Charles Meyrick Pritchard would die on the Somme in August with 12th SWB, leading a raiding party to take prisoners for intelligence purposes. He had been in the pack that had battled the Original All Blacks and hung on for their famous victory. Birdie Partridge, writing to his family, called him a 'fine example of what a British sportsman should be'. To his left in the picture, artilleryman Phil Waller also stayed behind in French soil after the war, killed with his South African battery commander by a stray shell.

The thirteen Welsh internationalists who died in the Great War are called to remembrance by the detailed research and passionate prose of countryman Gwyn Prescott, which readers are recommended to seek out. But there is another story which encapsulates the scale and complexity of wartime service and the contribution of Welsh rugby in one Bridgend family. It is the history of six brothers: Stanley, William, Edwin, Charles, Frederick and the most notable of all, Ben, who stands with Pritchard, Waller and Hop Maddock in the photographic souvenir of St Helen's in 1910. They were the sons of William and Ellen Gronow (rhymes with Jonno) of 18 Cheltenham Terrace, who had nine children in all. Fighting and sport were in the Gronow genes: the boys' late father was Private William Gronow of the Regular 1st Worcestershires, who had served overseas in India and Malta and was reportedly one of the best cricket players in the army. He died in 1908. All six of his sons would fight, four would survive, and two died; for the rugby-playing Gronow family, their fatal fraction would yet again be the infamous third.

Edwin, like his father, was an older soldier who wore two medals from his service in Afghanistan, and now returned to war with the 8th Welsh Regiment. Frederick was discharged from the 7th Welsh through ill-health. Charles, Private 14164 of the 5th Battalion, South Wales Borderers, was killed aged just 20, on 12 November 1916, as the Battle of the Somme finally thrashed itself to a standstill, with both sides exhausted and floundering in winter mud. The battle would be officially 'closed down' a week later with over a million dead or wounded on the two sides. Haig insisted in his post-match despatch that 'Verdun had been relieved; the main German forces had been held on the Western Front; and the enemy's strength had been very considerably worn down. Any one of these three results is in itself sufficient to justify the Somme battle.' Modern military historians compete to agree with his self-justification; Charles, who is buried in Pozières British Cemetery, Ovilliers-la-Boisselle, might have another view, but remains silent on the matter.

His older brother, Lance Serjeant (Corporal) 290054 Stanley Gronow was 26 and married to Winifred, so had moved from the family home at No. 18, just across the street to No. 25. Unlike kid brother Charlie, Stanley returned home: he is buried with thirty other Commonwealth War Graves dead at Bridgend Cemetery. It was some small consolation to his wife and widowed mother. Both Charles and Stanley are commemorated on the Cenotaph at Dunraven Place, Bridgend. Stanley is also on the exquisite Celtic Art Nouveau memorial plaque at Nolton Church,

Bridgend, to thirty-six men of the parish who fell in the Great War (for some reason, Charles is not). Stanley's name was also read out by Mr W. Bradshaw, President of Bridgend RFC, at its August 1919 Annual Meeting ('five years next Monday since the last') among their twenty-five fallen, including their most famous son and first mentioned son, Dick Thomas. Also mentioned that day was Stanley Thomas, killed with the Canadian Highlanders at Ypres, who played for Bridgend and Llwynypia, before emigrating to Canada.

Stanley Gronow served with the 7th Welsh Regiment and played rugby for its D Company rugby team, formed mainly of Bridgenders. Whilst in training in Scotland, they played a first match against Montrose Academy on 9 October 1914. It was a 'grand day' as they won 17–3: 'Montrose are a smart team but it was the dummy pass that beat them.'[7] It was a shell fragment that beat Stanley almost four years later: he died aged aged 26 at St George's Hospital, London, on 4 July 1918, having been wounded in the *Kaiserschlacht* spring offensive.

William – Private W.J. Gronow, or 'Bill, as he is familiarly known in football circles' – was vice-captain of Bridgend FC. A Rhondda collier on his enlistment, he served with the South Wales Borderers' 4th Battalion and was awarded the DCM in 1916,[8] proudly reported by the local press: 'Footballer D.C.M. Distinction for Former Bridgend Player'. In his later account of his 1915 Dardanelles campaign, Wilfred Jesson of Sherborne School, a Rosslyn Park and Surrey half back and county cricketer for Hampshire, related an unexpected reunion at Gallipoli with William:

> . . . Pte Gronow, a huge Welsh miner with whom I had come in contact on the rugger field more than once, and such meetings one does not forget. I asked him whether he felt like rugger and he grunted there would be some dirty rugger work if he got amongst them and I knew he spoke true.[9]

Bill's decoration and leadership qualities saw him promoted to sergeant and he didn't stop there: he was commissioned as a lieutenant and awarded the DSO and an MC and Bar.[10]

If Bill had the distinguished military career, it was his brother Ben who was the rugby superstar. Ben Gronow, a stonemason with huge hands, was born in 1887 and began his rugby career with Bridgend Harlequins, following a well-worn path to the senior Bridgend Football Club. In 1908–9, he captained them and made sixteen appearances for Glamorgan County. At Newport in December 1909, the full back so impressed the selectors with his size and goal-kicking in his trial that he was picked for the forthcoming game against France – as a forward. Not yet 23, he played with Pritchard and Waller at Swansea on New Year's Day 1910, scoring a try in the 49–14 victory. The next game up was away to England and the inauguration of Twickenham as an international ground, after Harlequins and Richmond had first tested its turf.

The date was 15 January 1910; a capacity crowd of 18,000 was a third of the number that Swansea or Cardiff could command, but it did include George, Prince of Wales, shortly to be king. The settled Welsh had not lost in the championship for three years. Scots referee James Dallas had been in charge on the day they beat New Zealand. England had eight new caps and their fifteenth man, centre Bert Solomon, arrived from Cornwall in the nick of time by the delayed milk train. The mercurial Harlequin Adrian Stoop won the toss and elected to receive the kick. Ben Gronow of the magnificent boot, launched the ball into the air. It went not to the forwards charging down the touchline, but straight to Stoop; instead of returning it, as everyone expected, he set off on a long diagonal run. As he reached the Welsh 25, he kicked cross-field behind their backs; Gent picked up the bounce and four passes later, Chapman touched down in the corner. No Welsh hand had touched the ball. England won the game 11–6, their first victory over Wales in twelve years and a tectonic plate had shifted in British rugby.

Ben completed the championship season, but another earthquake shook South Wales as he went north, for a fee of £120, to play League for Huddersfield. On 3 September 1910, he made his debut against Ebbw Vale (when the Welsh team was part of the Northern Union) and won his first rugby league international cap when Wales played England at Coventry. Ben went on to 395 appearances for Huddersfield, scoring 80 tries and kicking 673 goals, for a tally of 1,586 points. He was part of the 1914–15 'Team of All Talents' under Harold Wagstaff which won all four trophies: the Challenge Cup, Rugby League Championship, Yorkshire League Cup and Yorkshire Cup in wartime.[11] As with Association, League professionals carried on while Union enlisted; but in 1915 Ben, with Wagstaff, joined the war effort in the Army Service Corps (Motor Transport) at Grove Park and rose to sergeant. His 'active service' initially consisted of rugby in London for Major R.V. Stanley's conquering ASC side, unbeaten except by a United Services team packed with internationals. If Edgar Mobbs was critical, there was risk of even harsher words from heroic brother William, Ben finally went overseas in charge of a transport depot at Ypres.

He survived to play on after the war, for Huddersfield and a small-town club, Grenfell in Australia, before retiring.

On 17 January 1919, as the oval ball again appeared on Welsh fields, a single game salvaged another season lost to war. Bridgend & District played a 'Picked Military Team' in aid of the Bridgend Reception Fund to celebrate the return of the troops. Both William and Frederick Gronow took the field; Charles and Stanley watched from the grandstand in the sky.

For Wales, the last words rest with another dual-code international player from Bridgend. Gareth Thomas, above all a proud Welshman, deeply moved by Mametz Wood, said: 'It all comes down to duty, loyalty and other old-fashioned values. Just because it is the old way doesn't mean it is the wrong way.'

France

Allons enfants de la patrie
La jour de gloire est arrivée.

The world knows the Basque city of Bayonne for two local specialities to which it has given its name: one is its justly famed and delicious *jambon de bayonne*; the other is the notorious and less palatable *baïonette*, which gave a savage edge to the trench fighting of the Great War.

The ancient port of Bayonne is situated at the confluence of the Nive and Adour rivers; these waterways were vital to its early commercial success, including the armaments industry that created the bayonet. By the end of the nineteenth century, rowing was more exercise than commerce, and a sporting club dipped its less deadly blades in the rivers for recreation. In 1904, the rowers decided, like their Vancouver counterparts, to keep themselves fit in the winter months by playing rugby; like the Canadians, these oarsmen kept the same name for their rugby section – Aviron Bayonnais. Among them was Fernand Forgues, French rowing champion in 1905, who had helped to found rugby club Olympique in neighbouring Biarritz in 1904. Two years later he joined the new club at Bayonne.

Tucked into the southwestern corner of France, 40 kilometres from the Spanish border, Bayonne could hardly be further away from Paris if it tried – being fiercely Basque, it probably has. But on 20 April 1913 provincial Aviron Bayonnais came to the capital to play Sporting Club Universitaire de France (SCUF) for the French rugby championship. Competitive rugby was a comparatively recent affair: the first championship in 1892 was a straight Parisian challenge between Stade Français and Racing Club, refereed by Baron Pierre de Coubertin, who went on to bigger things. This was the same year that Rosslyn Park became the first English club to play on the Continent, defeating Stade; rugby tours crossed the Channel with increasing frequency, spreading the popularity of the 'English' game.

The provinces had broken the hegemony of Paris when Stade Bordelaise (SBUC) won in 1899, the first year the championship was opened to clubs outside the capital. SBUC from Bordeaux were a dominant force in the first decade, winning five '*boucliers*',[1] but Lyon and Toulouse also carried the title south; these were all major cities compared to Bayonne. Crowds had grown from 2,000 in 1892 to ten times that for the 1913 championship final. The Springboks had attracted 20,000 to Bordeaux at a time when French soccer internationals in Paris drew only 4,000 spectators; the crowd's understanding of the game did not always match their enthusiasm.

SCUF were favourites in 1913, having been losing finalists in 1911 and boasting five capped French players, albeit that 'one-cap-wonder' Joé Anduran, a Bayonne-born hooker, was among them. His art gallery happened to be near the Gare du Nord as the French found themselves a man short on the way to Swansea in 1910 to play Ben Gronow's side; Anduran was 'selected' on the spot by Cyril Rutherford for his only cap, on New Year's Day. The Aviron Bayonnais captain on Final day in 1913, seven years after he joined the club, was Fernand Forgues. His pedigree was impressive with nine caps at flanker for his country (he would win eleven in all, two as captain); he had already faced Scotland, Wales and the Springboks, at Le Bouscat, Bordeaux, that season.

The Stade Yves du Manoir at Colombes was his lucky ground: it was here that he had made his debut for France on the triumphant day in 1911 that they first won an international, against Scotland 16–15. He would never be on a winning French side again, and the lucky Colombes charm ran out in his last game against Poulton-Palmer. Or perhaps it didn't. Forgues would survive the war to become chairman of Aviron (and three-time pelota champion of France in his forties) and win Bayonne a second title as coach in 1934. But his brother and fellow prop, Jean-Charles, was killed in action in 1918, and another brother, Jules, followed in 1919 from influenza. Six team-mates died, of whom three were French caps, all with visible Basque roots: Maurice Hédembaigt, Emmanuel Iguiñiz and François Poeydebasque. Albert Chateau (or Chatau) struggled on with his wounds until his death in 1924. Aviron Bayonnais' is the story of the proud rise of a small-town team and the correspondingly deep pain it suffered in the Great War.

Three *frères* Forgues appear in a postcard of the 1912–13 team: Fernand, Jules and Jean-Charles. Jules and Marcel (a fourth brother who played in Aviron's two-time championship runners-up after the war) reveal another intriguing trait in French rugby's development: the British, or specifically, Welsh connection. Jules played for Penarth and Marcel later for Swansea and Cardiff, but there was more to it than that. In the same photograph sits a player captioned 'Roé'. Despite his frenchified surname, he was a

Welshman called Harry Owen Roe; the 'panache from Penarth' was the secret of their success on the road to the Colombes final. The Welsh shipping clerk and compact stand-off (he was 5ft 7in) was recruited in 1910 by Fernand when visiting brother Jules, who was working and playing rugby in Penarth; Harry arrived to be player/coach at Bayonne in 1911, aged 25, and only retired when he was 44.

He brought in his trunk a manual by Cardiff and Wales star centre Gwyn Nicholls: *The Modern Rugby Game*. From its pages he drew a playing style of 'total rugby' where backs and forwards combine, which had been the signature of Wales' Golden Decade. He noted the dexterity and ball skills of the local *basquais* pelota players, and youngsters who practised bullfighting by dodging young bulls; he instructed his new charges that there were to be no rucks or mauls, but a fifteen-man handling game. It became known as the *La Manière Bayonnaise*. Or in Basque, *Le Manie Galois* – the 'Welsh Way'.[2] The brothers Forgues, like Gallaher and Stead before them, would publish the secrets of their open passing game for all to read, if not always to follow.

There was a commercial exchange that sustained the Roe move: prized Welsh coal was need by Bayonnais metalworkers at Boucau to smelt iron ore from Bilbao; the pine forests around Bayonne provided resinous pit-props that did not rot in the damp South Wales coalmines. Harry and Jules arranged the contracts and the shipping. Harry met and married a local girl and settled down, playing again after the interruption of war. Despite Roé's newly acquired accent, in forty years, he only ever got to grips with one new language, which was Basque rather than French.[3] He was certainly not up to writing a coaching manual about his methods.

The Bayonnais swept all before them, racking up 600 points in the 1912–13 season; in the qualifiers that led to Paris, they scored 171 points to 6 against. The playmaker Roe had topped the scoring tables, and was renowned for his drop goals. The SCUF Parisians clung on for 13–3 at half-time, but were washed away by a wave of tries in the second half, which showed 'stunning brio, amazing audacity and staggering skill', according to Gaston Lane.[4] The 31–8 final score included six tries from forwards Jules and Fernand, Eugene Ellisalde, Paulin Bascou and Jean Domercq, with winger Victor Labaste scoring one for the backs. Harry Roe converted four of them. One of many souvenir postcards printed of the successful team acclaimed them *Les Gallois de France* – the Welshmen from France. For Aviron players like Felix Lasserre and Jean Domercq, fortunate enough to survive the coming conflagration, Roe's coaching would give them a versatility that would prove invaluable to their careers.

The year 1913 had started less triumphantly for Forgues, and one game exposed a flaw that would bedevil French rugby, but not on the pitch. With his international cap on, Fernand had faced Scotland on New Year's Day at Parc des Princes, the fourth meeting between the two and his second. The Colombes encounter of 1911 was still France's only Test victory; a partisan home crowd of 20,000 hoped for a repeat performance. The French, under the captaincy of Gaston Lane, played well, and Forgues's pack had the better of the second half, but they did not take their chances. They were improving by the year, but still lacked composure.

The referee was James 'Bim' Baxter of Birkenhead Park, an England cap in 1900 and RFU President in the twenties. As 1930 Lions manager in New Zealand, he would loudly condemn the All Blacks' rover role perfected by Gallaher: it was subsequently banned in 1932. He frequently penalised the French; the crowd, more passionate than knowledgeable about the game, became restive. As his whistle finally blew for a 21–3 defeat, spectators stormed the pitch. Some of the Scots were hit by flying stones, Baxter himself was attacked and at least one assailant arrested by gendarmes.

Condemnation of the crowd's behaviour came swiftly, not least in France. The French Union deplored the incident and sent an emissary to the International Board in Glasgow with a formal apology. The Scots were unforgiving, and refused further matches. In a letter to Cyril Rutherford (ironically a Scotsman), secretary to the Union Sportive Française des Sports Athlétiques (USFSA), it was noted in particular that the pitch invaders were not solely those in the cheap seats. The two sides did not meet again until after the war; the Paris mob would find new targets in 1924.

France wept for 1.4 million men who died in their *Grande Guerre*, almost twice as many as Britain. French international rugby teams were hard hit: their 1910 *quinze* against Wales at Swansea lost six men, as did the Colombes XV that succumbed to Poulton-Palmer and Lowe. In all twenty-one capped players were killed, a high toll when we consider that France only began playing international rugby in 1906 against the All Blacks and had capped only 114 players by 1914. Almost a fifth of *les bleus* were 'napoo', as Tommy would have it. With death came the consolation of glory: the 'omnisport' Racing Club de Paris lost 215 members, but collected 34 Médailles Militaires, 95 Légions d'Honneur,

405 Croix de Guerre and 1,200 *citations* (French mentions in despatches). In March 1918 alone, its former 1st XV members collected 56 *citations*.

The first capped Frenchman to be killed was Alfred Mayssonié, known as 'Maysso', a founder member of Stade Toulouse, as Forgues was at Biarritz and Bayonne. This generation of players was building French rugby from its very foundations: it was still young and an *enfant terrible* tendency would creep in both on and off the field. That so many senior figures were killed in wartime may partly explain its troubled adolescence in the 1920s. Maysso was the first player from Toulouse to be capped, in 1908, and played Wales – Gronow, Pritchard, Waller, Maddocks *et al.* – at Swansea when France were first officially admitted to a 'Five Nations' championship in 1910.

He joined the 259e Régiment and died, as so many compatriots did, on his own French soil. His French Army was no expeditionary force like its British imperial allies: it was defending his homeland and the *liberté* his country held so dear. Dressed still in *veste* of bright blue and scarlet *pantalons*, they were mown down in tens of thousands in the first month: on the single day of 22 August, 27,000 Frenchmen were killed. Maysso met his fate on the second day of the Battle of the Marne, in desperate defence of Paris, on 6 September 1914. He was the first rugby internationalist to fall, a few days before Scots Simson and Huggan. His Toulouse captain, lock Paul Mounicq, who had played with Forgues in that infamous Scotland game, retrieved his body; three days later a Toulousain party accorded him a proper burial facing Toulouse, and fashioned a *rouge-et-noir* tie from their red leather tobacco pouches and black notebook covers. Maysso wore his team colours even in death.

Aviron Bayonne took two grievous early blows: on successive days in September: first Emmanuel Iguiñiz (or Iguinitz), then François Poeydebasque, fell on the killing fields of the Aisne at Craonne. This village on the plateau de Californie would be bitterly enshrined in the *'Chanson de Craonne'* of the French mutineers after the disastrous Nivelle offensive of 1917.[5] Gaston Lane had been well qualified to praise their play for Harry Roe's team: a Racing Club centre, who began his international career against the All Blacks, he was the first Frenchman to ten caps (with Marcel Communeau) and also wrote for the French magazines *Sporting* and *L'Equipe*. He was next to die on the 23rd with his 346e Régiment. Three *bleus* in four days; another week and it was four, as singleton cap Joé Anduran perished on 2 October. From November, the French infantry were issued with new uniforms in a *bleu d'horizon* which looked remarkably similar to the pre-war French national team's rugby shirts. The coincidence had more to do with the stopping of aniline dye imports from German BASF, but was nonetheless an ill omen for rugby.

It is impossible that with so many French casualties from August onward that they did not include many hundreds of rugby men. Young and fit like their British *confrères* they were first in line for the fight, although, like their German foe, more were conscripts than volunteers. One who did volunteer, and may have been the first French rugby player to die in the war, was Robert Bergeyre, of the Sporting Club de Vaugirard (SCV), founded appropriately enough for a rugby team, in the *15e arrondissement* of Paris in 1897. In 1911–12, SCV were third ranked to Racing and Stade in the top tier of Paris clubs. In 1913, winger Bergeyre, who had joined SCV from his school, the Lycée Michelet, volunteered for army service. With his clubmate Maurice Allemant, he joined 103e Régiment d'Infanterie, a unit that actively espoused rugby for its fitness training. This was by no means a universal view, as military officialdom favoured the discipline of *la gymnasie,* or individual gymnastics, over team sports.

Robert's regimental team reached the final of the Paris military cup at Colombes; he was one of five soldiers in the XV selected to represent Paris against a London team in March 1914. Corporal Bergeyre had just turned 20 when he was killed on 22 August at Ethe in Belgium; his regiment lost 60 per cent of its effective strength on a day of unimaginable carnage. Almost four years to the day after his death, a new multi-sport ground was opened at the Buttes-Chaumont, Paris, which could accommodate 15,000 spectators in moveable stands. It bore the name of the first club player to fall in the 'field of honour': Robert Bergeyre. In 1920 it hosted the French football cup final and – in 1924 – Olympic matches, before being demolished in 1926.

Bergeyre's SCV club survived the war through a series of alliances, one with SCUF, which was named *les deux Sportings* (S2). In the absence of senior players at the front, club rugby remained full of hope for the future with a *Coupe de l'Espérance* in place of the national championship, contested by youth players who had not yet been drafted. This fulfilled the same function of fitness and preparation for military life as the public-schools games in Britain, but also helped sustain the clubs through the lean years. Although familiar names like Toulouse, Racing and Stade Français appeared in the finals, so did FC Grenoble and Stade Nantais. In 1919, Stadoceste Tarbais and Aviron Bayonnais contested the final, sign of a youth development policy that would pay off after the war.

Rugby behind the lines was not always well received and rugby players not at the front were thought by some to be unpatriotic. At a quarter-final between Perpignan and Toulouse, there were catcalls of 'cowards and thieves' from the crowd. Stung by the abuse, Dr Paul Voivenel, who had been with Maysso and Mounicq on the Marne and was now a military flyer, wrote an enraged letter to the press, countersigned by Mounicq and 'champions de France' from the two teams:

> In sport we recognise only one goal: training for the defence of our country. All the rest is 'gravy'. There is sport to the east and north. The only opposition is the Boche. The only whistle is from bullets.[6]

Harry Roe's military service in this war remains a mystery, although he sensibly fled the Nazi occupation of France in 1940 and served in the Home Guard in Wales. Another Welshman, Rowland Griffiths, of Newport and the 1908 Anglo-Welsh team, coached Perpignan in 1912 and 1913. But another trainer for a French club, Major Edward Marie Felix Momber, born in Biarritz of an English father and French mother in 1888, served with the British Royal Engineers, winning the DSO and MC. The *Army List* of 1911 shows him 'Qualified as 1st Class Interpreter in a Modern Language', always useful when you are coaching Biarritz Olympique, as he was in 1912, and where he is commemorated on a plaque at the stadium under the name 'Monbert'. More unusually, he has two mine craters correctly named after him at Vimy and Railway Wood, near Ypres: it is no surprise to find that he is unique in this honour.

Momber, an absurdly talented swimmer, fencer, rider and rower, represented Hampshire, the Army and United Services at rugby, as well as his military colleges at Woolwich and Chatham. In 1914 he returned to fight from Hong Kong, where he was stationed. In November 1915, with the low cunning that becomes necessary in wartime, he won his MC near Givenchy:

> ... when, by firing a small charge, he induced the enemy to occupy the crater in considerable force. Two large charges were then at once fired, by which about fifty of the enemy are believed to have been killed, and much damage was done to the German parapet and galleries.

At Vimy Ridge in 1916 he was awarded the DSO (and his first crater) for 'conspicuous gallantry and skill in connection with mining operations'.

He was blown up, wounded and deafened by a trench mortar bomb; on his return from hospital, he became OC of 177 Tunnelling Company in February 1917 and commanded it through a time of desperate underground warfare beneath the Bellwaard Ridge. This is *Birdsong* territory. Momber prepared and fired the Wijtschaete mines on the Messines Ridge, which launched one of the most decisive actions of the war. A few days later he was admitted to No. 2 Canadian Casualty Clearing Station with severe hand and head injuries, dying on 20 June 1917. He has another rare distinction for a British officer in that he is named on the 'Monument aux Morts Pour La France' at Biarritz.

The intensity of Verdun and the Somme left little time for military sport (and precious few men to play it). It seems no coincidence that within a week of the close of the Battle of the Somme, on 26 November 1916, a match was held between Stade Français and a 'British' military team, made up of Home Nations' and Dominion players: the French won 8–6. After the near catastrophe of the widespread mutinies of 1917, Marshal Pétain and the French military realised the value to morale of recreation and sport (as well as better food, fewer punishments and more time out of the line). The presence of British and Dominion military teams whetted a renewed French appetite for competition, and a desire to prove themselves as a sporting people. France played nine 'official' international games (as endorsed by USFSA) between April 1917 and the Inter-Allied Games organised by the US Army in June 1919. In Rugby Federation (FFR) records, fifty-six players are recognized as '*internationals de guerre*' – they were not accorded the status of full international caps, as USFSA officialdom protected its patch against military encroachment.

The original American in Paris, Allan Muhr of Racing Club, now reappeared as a key driving force. This 'slave to his passion for rugby' had been capped in the first ever French game against the All Blacks in 1906 and was now a bilingual US Army officer; through him, as early as 1916, French soldiers played American volunteer ambulance men. In January 1917, he set up a team called 'Lutétia' (after the Latin name for Paris) combining the best players from Paris clubs 'to make beautiful sport and win the interest of the public'.[7] It was also designed to attract young men who would come of draft age in 1918 and 1919. The side was built around Maurice Boyau, the pre-war France flanker from Stade Bordelais. The career soldier (whose name means 'trench' – *incroyable*) was now flying with Escadrille N77, known as 'les Sportifs'; the flamboyant aviator painted a dragon writhing across the fuselage of his Nieuport aircraft.

1. 'Forever England'. The last pre-war England XV in April 1914 at Colombes, remembered in a commemorative painting by Shane Record, commissioned by the RFU. Six players who died have their red roses 'greyed', from back row left: **Arthur Harrison VC, Robert Pillman, Jimmy Dingle, James Watson, Ronald Poulton-Palmer, Francis Oakeley**. Only Bruno Brown (right of R.P.P.) would play in the King's Cup in 1919. *(RFU and Shane Record)*

2. The silver ACME Thunderer presented to referee Gil Evans in 1908, which has whistled the start of every modern Rugby World Cup. *(New Zealand Rugby Museum)*

Names in **bold** in picture captions indicate players who lost their lives during the war.

3. The French team of April 1914: *back row L to R*: Jean-Louis Capmau, **Jean-Jacques Conilh de Beyssac**, Fernand Forgues, **Paul Fauré**; *middle*: Marcel-Frédéric Lubin-Lebrère, Robert Lacoste, Gilbert Pierrot, Maurice Leuvielle, Lucien Besset, Paulin Bascou, **Emmanuel Iguiñiz**, Geo Andre; *front*: **Jean Larribau**, Jean Caujolle, **Marcel Burgun**. *(Frédéric Humbert)*

4. Recruiting poster from early 1915: 26 England internationals would die and a 27th, Reggie Schwartz, succumbed to flu in late 1918. *(Library of Congress)*

5. This hard-hitting poster reveals the bitterness felt at football's continued season; both players and crowds are caught in the same resentful stare. *(Library of Congress)*

8th Battalion The Cameronians (Scottish Rifles)
WAR STATION.   DECEMBER 1914.
OLD GLASGOW ACADEMY BOYS.

A. C. BRUCE, O.P.,
Naval and Military Photographer

B Annfield,
Newhaven, LEITH

Lieut. H. M'Cowan.   Lieut. W. N. Sloan.   2nd Lieut. W. Maclay.   2nd Lieut. T. Stout.   Lieut. E. Maclay.   Capt. Chas. J. C. Mowat.
Lieut. A. D. Templeton.   Capt. W. C. Church.   Capt. A. B. Sloan, R.A.M.C.   Capt. J. W. H. Pattison.   Capt. E. T. Young.

6. 8th Cameronians (The Scottish Rifles), all former Glasgow Academy boys. Eight men here, including Accies rugby players **Templeton, Stout, Church** and **Young** would die on the same day at Gallipoli, 28 June 1915. *(Glasgow Academy)*

7. The First Wallabies 1908, featuring captain Paddy Moran, Tom Richards, Danny Carroll and Syd Middleton. *(World Rugby Museum)*

8. A more formal shot of the 1908 Wallabies tourists taken before leaving Australia. *(World Rugby Museum)*

9. The 1905 All Black Originals prior to their first stunning victory over Devon. Captain Dave Gallaher holds the ball. *(New Zealand Rugby Museum)*

NEW ZEALAND FOOTBALL TEAM. 1905.   G.W.S.M.

10. The 1905 All Black Originals in informal pose, less intimidating in boaters. *(Alexander Turnbull Library)*

11. New Zealanders playing rugby at the front near Fontaine. No rugby kit, just what they stood up in. (*Royal New Zealand Returned and Services' Association Collection, Alexander Turnbull Library*)

12. The Horowhenua Māori side of 1913, featuring brothers Jack and Charles Sciascia. (*Alan Sciascia*)

13. The Vancouver 'Rowers' with the Miller Cup in 1911. Reggie Woodward, club founder, who lost his son Tommy, is back left, next to Scots internationalist **Andrew Ross**. To his left, Nelles Stacey and **Russel Johnston**. Captain T.E.D. Byrne holds the ball. (*VRC*)

14. Rowers' 1913/14 squad. Malcolm Bell-Irving sits centre in the plain jersey. **Owen Sawers**, killed at Ypres in 1915, is the second player from the left in the back row. (*VRC*)

15. California dreaming: American optimism in 1910 as a Stanford/UCal Berkeley student squad tours Australia and New Zealand. *(Library of Congress)*

16. American disillusion sets in as Australia narrowly beat the USA in 1912. *(Library of Congress)*

17. USA Olympic finalists 1920: Rudi Scholz (*standing 5th from left*) is next to the Australian dual internationalist and 1908 Olympic champion Danny Carroll (*7th from left*). *(Author)*

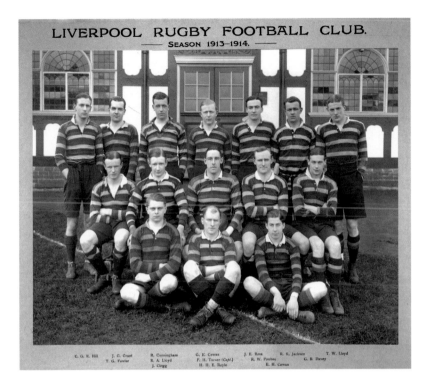

LIVERPOOL RUGBY FOOTBALL CLUB.
— SEASON 1913–1914. —

C. G. R. Hill   J. G. Grant   R. Cunningham   G. K. Cowan   J. E. Ross   R. K. Jackson   T. W. Lloyd
    T. G. Fowler   R. A. Lloyd   F. H. Turner (Capt.)   R. W. Poulton   G. B. Davey
        J. Clegg   H. H. E. Royle   E. H. Cowan

18. Liverpool FC's great 1913/14 side with three international skippers: Dickie Lloyd and **Ronald Poulton-Palmer** (named as Poulton on the team list) sit beside club captain **Freddy Turner**. *(Liverpool St Helens RUFC)*

19. **Edgar Mobbs** skippers the combined East Midlands/Midlands team in France in 1913. Australian rugby troubadour Tom Richards is back left. *(Author)*

20. Recruits for D Company, 7th Royal Dublin Fusiliers, at Lansdowne Road, September 1914. Sergeant Major Guest and **Frank Browning** at front. *(Lansdowne FC)*

21. The 'Combined Irish' against the Springboks in 1912. **Robert Burgess**, winning his single cap in this game, stands under the letter D, which seemingly held fatal significance for rugby players in this war; he was killed by a shell while cycling through Armentières. *(Patrick Casey)*

22. The 1910 Welsh team to play France at Swansea, captained by Billy Trew, including Ben Gronow, **Charles Pritchard**, **Phil Waller** and Hop Maddock. *(Frédéric Humbert)*

23. Fernand Forgues again led the 1913 French champions in the final season before the war and would face England at Colombes in the last International. *(Frédéric Humbert)*

24. Aviron Bayonnais (with most of the team in Basque berets) are hailed by *Le Plein Air* as 1913 champions of France with the Forgues brothers, Harry Roe and the doomed **Hedembaigt**, **Iguiñiz** and **Poeydebasque** in the line-up. *(Frédéric Humbert)*

25. Captain **Alec Todd** (*3rd from left*), British Lions and England forward. A lost letter describes meeting 'ruggers' at the front; these unidentified men of different ranks and regiments may be that meeting; on the right may be Dickie Lloyd of Ireland and Liverpool Scottish. Todd was fatally wounded at Hill 60 in April 1915. *(David Byass)*

26. **Blair Swannell**, the Northampton-born forward for Britain and Australia, killed on the first day of the ANZAC landings at Gallipoli. *(World Rugby Museum)*

27. The Australian Imperial Force Trench Team in France in March 1917, looking as rough and ready as you would expect in wartime. *(Frédéric Humbert)*

28. After the Armistice the winter of 1918/19 was hard, but did not stop the Australians playing rugby. The *Chaufferie entrée interdite* behind them must have been a sore temptation. *(Frédéric Humbert)*

29. Major R.V. Stanley and his all-conquering Army Service Corps (Motor Transport) Grove Park team: Ben Gronow, with distinctive lugs, stands behind General Burn, with Harold Wagstaff next to Stanley. *(Huddersfield Rugby League, a Lasting Heritage – www. HuddersfieldRLHeritage.co.uk)*

30. 'The Battle in the Football Field': the ASC defeat a NZ team by 21–3. This is more likely to be the UK HQ team than the fearsome Trench Team. *(Frédéric Humbert)*

31. Rugby grew in popularity in the French military. Here the players of the 24e Régiment d'Artillerie de Campagne. *(Frédéric Humbert)*

32. The AIF Reserve team, captained by Peter Buchanan, which toured Britain during the King's Cup. *(World Rugby Museum)*

33. New Zealand playing the South Africans at Twickenham, 29 March 1919. The sparse crowd on a bright but chilly day is mainly military. *(New Zealand Rugby Museum)*

34. King George V presents his cup to James Ryan, captain of the New Zealand Services Team before the France game at Twickenham. *(Royal New Zealand Returned and Services' Association Collection, Alexander Turnbull Library)*

35. The New Zealand Division rugby team visit Versailles; with these men outside the windows, peace was swiftly concluded. *(Royal New Zealand Returned and Services' Association Collection, Alexander Turnbull Library)*

36. New Zealand Services rugby team performing the *haka* before a match in France, 1919. *(Royal New Zealand Returned and Services' Association Collection, Alexander Turnbull Library)*

37. The King's Cup. For reasons unknown, Charles Brown is shown as captain, not James Ryan. The engraving may have been done after the return home, by when Brown had captained the team in South Africa. *(New Zealand Rugby Museum)*

38. The memorial to London Scottish and Richmond's fallen at the Richmond Athletic Ground. *(Author)*

39. Hope for the future: Afghan children playing rugby in 2015 before the ruins of the presidential palace built in 1920. *(Asad Ziar)*

Boyau's Lutétia beat an Anzac side 9–6 in front of 5,000 at the Parc des Princes. In March 1917, nine days after he notched his first aerial victory (the first of thirty-five, of which twenty-one were balloons – much harder than it sounds), Lutétia played a double-header at the Parc: its reserves (draft years 1918–1920) against an 'Australian Hospital No. 1' team, and its 1st XV against Aviron Bayonnais. He earned a dramatic Médaille Militaire when he was forced to land behind enemy lines with engine problems after shooting down a heavily defended balloon. As German troops raced to take him prisoner he made hasty repairs and took off again, bullets flying around him as they arrived seconds too late. Boyau was killed on 16 August 1918, as the fifth most successful French ace. He had also won the Légion d'Honneur. The sportsmen of France subscribed to buy him a diamond and platinum cross. It was never presented.

Most significantly for Boyau and military rugby in France, for the first time in its history, the French Army fielded a representative team, to play the New Zealand Army Corps on 8 April 1917 for a *'Coupe de Somme'*. Although eight capped internationals were included, the French team was hastily assembled. An emergency letter was sent to twenty-three generals the week before, requesting immediate release of players; at 5.30 p.m. on the eve of the match, Alfred Eluère, of Nantes and now a *capitaine* in the 64e Régiment d'Infantérie, was still in his trench at the Chemin des Dames, where the French had returned after the German withdrawal to the Hindenburg Line. As well as the prospect of rugby, there were other reasons to be cheerful:

> The news of the declaration of war against Germany by the USA has just come to hand and the tricolour was fluttering in every street in Paris and in every town and village behind the battle zone.[8]

The opposition, with seven All Blacks, prepared with the thoroughness familiar since the days of the Originals. For three months since Christmas, they had kept a rigorous daily regime: PT, followed by bayonet and bombing practice in the morning; rugby training and games in the afternoon; extra rations and sleep and evening gym sessions in a local school. On the day of the match, the USFSA decision to give free entry, helped by sponsorship from *Le Journal*, attracted a vast crowd of 40,000 to the Vincennes velodrome. Despite a crushing home defeat by 40–0, the event was deemed a huge success:

> In the middle of war, sport was victorious before an audience so large that it was impossible to count the number. All sportsmen

should thank the thirty champions who carried off the match with energy. The crowd, this great Paris crowd, hailed the splendid efforts, and . . . New Zealand made a point of demonstrating what sports in general, and rugby in particular, were worth as training in human energy . . . Let us hope that the hard sporting lesson given by the New Zealanders has borne fruit and that the fine rugby played has been an example to the young players . . . that the thousands of non-believers filling the stands have been able to discover the beauty of our noble oval ball game.[9]

The journey back to Paris was a triumphal procession. Women rushed to kiss the New Zealanders, they were banqueted, invited to clubs, had theatre seats reserved. *Le Journal* presented them with a bronze statue by sculptor Georges Chauvel, designed while he was in the trenches. There was more:

Each of the 'athletes and heroes' received a beautiful medallion in frosted silver on which is the famous figure in relief of La Marseillaise from the Arc de Triomphe. They were also given tinder boxes of solid gold or gold and silver. They had the time of their lives.[10]

War brought them back to earth: New Zealand Army Corps flanker Reg Taylor, who had scored on his All Black debut against Australia in 1913, was killed on 20 June at Messines with his Wellington Regiment. In the same battle, fellow All Blacks Baird, Sellars and McNeece all died.

In 1918, in a winter lull not yet broken by the whirlwind German offensive of March that would threaten Paris for the first time since 1914, it was decided to repeat the exercise on Sunday 17 February. The USFSA took this second challenge much more seriously: it organised trials, training and a warm-up match against a Royal Artillery team with five capped England players, which the French won 15–14. The team of soldiers and airmen which paraded at the Parc des Princes was almost fully international and included Fernand and Jules Forgues, Lasserre and Domercq from Bayonne, Conilh de Beyssac from SBUC,[11] Nicolaï, Struxiano, Strohl and Thierry, whom we shall see again, the dazzling winger Adolphe Jauréguy and Géo André, Olympic athlete and fighter pilot.

New Zealand, captained by George Murray, fielded seven All Blacks including Alec Macdonald, an Original and captain of the 1913 USA tour, Charlie Brown, Arthur Wilson and a Sergeant James Ryan in the centre. This last trio would play another French military team a year later, in the peace of which they all dreamt. Allan Muhr refereed eccentrically: he whistled for half-time after only thirty minutes, so extended the second period to forty-five. This time the result was a close 5–3. The USFSA offered a spring tour, which the New Zealanders were pleased to accept 'on condition that military events did not stand in the way'.[12] Once again, the Kaiser had different plans: an artillery bombardment began at 0440 on 21 March over an area of 240 square kilometres, the biggest of the entire war. Over 1.1 million shells were fired in five hours onto British troops in the Somme sector. It was springtime for Ludendorff and Germany; rugby took a long break.

From another spring four years before, Marcel Burgun, the fly half with eleven caps who had faced England in that last Test at Colombes, was long dead, shot down in 1916 whilst earning a posthumous Croix de Guerre; he had joined the Aviation Militaire to avenge his brother. His half-back partner, Jean Larribau from Biarritz, was by now a pile of bleached bones at Verdun and would be named on the Biarritz Monument Aux Morts alongside his coach, Momber. Hooker Iguiñiz was killed within five months of his French debut. Tank commander de Beyssac died of his wounds in an ambulance on the way to Compiègne in June 1918. Paul Fauré, of Tarbes, invalided by a leg wound, died of influenza at home in Aureilhan, Pyrénées, in September.

As German morale and resistance crumbled as their advance was halted and then decisively driven back, release from the front became easier. A Paris team beat the Australians 9–6 at the new Stade Bergeyre on 20 October. New Zealand's soldiers played in Paris on 27 October, and Tarbes and Bordeaux in early November. Playing before a capacity crowd at the Parc, the New Zealanders had no Māori players, so a young corporal in the uniform of the Māori Pioneer Battalion led the *haka*. At the Armistice, sport replaced fighting, but kept a similar tempo, with many more games against British and Dominion teams.

French rugby emerged from war considerably stronger than in 1914. The military had embraced the sport and frequent encounters with British and Dominion sides had improved the French game. Many of its veterans were dead, and it would start to rebuild with new blood. The notoriously tough sixties forward Walter Spanghero once said: *'Un match qui ne fait pas mal est un match raté.'* Or 'A game which doesn't hurt is a bad game.' On that logic, this had been a very good game for rugby.

No Side

When this lousy war is over, no more soldiering for me
When I get my civvy clothes on, oh how happy I shall be.

Friday 8 November 1918. 'Somewhere in France':

> Night has fallen, the weather is awful. Although a drizzle is
> falling it is unable to dispel a thick fog. Finally, the sentries
> can see a halo of light and hear a few notes of the trumpet call
> 'Cease Fire'. A few seconds later a convoy of cars moving very
> fast appears on the road, their headlights ablaze. On the bonnet
> of the first car, a large white flag looms from the darkness.
> Standing on the running-board, the bugler keeps on blowing
> his call. Someone motions the cars to stop. A 25-year-old captain
> comes forward: he is Captain L'Huillier of the 171e Régiment
> d'Infanterie. He identifies the bearers of the flag of truce and
> gets into the first car. Corporal Sellier takes the place of the
> German bugler and sounds the 'Attention', the call of four years
> of fighting and suffering.[1]

So recalled French General Weygand. And so began the end.

At the station in the small town of Tergnier, Picardie, 20 kilometres
south of Saint-Quentin, a train waited at 0300. The town was in ruins,
the station, 'lit by torches. On the platform a smart company of riflemen
presented arms in a fairyland setting.' The German delegation left its cars
to board the train; its saloon draped in green satin still bore the monogram
and crown of Napoleon III, defeated by the Prussians at Sédan. A clank
and a lurch and a hiss of steam, and the train departed for an unknown
destination. The night was pitch-black and the carriage windows had their
curtains drawn.

At 0700, the train stopped, its passengers wondering where; the
windows were now uncovered but in the words of their accompanying
French host, Major de Bourbon-Busset, they saw 'nothing but a marshy
copse, and a lowering sky of leaden clouds'. A few yards away stood

another train, wrapped in the morning mist. A gendarme disclosed the secret: they were in the forest of Compiègne.

The two trains had been shunted onto sections of track leading from Rethondes station on the Aisne into the cover of the trees; these spurs had been used by heavy artillery firing on the German lines towards Noyon to the northeast. The wooded location was chosen for its calm and isolation, but also out of respect to a defeated enemy. The Allied Commander-in-Chief, Marshal Foch, preferred it over his headquarters at Senlis, whose mayor and other hostages had been shot by the invading Germans four years ago; the town was unlikely to be magnanimous in victory and was also too close to Paris, with its journalists and sightseers. So the forest clearing was chosen.

Between the carriages, the ground underfoot was so bad that duckboards had to be laid, an apt reminder of the pulverised front-line terrain. From his carriage 2419D, newly refitted as an office by the Compagnie des Wagon-Lits, Foch sent word to the German delegates that he would see them in his train at 0900. Negotiations commenced, although the terms were unconditional; the deadline given was 1100 Monday 11 November. In the small hours of the 11th, the Germans announced they were ready to conclude the talks; they were shown at once into the Marshal's carriage and the final session opened at 0215.

In the midst of the forest there was darkness. The men talked and when they had finished talking, a new light was dawning. At 0510 Foch was the first to sign and then left for Paris carrying the Armistice agreement. Its twenty-four articles specified the cessation of hostilities six hours after the signing, but Foch refused the German request for an immediate ceasefire to avoid more wasted lives. Another 11,000 men were killed or wounded in those six hours. Canadian Private George Price, from Moose Jaw, Saskatchewan, was the last soldier of the British Empire to die, shot in the chest by a sniper at 1058. He is buried at St Symphorien cemetery, where also lie the first and last British soldiers killed during the Great War, respectively John Parr and George Ellison. The final fatality was US soldier Henry Gunther, from a German-American family in Baltimore, just one minute before the eleventh hour of the eleventh day of the eleventh month.

'Cease fire' sounded along the Western Front. This was the final whistle to a game that had lasted four long seasons. It was not yet a peace, merely a 'stay of arms';[2] this Armistice was set to last just thirty-six days and had to be renewed three times, on 13 December, 16 January and 16 February, while the peacemakers did their work. The Paris conference began on 18 January 1919. Not until 28 June – twenty-four weeks later and five years to the day since the Archduke Franz Ferdinand was assassinated at Sarajevo – would the treaty with Germany finally be signed at Versailles in the Hall of Mirrors, where at least they had time for reflection. Section 231 laid the guilt for the war on 'the aggression of Germany and her allies' and paved the way for punitive reparations. The peace would last only another twenty years.

That November Monday, notices were pinned to the doors of any churches still standing behind the front line: '*Onze heures du matin, la guerre est finie.*' Orders were passed to the troops:

> Hostilities will cease at 11:00 hours on November 11th – Troops will stand fast on the line reached at that time which will be reported to Corps Headquarters – Strictest precautions will be maintained – There will be no intercourse of any kind with the enemy.

Some made a final 'gesture of intercourse' to their enemy and played hard right up to that final whistle, whether out of duty, habit or simply to save carrying away heavy ammunition. They sent up a lethal daylight fireworks display, as Colonel Nicholson of the Suffolk Regiment recalled:

> A German machine-gun remained in action the whole morning opposite our lines. Just before 11 a.m. a thousand rounds were fired in a practically ceaseless burst. At 11 a.m., there came great cheering from the German lines and the village church bells rang. But on our side there were only a few shouts. I had heard more for a rum ration. The match was over – it had been a damned bad game.

Frank Mellish was having a second slice of bread and marmalade. The previous day, 'we had travelled through little villages which had been occupied by the enemy for over four long years':

> Our welcome from the parish priest to the youngest inhabitant had been tumultuous. We could take lots more of this sort of thing, and the joy we were bringing began to make amends for the losses we had suffered and the misery we had endured. There were still mines and booby-traps to be negotiated, but we felt the worst was over.

When a despatch-rider arrived with a message, his battery major 'threw it across to me and said':

> 'Tell the men, Frank, I can't.' It baldly announced that hostilities would cease at 11 am, that there was to be no fraternising with the enemy and we were to remain wherever we were until further orders. You will have heard the expression 'A slap in the face with a wet fish' . . . I just could not believe that after having lived for four years in desolate and torn-up country, there should be no retribution and that our cunning, fierce and ruthless enemy should be allowed to pack up his souvenirs and go back to his practically untouched and unblemished homeland.

That evening a party went to the Officers' Club in Lille, where 'we proceeded to get exceedingly intoxicated and where the largest rugger scrum ever to have been formed took place. There must have been three hundred a side and by the time the mythical ball was heeled, the place was a veritable shambles and the party over.'

On other sections of the Western Front, the great world war ended less with a bang than a whimper, according to a corporal of the Honourable Artillery Company: 'It wasn't like London where they all got drunk. It was all very quiet. You were so dazed you just didn't realise that from now on, you could stand up straight and not be shot.' From Downing Street, Prime Minister David Lloyd George made a formal announcement, largely reiterating what the church doors had said in France:

> At eleven o'clock this morning the war will be over. You are well entitled to rejoice. The people of this Empire, with their allies, have won a great victory. It is the sons and daughters of the people who have done it. It is a victory greater than has ever been known in history.

A young New Zealand officer, Leslie Averill, who had just distinguished himself in scaling the fortified walls of Le Quesnoy by ladder, was more concerned with dwindling opportunities for wristwatch trophies:

> A few souvenirs would have come in very handy especially as it appears there won't be any more prisoners. Peace looks very close now. The official news today is that the German fleet is out. Mutinied, & the German Peace Delegates meet Foch today, so it's quite on the cards that the war will be finished by Xmas.[3]

Most soldiers celebrated the end of fighting and the prospect of finally going home. Frank Cobb, with the 1/4th Northamptons in the Egyptian Expeditionary Force, wrote to the *Rushden Echo* on 12 November, from Abbassia Command Depot, Cairo:

> . . . we are having a royal time out here, celebrating the Armistice. I had the honour of playing the glad tidings on the piano. We had a tableau on the stage, including all flags of our Allies. As each flag was presented cheers were given by a very large audience, and I played the National Anthem as each one was presented. The boys gave vent to their voices; in fact, they sang till they were hoarse. I played all popular patriotic tunes, which suited immensely, but I think the two most popular ones were 'Take me back to Blighty, and 'I want to see the dear old Home again'. There are numerous boys here from our county, so you can imagine we had a decent night together.

In peaceful Oswestry, far from Cairo, Mrs Susan Owen was surprised to hear the unexpected peal of church bells from nearby St Oswald's on a Monday morning. Much louder was the knock at the door as a telegram boy brought news that her Shropshire lad who had marched away in 1915, had been killed just seven days before, almost to the hour, at the Sambre–Oise Canal and would never return home. What passing bells.

In London, before the news arrived (and the drinking started), the sports pages reported the results of Saturday's rugby matches between the military teams in the capital's multi-national melting pot. South Africans beat London Canadians heavily at Richmond 27–0; Royal Military Academy beat Guy's Hospital at Woolwich; a Machine-Gun School side bullied a Public Schools Services side 29–0 at a busy Richmond ground; and New Zealand Headquarters Staff beat Australian Headquarters Staff at Herne Hill. The fixtures reveal just what a world war this had been.

It was not a planned peace: in October, the War Office was actively making plans for another two years of war. They had expected to continue fighting, but the collapse of German morale was swift, with whole regiments surrendering en masse; this later gave rise to the Hitlerian myth of the brave German soldier being stabbed in the back by faint-hearted (and Jewish) cowards at home. Liverpool FC's Henry Royle, wounded in 1915 and gassed at Passchendaele in 1917, rejoined his KLR battalion, ready to fight again. Thankfully for him, it was seven days after the Armistice; he had to wait until 25 January for his battalion to disperse.

With no prospect of any resumption of regular rugby at home, the situation for clubs was parlous. Rosslyn Park's Harry Burlinson, redoubtable organiser of the Old Deer Park Public Schools and Services games, sent out another arm-twisting circular appealing for subscriptions:

> ... since the commencement of the War nearly one hundred subscriptions have lapsed owing to the very heavy casualties amongst the members on Active Service, and no new members have been enrolled for the past four seasons. The Annual income, therefore, is greatly reduced, and to add to the anxiety everything has increased in cost.

Even in those days of amateurism, money mattered. We know it was not the first time 'Burly' had written: in October 1915, Rifleman Jack Bodenham came out of the front-line trenches near Ypres to find a letter from his rugby club, requesting a guinea and a photograph ('I don't know what they can want with it & hope it is not for the police', he quipped). He wrote to his father:

> I should be grateful if you would pay the subscription of £1. 1s which I should like to go forward with this, but money orders are difficult to get here & I am afraid I must ask you to trust me for it till I can return it later on.

He would never pay his father back: he was killed on the first day of the Somme, his bodily remains churned into the battlefield by a second passage of slaughter in 1918, with only his name on the bulk of Thiepval to recall him.[4]

For some troops, their war went on; they just moved to a different front. While haggling went on at Versailles, old wounds reopened: the Third Afghan War started on 6 May 1919 and lasted until 8 August. The RAF's 31 Squadron was there in 1919; they were the last to leave in 2014. Pre-war Eastern Counties skipper Lieutenant Colonel Barry Wells, commanding his 4th Essex battalion found himself in Murmansk, Russia, fighting Bolsheviks, as did Ira 'Taff' Jones, the Welsh fighter ace from Carmarthen. The Canadians sent a Siberian Expeditionary Force to the other, eastern extreme of Mother Russia's vast bulk for the same purpose. Most came back, although Wells lost men when some of his allied 'White' troops mutinied, murdered and went over to the Reds. Many South Africans, including the commanders of both 1st and 4th infantry regiments, preferred to volunteer in support of the

Whites, rather than returning home, and were awarded Russian service honours.

Naval stoker Jack Finnis, one of thirty-eight Wasps to die, would stay another nine years before what was left of him returned for burial in Portsmouth. His submarine *L55*, launched too late for the Great War, was in the Baltic in June 1919. She engaged two Bolshevik destroyers laying mines to guard Petrograd; her torpedoes missed, and she was pressed towards an area sown with British mines and sank. Although the Bolsheviks claimed the kill, *L55* may have fallen victim to 'friendly mines'. The remains of its forty-two officers and men would stay in their tin-can coffin until *L55* was discovered by a trawler in 100 feet of water and raised in 1928. Since Britain had no diplomatic relations with Communist Russia, no British warships were allowed in its waters; the skeletons were handed over to a merchantman and transferred to HMS *Champion* in Tallinn, Estonia, before returning for burial at Haslar, Portsmouth.

The killing was over but the dying was not yet done. Wellington's apocryphal boast that the Battle of Waterloo was won on the playing fields of Eton must be balanced by his verified observation, on surveying the carnage, that 'next to a battle lost, the saddest thing is a battle won'. England's Reggie Schwarz, MC, Richmond fly half and leg-spinner for South Africa, died aged 43 at Étaples camp from 'Spanish' influenza seven days after the Armistice was declared. Fred Perrett, Royal Welch Fusiliers, a Neath and Wales forward who had turned professional with Leeds, died of his wounds on the first day of December. James Gibson Grant, of Liverpool FC's great team, died of tuberculosis in February 1919, in a sanatorium at Banchory, Aberdeenshire. He had twice been invalided from the front through illness and resigned his commission in November 1917, when his health broke down irreparably after three years of fighting. His entry on Loretto's Honour Roll blames 'hardship and exposure on service'. In the same February the wounded Major William Beatty of Ireland succumbed to pneumonia at a casualty clearing station at Charleroi.

Hop Maddock was awarded the MC in April 1918 for covering the retreat of his unit from Le Mesnil. Although practically surrounded, Maddock continued firing until all had crossed a bridge and was the last man to retire to safety. He saw out the war but never fully recovered from his Somme wounds from 1916. He died in Cardiff in December 1921, still young at 40: London Welsh wore black armbands in his honour. France's Albert Chateau, the talented Aviron Bayonnais back from their

1913 championship team, succumbed to his war wounds in 1924, six years after hostilities ended.

As if to add insult to injury, the Armistice came as wintry bleakness was again settling on northern France and Flanders. The mizzle and gloom of the Compiègne forest in November presaged another harsh winter. Few soldiers would have lived through all four since 1914, or survived the killing seasons that began in spring. Bad weather had its compensations: it had slowed movements of men and munitions and so afforded some brief, if frozen, respite from bloody mass attacks. This was not yet a peace, but a cessation of hostilities, which could break out again: the enemy had to be disarmed and occupied territory retaken. There was still work to be done, albeit no longer under fire.

The Allied war machine had built an astonishingly efficient logistics system to move unprecedented masses of men and matériel to the front, but it had not been much used in the opposite direction. There were not enough trains and boats to get millions of men back to Blighty, let alone distant Dominion homes. There was also the ticklish problem of battle-hardened men who had accumulated – to paraphrase Liam Neeson – 'a very particular set of skills, acquired over a very long war' and might not have purged the instinct for lethal violence from their system. After six-month tours in Afghanistan, twenty-first-century British soldiers spend weeks 'decompressing' in Cyprus, where the stresses of combat can be released through a unit-based safety valve, before returning to the unfamiliar normalcy of home. In 1918, after four years of fighting and little leave, it was vital to occupy a massive Allied force in productive and harmless activity: sport was one answer.

Burlinson had pointed out the value of the 'great amount of Rugby Football now played, in fact the military authorities attach much importance to it, and recognise it as great help in training and keeping men from getting stale, and do everything possible to encourage it.' In the sudden, unexpected silence of peace, the military authorities would again discover the importance of sport. After the Armistice it came into its own, as Australian Lieutenant G.H. Goddard put it, in 'keeping a couple of hundred thousand home-hungry men contented'.[5]

They had lived. It was time to make life-affirming choices. War was over; now it was time to play rugby.

The Return of the King

Send him victorious,
Happy and glorious.

War has many unintended consequences, very few of them happy.
But the 'greatest imperial emergency' and the influx of Dominion
troops into Europe made the period 1916–19 a golden age for international
rugby – or at least a gunmetal one. The gilding, by royal patronage, would
come in the spring of 1919.

In January 1919, the War Office decided on a rugby competition
in Britain for the Services and Dominions or, in the language of the
hated trench stores return, an 'Army Football Competition (Rugby)'.
On 8 February, representatives met at the Junior United Services Club,
London, with General Harington, a senior War Office figure, presiding,
to finalise arrangements, grounds and fixtures for an 'Inter-Services Competition', to be played under the auspices of the Army Rugby Union. The
event was given the royal seal of approval – and a snappier name – by
the offer from His Majesty of a cup to be presented in his name. This
would be the only 'international' rugby played in Britain in a 1918–19
season whose first half was spent overseas on shell-pocked pitches under
raining lead.

The King's Cup would be the jewel in an extraordinary crowning of
rugby, as touring military teams from the Dominions took on renascent
clubs and home units awaiting demobilisation. In wartime, rugby was
approved therapy for shattered men from the front; it would now play a
part in the entire nation's recovery. In this new, uncertain peace, it was an
opportunity to restate the values that had carried the Empire through the
conflict – this, after all, was the game that won the war, in the view of one
headmaster who urged on 26 February that:

> It is timely to press forward the claims of the greatest game of
> all. It is not only national but imperial; it is the game of the most
> vigorous of our Colonies; it is the game of the Army that has won

the hardest and grimmest of all wars; it should be the universal game of our new educational system because it is a maker of men.

At Richmond that afternoon, spectators might read his letter whilst perusing the morning *Times* over a pint while awaiting kick-off. 'Hear, hear!' they would murmur before enjoying a double-header of New Zealand and Australian Services A and B teams, in final rehearsal for the royal command performance of the King's Cup.

Australia's representative at the meeting was Major Walter 'Wally' Matthews. This versatile man was a qualified doctor, pre-war Sydney University and NSW player, and former mayor; he would not only manage the AIF team and be team doctor, but would also turn out at half back against South Africa at Newport, aged 35. When the whizz-bangs fell silent in 1918, the energetic Australians had wasted no time in setting up a Sport Control Board in France, with sub-committees in charge of staging events for each sport, funded by the Comforts Fund. The rugby organisation was led by Major Syd Middleton, DSO, 17th Battalion, and rangy back-row for the Olympian Wallabies, with Moran, Richards and Carroll. He was an impressive physical specimen at 14 stone and over 6ft, and seemingly tireless: he played the first eighteen tour matches of 1908 on the trot. Against Oxford, to his lifelong regret, he became the first Wallaby to be sent off. His skipper Moran, watching injured on the sidelines, recounted in 1939:

> Suddenly on a line-out I saw one of our biggest forwards swing a blow that hit an opposing forward. A.O. Jones promptly sent our man off; what else could he do? The man who committed this offence was a magnificent athlete, rower, boxer and footballer, and actually a very good sportsman, but irritable and hot-headed. I followed him into the dressing-room with murder in my heart for one who was and is still a firm friend. But when I saw his bowed head I said nothing and walked out. He is still paying for that indiscretion. It has pursued him for thirty years. It followed him to the war and it still pops up, every now and again, when the striker and the struck meet socially in London, where they both live.

Syd had taken offence at being called a 'convict' by one of the students. Was practical joker Freddy Turner the line-out sledger who provoked him? Red mist moments still haunt players today, at least in the media if not always, like Middleton, in their own minds.

It's worth pausing to consider the horrors Syd later saw on the battlefield. Richards encountered him at Ypres after a shell had fallen in his trench:

> . . . the wounded are patched up and after separating the 'brain from the guts' the identification disc and pay book are found and then all hands throw the body up over the parapet to strengthen it. Oft-times a shell will throw a body back into the trenches after it has been lying there for some days and is an awful proposition to handle.

Syd came close to death on numerous occasions: 'He was practically buried five times in one day, his stars were shot away from his shoulder on one side, the heel of his boot was dinted and his foot wrenched, a piece of shell penetrated his side.' Yet it was his momentary fall from grace on the field of rugby that troubled him more.

The chastened Middleton had no interest in joining the defectors to League on returning to Australia in 1908; his loyalty to the amateur code was rewarded when he twice captained NSW against the All Blacks, and twice more against the Māori. He then led the national side in three Tests against NZ, including a prized victory. In a rare Olympic double, he rowed at the 1912 Stockholm Games for Australasia, a joint team of 'Anzac' oarsmen, who took home silver; it is no surprise that his seat was in the engine room at six. Middleton fought at Gallipoli and in France was mentioned in despatches in 1918. His DSO citation for his action during an enemy attack near Amiens on 14 May recorded that 'The battalion owes much of its success to the splendid example set by this very fine type of officer . . . the manner in which he handled the situation and quickly restored the line showed great initiative and leadership.' Was it his initiative that winkled out his 1908 tour-mate Danny Carroll from the US Army to play two games in the King's Cup? For good measure, Syd also took home with him an OBE and a second King's Cup for rowing from the Peace Regatta at Henley.

Under Syd's guidance, a 'Trenches Team' of sixty players went into camp at a newly created School of Physical and Recreational Training at Barbençon in Belgium, close to Maubeuge, the original rendezvous for the Franco-British force in 1914. Within weeks, a corps rugby team was 'sent to Paris to try conclusions with a French Army XV' eager to test its mettle against the southern stars of the Anglo-Saxon galaxy, and emboldened by a strong showing in defeat to New Zealand in April. Australian victory by 6–3 apparently belied the AIF superiority as Lieutenant Goddard, in his official account, showed promise as a monocular Aussie sports journalist:

> The Australians were on the offensive during the greater part of the game . . . only their lack of properly concerted action and their inability to take full advantage of opportunities offered, due to the shortness of the period of their training . . . prevented them from making the score much bigger. Credit must be given to the Frenchmen for their splendid defensive game, and for the numerous occasions on which they repulsed the onslaughts against their line.[1]

After Verdun, this was second nature to the French Army. But see how seamlessly the soldier's language of warfare slides into rugby reportage. The Trench Team then crossed the Channel to play its Headquarters comrades in England, and varied civilian and military sides.

The AIF ran a rugby competition from March in a round-robin of six teams, one from each of the five divisions and one from corps troops. Although the divisions were widely scattered through the French countryside, 'each team was concentrated on a central village' and 'trained assiduously'. Conditions (and the team bus) were not ideal:

> One day a game would be played on a field covered with a couple of inches of snow. At another time the snow would give place to a similar depth of mud, and yet again the ground would be frozen hard . . . the teams often had to undertake journeys of 20 to 30 kilometres, and even more, over bumpy roads, and return after the game. The Army wagon was not by any means a well-upholstered or well-sprung conveyance, and it had no central heating arrangements.

In occupied Cologne, a combined corps team defeated the British Second Army team and the RAF. Now they sought challenges on pastures new, which conveniently materialised, wrote Goddard, 'When the idea was first mooted of giving Australian athletes who were serving in the AIF, an opportunity of pitting themselves against European nations, it was eagerly taken up.' What most concerned the competitive Aussies, however, was how 'to choose the best possible side to represent Australia' in the crunch inter-services contest. Goddard got his excuses in early:

> This was not such an easy matter as it seemed. There was Headquarters Team in London that had played a few matches

and done rather well. There was also the Trench Team, which had come across from France, after having notable victories. Neither was a really first-class combination, although there was a lot of excellent material. The four and a half years of war were responsible for a loss of many of the finer tactical points of the game which had always characterised Australian Rugby.

Such was the eagerness to play, however, that two teams were formed, separately managed by Watson and Lieutenant Seaborn, MC; both would criss-cross the country by train, bringing an exotic brand of rugby to starved pitches. They independently toured Wales and the Southwest, with occasional sorties to the Midlands, sometimes bumping into the two NZEF teams engaged in their own travelling rugby circus. But it was the 'AIF First Rugby XV' that would compete for the King's Cup, now grandly billed on match-day tickets as the 'Inter-Services and Dominion Forces Championship', for a 'Rugby Football Challenge Cup'.

Every aspect of this sporting celebration was carefully considered. This was the world's first genuinely international tournament for team sports. The Olympics were primarily about individual endeavour, and the amateur principle excluded professionals. Team sports rarely saw more than a few entrants: 1908's rugby saw just two contesting an immediate final. Cornwall drew the short straw to face Australia, after Scotland, Ireland and France had all turned down the RFU's invitation. Nor were there fully representative national sides: Great Britain's 1900 rugby side was 'Moseley Wanderers', a composite team of Midlands clubs and old boys' associations. There was no rugby at Stockholm in 1912, and little enthusiasm was displayed in 1920 and 1924, other than aggressively by America and France, towards each other and hapless Romania. War's insatiable demand for manpower, however, meant that – if not already dead or wounded by 1919 – the best sportsmen in the Empire were in uniform in Europe at the same time. If they were good enough to fight for their country, they were certainly fit to represent it at rugby.

The King's Cup, it was decided, should be an opportunity for all of Britain to applaud the Dominion troops who had defended the Empire and British values. Venues were chosen to reach a wide population – not easy when clubs had closed grounds when rugby ceased in 1914. A commitment was made to rugby grounds: no need to press into service football or athletics stadia, like Stamford Bridge or White City, with their greater capacity. In total, sixteen games were played at eight venues by the original six teams, plus a seventeenth against the French. This was an early template for what we now recognise as the World Cup format. Not until 1930 did fast-growing association football play its first tournament, and it was not much bigger: thirteen teams played eighteen games, but all in one city, Montevideo.

It would have been quite possible to concentrate the tournament into southwest London's 'rugby triangle': it boasted perfectly adequate grounds, like Queen's Club, Old Deer Park and Richmond Athletic Ground – all had staged pre-war Tests and wartime charity matches – and 'Billy Williams's cabbage patch' at Twickenham. Crystal Palace and Blackheath offered southeasterly capital options. Instead, the fifteen matches in the qualifying round-robin format were played over six weeks in different cities around mainland Britain, with the final decider to be played at Twickenham.

In Scotland, Inverleith hosted two matches, as did Swansea's St Helen's and Leicester's Welford Road. Newport's Rodney Parade, Gloucester's Kingsholm and Portsmouth's United Services Club – presumably with a loyal War Office nod to the Navy – each held one game. On some weekends, simultaneous fixtures were played: Saturday 29 April saw all six teams in action at Edinburgh, Gloucester and Twickenham – no problems with scheduling then, as Logie Baird's 'televisor' would not broadcast its first experimental moving pictures for another six years.[2] By the combined miracle of the cinematograph and internet, some flickering moments of these games can still be glimpsed today.[3]

The RFU's Twickenham ground, not yet a fortress, had the English lion's share of the fixtures, with seven in total; careful planning gave every side the chance to play on the hallowed turf. The scheduler's art is a fine mystery, but it is perhaps a further sign of South African favour with the RFU that they were accorded three fixtures at 'HQ', one more even than the home Mother Country. The stadium built in 1908 at a cost of £8,812 15s, had stands East and West for 3,000, a south terrace for another 7,000 and an open mound to the north, giving a total capacity of some 20,000. With club rugby for its Harlequin tenants suspended in wartime, and Richmond's transport connections being more convenient for spectators at charity games, the stadium had been used as a grazing enclosure. Both stadium and surrounding area have been built up a little since: Twickenham stages the 2015 World Cup Final as an iconic temple with a capacity of 82,000.

Poulton-Palmer had been widely mourned in 1915 and poet Alfred Ollivant composed a popular elegy to 'RWPP: Killed in France'. His last words are said to have been: 'I shall never play at Twickenham again.' It seems unlikely that a sniper's headshot would have allowed him time for such theatrical expiry. But the fallen England captain's words helped turn the cabbage patch into a rugby Colosseum and Valhalla combined. In 1919 it was quickly restored as a rugby ground, with equine deposits removed and new turf laid. Its suburban, almost rural location was then one of the abiding mysteries of early RFU decision-making and transport problems abounded, as Grierson commented:

> The spectacle of some forty thousand people on foot and in cars and taxis trying to make their way down the Twickenham bottleneck is a sight such as one can only compare with the first cup final at Wembley, and were it not for the inherent discipline and good behaviour of the crowds who frequent Rugger Internationals scenes would have occurred long ago which would have forced the RU to take drastic action in the matter! No first league soccer club would have dared to build a ground for its patrons with such inadequate means of access and egress.

Little has changed. He would be pleased to know that the same good nature under trying conditions is still exercised by rugby crowds today; trips to HQ are as revered as pilgrimages to Lourdes or Santiago de Compostela, and almost as long.

Grierson, writing in 1924, may seem an old buffer, but he wrote brilliantly for the satirical trench journal *The Wipers Times* under the by-line of 'PBI' (Poor Bloody Infantry) so deserves respect. He was also a veritable rugby visionary, recommending the scoring system of five points for a try (and two for a conversion) all of sixty-eight years before the International Rugby Board[4] finally made it happen.

His Majesty King George V was a great rugby fan: as Prince of Wales he saw Ben Gronow kick off the first ever Test at Twickenham. He was also cannily conscious of the political symbolism of sporting occasions. The 1914 Valentine's Day encounter between England and Ireland at Twickenham, his first international since his 1910 coronation, was chosen with deliberation. His attendance with Prime Minister Herbert Asquith by his side, at a time when the debate over Irish Home Rule raged in Parliament, was a finely judged gesture of conciliation. Tensions about extremist demonstrations at the ground proved unfounded. Three weeks later, the king made up for lost game-time in his first four years by attending the match between the Officers of the Army and the Navy, at the perennially fogbound Queen's Club. Still at this stage a Saxe-Coburg-Gotha, the king proved himself a man of his English people, by sitting throughout the rain-soaked match without benefit of an umbrella, which would have obscured the view of those behind him. 'Mustn't grumble,' he probably thought, as he received appreciative applause from his sodden subjects.

So it was no small matter in 1919 that His Majesty chose to return to Twickenham. This was about more than watching rugby: this time it was the future of the Empire that concerned him and the need not only to thank his Dominions for their role in the victory, but also to hold together these vigorous colonial partners who were straining at the Imperial leash. As the tournament progressed, the Paris peacemakers were deep in talks: for the first time, in recognition of their part in war, former colonies participated as nations in their own right at an international conference to make peace. When New Zealand, along with Canada, Australia, South Africa and India, was awarded a seat on the new League of Nations, fashioned by the Versailles Treaty in 1920, Prime Minister William Massey said it joined as 'a self-governing nation within the empire'. This echoed the language of the 1917 Imperial War Conference when the Dominion premiers had called for full recognition as 'autonomous nations of an Imperial Commonwealth'.

The spoils of war, won by the sacrifice of so many sons, brought them a new international role in a world that no longer seemed so distant and remote. The astute George, by donating the King's Cup for the champion of the Inter-Services Rugby Tournament, was offering another hopeful symbol of Imperial unity and military teamwork. Never slow, the press cottoned on, although they could not manage the new-fangled transition of C-words, from Colony to Commonwealth:

> It is a most practical means of continuing and strengthening the bonds of interest between us and our relations scattered over the world. War has brought all parts of the Empire closer . . . Often in the past the ties between this country and the colonies have been slender and the strongest of them is the common interest in British games.[5]

As further gesture of kingly benevolence, George also sent down his sons from on high at Buckingham Palace to grace the Twickenham turf; the Chertsey Road would suffer more bouts of congestion by royal entourage.

In another move laden with political messaging, the British Army team, uniting the home nations in rugby as in war, played under one banner as the 'Mother Country'. There had been plans for separate teams from Army, Navy and RAF, but the sailors could not field a competitive side; predictably, Celts grumbled over the lack of RFU consultation. The term 'Mother Country' was already tinged with nostalgia for Imperial stability, long presided over by the maternal Queen Victoria, which was so irrevocably rocked by the Great War. It looked positively odd when typesetters compressed it to 'Mother C.' or 'M. Country' in fixture lists and match reports for the King's Cup. Not to mention providing a fruitful source of abusive shortenings to be thrown at the British by their opposite numbers, particularly the Anzacs – let's not forget these were blunt, rugby-playing soldiers, with four years study of the Trench Thesaurus under their belts and a talent for inventive swearing. Tom Richards, no respecter of the British officer class, refers to the special treatment meted out in one 'friendly' at the front: 'I had a lot to do at full back and could hardly stand up at the finish of the game. Three of our officers played and were handled with a little more despatch than the others.'

The blood of many mates at Gallipoli was laid at Britain's door; surely the rankers in the Dominion teams would not have missed this supreme chance for a quiet word in the ear of the officers facing them (even if one was a man of God, the Reverend Bill Havard, of Oxford and Wales, chaplain to the Guards Brigade). The Mother Country front row could not have been a happy place.

Matters almost got out of hand in the match against Australia at Welford Road. Wing forward Sergeant Bradley, a North Sydney rugby league player, so annoyed the crowd with his obstruction of scrum half Pym that there were calls for him to be sent off. This would have been unprecedented in a representative match in Britain – although Syd Middleton's disgrace was probably invoked by those with memories of 1908 – and would have disturbed the harmony of the Imperial celebrations. The referee tried to defuse the tension by putting the ball into the scrum himself, a stratagem that was later repeated when France played Scotland in 1920. Ironically, New Zealand, arch-exponents of the wing forward's dark arts, formally proposed this in August to the RFU. In the wake of endemic crooked feeding, there are calls for it again.

The contents of King George's chalice may have soured over ensuing decades, as the tight Victorian bonds of Empire loosened into a Commonwealth of Nations. Not until 1939 was the next Wallaby side invited to Britain; unfortunate timing, as the second war erupted before a game was played. But guess who's still coming to the Rugby World Cup party in 2015? In a century of astonishing political and technological change, more global strife, and the rise and collapse of Reich and Soviet, the Commonwealth is an underrated achievement. Consider the changes in Russia's century: nine months before the King's Cup final, the Russians murdered their royal family at Yekaterinburg. Revolution and upheaval has seen a procession from Lenin, Stalin, Khrushchev, Gorbachev and Yeltsin to Putin; a colossal empire was set in concrete until, almost overnight, its walls crumbled and fell. Yet in 2015, we still have a United Kingdom (phew), King George's granddaughter sits on the same throne, while her daughter and grandsons take their box-seats as enthusiastic rugby fans and patrons.

It was a good moment, too, for the RFU to score some points. Historian Tony Collins has pointed out that from 1895 to 1914, rugby was in anything but union: almost continual crisis prevailed. League had split rugby at home and down under; Scotland clashed with anyone and everyone over professionalism; and Australian and New Zealand Unions openly challenged the RFU's authority. Only the South Africans seemed to play ball in the approved amateur way – which is why they were invited back before the war. In 1914, the RFU had initially instructed clubs to keep playing but admitted defeat in the face of wholesale enlistment and cancelled the season in September. Rugby enthusiasts like Tom Richards found a game at the front whenever they needed it, but by 1917 the official ball of the British Army on the Western Front was round, each company being issued with a football. Mythology has since accreted around the 1914 Christmas Truce and footballs kicked from trenches at Loos and the Somme, although the best story – sadly neglected – was the April Fool football 'bomb' dropped over a Lille airfield in 1917 which sent Germans scurrying for cover – until it bounced.[6] With twenty-seven wearers of rugby's red rose now lying amongst the poppies in Flanders' and other fields, the RFU felt justified in re-asserting the 'national value of Rugby Football'.

In another gesture of goodwill uncommon for the rugby authorities, a truce was declared and an olive branch extended to the professional League code. Out of practical necessity in wartime, Northern Union players had been 'amnestied' (as if they were outlaws) and allowed to play under 'proper' Rugby Union rules; Ben Gronow and Harold Wagstaff were prominent stars in the Army Service Corps team, which bore Mobbs's disapproval. This condescension was now extended by a dispensation for the King's Cup, albeit only for players still in the forces. Pointedly, only one League player was actually chosen.

RFU minutes show that New Zealand would also propose a relaxation of amateur regulations in August 1919; the RFU's pre-determined attitude in March was that 'they shall not pass' and it was not about to soften its stance by admitting League undesirables to the showcase event. But nonetheless an eighth ground was added – in the north. Allowing men to play (in theory) was one thing, but holding a rugby union match for the King's Cup in enemy territory was another. But this was not Bradford Northern or even Horton Park Avenue, a former bastion of League, now in Association hands, but Lidget Green, home of Bradford RUFC (where Yorkshire would later play the NZ Services). But it happened on 9 April (after a postponement of two weeks due to heavy March snow), with the mighty antipodean clash of Australia and New Zealand.

Australia's skipper was Lieutenant William 'Billy' Watson, who came up through the ranks. He ended his first war with MC and Bar and DCM on his chest and would add the DSO at Kokoda, New Guinea, in his second. Born in New Zealand, he was a 1912 Waratah who toured the Americas and faced the All Blacks in 1914. He enlisted on 8 August and so was 'not available for selection' in the last hurrah of Test rugby in Sydney the following Saturday. He served as a gunner at Gallipoli, then moved to the Western Front, where he was promoted to sergeant, won his DCM at the Somme and was commissioned in September 1917. Wounded in Flanders mud in November, he recovered and went on to win his MC in the push to victory that began at Amiens in August 1918. He just had time to add the Bar: at Foucaucourt on 27 August, Watson worked his way forward through enemy fire and directed three batteries to eliminate enemy machine-gun posts. He captained throughout the King's Cup; that he was on a rugby field at all in 1919 was a miracle.

The uncompromising Watson played in the front row, no place for the faint-hearted. But he would have suffered excruciating agonies in the scrummage, as he was covered in purulent sores resulting from a mustard gas attack in October. Major Matthews had to lance these festering wounds with a sterilised penknife before Watson took to the field, bleeding before first contact – read this at The Stoop and weep. Despite the pain, he would have the rare pleasure of turning over the Trans-Tasman arch-rival by a narrow 6–5 score, in their last game at Bradford. It was the only loss for the New Zealanders. Their soldiers had fought side by side in the ANZAC

Division at Gallipoli, and then the ANZAC Corps in France; now it was back to serious business. In July 1920, this lieutenant made of tough stuff would again be captain, this time of a NSW representative Test side, effectively Australia, as the Queensland Union was still suffering from shell-shock and had not yet re-formed. His AIF full back, Captain 'Jackie' Beith, hooker Quartermaster Sergeant Bond and wing forward Private Quinn would stiffen the spine of the NSW team; normal peacetime service was resumed, however, with a 26–15 defeat by the All Blacks.

Wing threequarter Sergeant Dudley Suttor played all five games of the Cup tournament with Watson. The New South Welshman, 'the crackerjack player of the side', was overlooked for the 1912 American tour. Such were the tensions in NSW rugby that his home town of Bathurst immediately seceded from Union in protest and swung over to League. 'Dud' toured New Zealand with the Waratahs in 1913. He won his international cap and was the leading try-scorer in the series with seven tries: 'Suttor as a winger is the ideal, a man who shoots off the mark like lead out of a Winchester, fast as zebra, and generally a reckless, daring smashing player.' A driver in the Australian ASC, he saw service in Egypt, France and Belgium, and then in the Trench Team. He was no 'dud' in the King's Cup, the prolific wing sharing honours with flanker Sergeant Bradley as top try-scorer.

A squad of some fifty players in the Australian XV, and the Reserves captained by Peter Buchanan of the Trench Team, trained at Chiswick in London. Warm-up matches included their own Flying Corps (shot down 50–0 in Gloucester) and Leicester County. They returned to Leicester for their first game against the Mother Country, played in front of 9,000 (not far off the Welford Road capacity at the time). As if to remind them of France, the March weather was bitterly cold. Although it was 'evenly contested', they lost 3–6 due to a 'lack of combined effort' – Goddard's earlier apprehensions confirmed. But a changed team, with Wally Matthews behind the scrum, turned it round against South Africa at Newport, with Suttor and Bradley scoring. Unaccountably, they then slipped up against the RAF, losing 3–7 at Kingsholm.

The Royal Air Force was newly formed in 1918 from a merger of the Army's Royal Flying Corps and the Royal Naval Air Service (RNAS). Their rugby side did not have ace Cyril Lowe, the coruscating 5ft 6in England winger and dogfight scourge of the Germans with nine kills,[7] and 'a demon at dropping goals' at Dulwich. But they did have wing forward William Wavell Wakefield, just 20 years of age, in the first two matches.

His youth had saved him from front-line immolation and his war, by his own admission, was largely spent in flying training and playing rugby at Cranwell and United Services. He would go on to captain England to consecutive Grand Slams in a 1920s heyday (as well as eleven years a Harlequin, an MP for almost thirty and subsequent ennoblement as Baron Wakefield of Kendal). He made his international debut against Wales in 1920, before going up to Cambridge and two Blues, the second as captain. His athleticism (he was RAF 440 yards champion) allowed him to redefine the loose forward role akin to that of a fighter pilot, hunting down stand-offs and making flying runs in support of the threequarter line.

Wavell Wakefield was at Scapa Flow with the Fleet when 'ordered to report to the Air Force Rugger side',[8] the highest ranking side of all – every one of the fly-boys held a commission. The RAF did, however, break ranks by including Lieutenant Billy Seddon, the only rugby league player in the tournament, at full back; Wakefield's insistence was vindicated when Seddon scored their winning four-point drop goal against Australia. Wakefield's first sortie as skipper was to take the nucleus of the side to France and Belgium in search of any RAF players stationed there who might have been overlooked. They practised against other units with little joy; the harsh winter meant living in freezing huts and playing on equally frozen ground. Instead, they tried, with little success to fend off the new enemy of influenza, which had already claimed England's Schwartz just a week after the Armistice, and would take its toll of the team in training and, by Wakefield's account, in their first below-par encounters with New Zealand and South Africa.

Wakefield recruited at a high level: Scots internationalist Flight Lieu-tenant Archie Symington was a man who had fought a busy war. Wounded at Bethune in 1914 with the KRRC, he was mentioned in despatches in 1915 and awarded the MC in 1916. A gas victim, he was discharged from service but rejoined into the RFC. Another clutch of Scots included George Thom, later capped in 1920, Robert Simpson, and Gerald Crole, Edinburgh Accie and Oxford Blue. Crole joined the 2nd Dragoon Guards, before transferring to 40 Squadron, RFC, winning an MC in September 1917 before his kite was pranged in October, forcing him to sit out the war as a guest of the Kaiser at Holzminden PoW camp.

Wartime flying attracted an international brigade of adventurers who lived short lives and died far from home. In Gainsborough cemetery in Lincolnshire, where the RFC Home Defence squadrons buried the pilots who plummeted to earth in their frail machines, Rosslyn Park aviator Jack

Harman lies next to three Canadians, two New Zealanders, one South African and an Argentinian. The RAF's rugby crew was fortified by ten South Africans, including the 1912 Springbok Godfrey 'Bay' Wrentmore and Cecil Thompson, DFC. 'From our point of view', wrote Mellish, 'it was a pity the RAF entered on its own as it meant several excellent players were lost to the South African side.'

The youthful Wakefield was thrust into the whirlwind of Dominion rugby on a rapidly ascending learning curve. The New Zealanders 'showed me the value of physical toughness and of keen following and backing up'. He was 'impressed by the size of the South African forwards and the difficulty of getting the ball in the line-out', and England's Barry Cumberlege, playing for the Mother Country, 'whipped the ball off my feet when I had gone away for a long dribble, for I was not used to meeting full-backs of his class'. Wakefield was learning at the feet of masters; the foundations of his England success were laid 'in these matches, which really gave me my first taste of representative football. I had a chance to put my theories into practice and I learnt a great deal.' Although his RAF team crashed and burnt in three of their games, most heavily against the Mother Country, 29–6, they did shoot down both Canada and Australia.

One unexpected RAF player was James Ira Thomas 'Taffy' Jones, a pre-war Carmarthen Harlequin.[9] At 22 the Welsh pilot had almost as many decorations as he had kills: he finished the war as Lieutenant (acting Major) Jones, DSO, MC, DFC and Bar, MM – 74 Squadron's leading 'ace' with thirty-seven victories in just three months. He was in every sense a tough bastard (his illegitimacy was a secret he kept all his life):

> My habit of attacking Huns dangling from their parachutes led to many arguments in the mess. Some officers, of the Eton and Sandhurst type, thought it was 'unsportsmanlike' to do it. Never having been to a public school, I was unhampered by such considerations of form. I just pointed out that there was a bloody war on, and that I intended to avenge my pals.

Whilst on leave he went to watch the RAF play New Zealand at Swansea on 3 March. As the team was a man short after South African Eugen Norgarb was felled by influenza, he was persuaded to play on the wing. 'Capt Jones, the Carmarthen man, did a lot in defence but was "starved" by his centre', reported the *Swansea Post* as the New Zealanders won 22–3. The *Wanganui Chronicle* was more critical: 'Their passing was haphazard, and the marked neglect of their right-winger, Jones, certainly robbed them of more than one excellent chance to score.' It was his only game in the tournament. He then went back to war in Russia.

The Canadians went about recruiting their team in a less scientific manner. Welsh-born sapper Jimmy Pritchard, who played for the Winnipeg Welsh before enlisting in the 101st Battalion, recalled in 1974:

> While walking by the sports field at Shoreham one morning, I saw a rugby practice and as I approached a group of soldiers who were watching, one of them said to me: 'Jimmy, where have you been? I've been looking for you. Do you want to play rugby for Canada in the tournament?'[10]

The speaker was Bob Lewis, Canada's team manager, against whom Jimmy had played in 1914 and not seen since. Pritchard joined his squad at its Metropolitan Water Board base in Honor Oak; he was given a brand new jersey by the army. As a left-winger starved of the ball, he was unimpressed by his centres who, 'never passed and always got tackled when they tried to run through our opponents'. After some crushing preliminaries, including a 43–0 hiding by Pill Harriers at Newport, they were first up for the Cup at Portsmouth against the mighty New Zealanders (albeit fielding their 2nd XV) *The Times*, with its customary condescension, damned them with faint praise in its match preview:

> The Canadians are improving very rapidly, but they are not a great side. Their real value is a missionary one, for it is hoped that they will instil into Canadians the value of the game which, despite climatic conditions, ought to be a real Canadian game.[11]

They kept the score to a creditable 11–0 loss. A scoreless draw at Honor Oak against United Hospitals did not bode well for the game against South Africa at Swansea. Snow fell before the game to make them feel at home, but to little effect: nine tries (including seven bombs from Captain H. Mills and Lieutenant W.J. Mills) were conceded in a 31–0 battering, on a day when the imposing Canadians dominated the scrummage but little else.

Their Twickenham debut came against Australia. Two Davies brothers, Sammy and Dai, both sergeant majors and friends of Pritchard from Winnipeg, filled the half-back berths for Canada. The sparse crowd of 4,000 rattled in the cavernous stands, a sad comparison with the 25,000 Scots packed into Inverleith the same day to watch New Zealand beat the Mother Country. The king was down with the flu and their royal audience was Princes George and Albert.

> With the Canadians wearing numbers, but unnumbered on the card, the Australians numbered on the card, but wearing no numbers, and both teams sporting blue, if of different shades, some time elapsed before the spectators could feel any confidence in their knowledge of the players.[12]

If royalty found the spectacle bewildering, think of the poor referee. But there was one spectator highly popular with the soldiers on the pitch: Princess Mary. The veterans might recognise her profile from the brass tins they had received at the front. Over 426,000 'Princess Mary's Gift Boxes' were distributed at Christmas 1914: it was her idea, when just 17, 'to send a Christmas present from the whole of the nation to every sailor afloat and every soldier at the front'. Another 1.4 million were distributed throughout the war, although production was delayed when a shipment of brass went down with the torpedoed *Lusitania* in May 1915. The 'Gift Box for the Troops' was filled with tobacco, a pipe or cigarettes (acid-drops for non-smokers, spices for the Indians), pencils, a Christmas card and a picture of the princess herself. Now they had a chance to thank her in person.

As for the rugby match, the result was as disappointing for the Canadians as the attendance, with another 38 unanswered points in the debit column. The Canadians proved the whipping boys of the tournament with no wins and a points difference of 110 (a solitary try by Lieutenant E.W. Watling against the RAF saw them take a short-lived lead). Rugby historian Owen Owen (so good they named him twice) was kindly in retrospect: 'although the Canadians lacked the long experience of the others, they proved no mean opponents'. Their Forces team ended its chastening overseas rugby adventure with losses to Llanelli and Gloucester, but two tries in each match were seized upon as signs of progress.

Three inches of snow at Bradford postponed the Australia v New Zealand fixture for two weeks and the tight schedule forced the match to be played midweek on 9 April, only four days – and a 200-mile train journey – after the trouncing of 'hopelessly outclassed' Canada at Twickenham in front of the princes. At full-time at Twickenham, their Highnesses came onto the field to speak to Watson's Australians and 'spent some time in conversation with the players. The Prince of Wales is a very popular man with the Diggers.'[13] The stadium, the royal presence and ten tries in 'really first-class football' clearly inspired them as they travelled north to play their black-shirted bogey-men.

As a microcosm of Empire, the teams revealed much about the rugby caste system in their respective societies. The New Zealand skipper, Regimental Sergeant Major James Ryan of the Otago Infantry, had under his rugby command two officers, eight sergeants and seven capped All Blacks, including his 1914 captain. Six more would wear post-war black caps, with Private Belliss captaining the ABs in 1922 and Gunner Alf West touring Britain as breakaway forward with the 1925 'Invincibles'. Rank and status did not matter: Ryan was the man for the job and RSMs are leaders of men. These were the boys who lived, and they had earned the right to choose who led them on the rugby field. The patrician Mother Country by contrast fielded twenty officers (including the reverend captain), one company sergeant major and not a single private soldier.

Ryan was one of the luckier of the 'Unlucky Otagos', serving throughout the war. One of seven brothers to play for the Petone club, he was 18 when he first wore black on the Wellington wing in 1905, the first of his eleven seasons for the province as a versatile, play-anywhere back. He added the silver fern to his jersey with the national side in 1910 and toured Australia in 1914. In France, he had played for the Trench Team before crossing to England and the Inter-Services team captaincy. Like the Canadian Davies boys, he had family for company – brother Eddie, otherwise Bombardier Ryan, played as 'a pacy three-quarter'. Eddie's hearing was permanently damaged by an explosion (an occupational hazard in the artillery) but did not stop him appearing for the All Blacks in 1921.

By this stage of the tournament, New Zealand had defeated all four of their opponents, including the host Mother Country, which had won its other three. Their Twickenham encounter with South Africa on 29 March was the first official meeting of the two titans of twentieth-century rugby (if we discount Gallaher's rumoured exploits against the Afrikaners on the veldt), although claims can be argued for their opener against the RAF and its ten South Africans. South Africa's own first game was also against the RAF and featured 'Boy' Morkel and Sergeant Wilhelm 'Bingo' Burger from the 1906 tour (rumoured to be a Saracen while in England after the tour). Despite the almost constant wartime games and a comprehensive series of selection trials and warm-ups, C.F.S. Nicholson wrote that the South African team was:

not evenly balanced and there were far too many changes that prevented teamwork and cohesion . . . we had a good leavening of Internationals, but several were just of good senior club standard. The team generally were good on the attack, but the defence was far from satisfactory, and some of the tackling was crude in the extreme.[14]

He singled out 'Buller' Scully, Frank Mellish and Boy Morkel for praise, but 'sound' was the best he could summon for other players. Morkel had been the star of the 1912 Springboks in Britain, but was handicapped by the flu; forward Mellish would stay on in Britain and win six caps for England during the winter of 1920–1. After trials (with firm friend Wakefield), he received a brief note, inviting him to a bring-your-own-shirt party:

> 'You have been selected to play for England against Wales at Newport on Saturday 20th January at 2.30 p.m. England plays in white. Herewith a rose for your jersey.'
>
> That was all. You wore your own club stockings, you bought yourself a pair of white pants and a white jersey and you got your girlfriend to sew on the rose. The cryptic message went on to say that if you required transport you were to inform the Secretary of your home station and he would send you a third class return ticket. And that I think is the charm of amateur rugby . . . we expected and were pleased to make some contribution towards our fun and enjoyed it a great deal more by doing so.

On his return to a southern winter in South Africa, he walked straight into the Springbok side about to depart on its first tour to New Zealand. He has the unique distinction of representing two countries in the same year in 1921.[15]

On 29 March, a beautiful spring day with a stiff breeze, 10,000 (mostly soldiers) watched 'easily the most brilliant exposition of Rugby yet seen in the competition'[16] against New Zealand on a firm field at Twickenham. The lengthy *Times* report noted: 'Save for one brief period until the end of the first half, the game was in New Zealand territory, but in this period New Zealand scored.' Sound familiar? The New Zealand forwards 'handle the ball like backs . . . very clever in picking up and barging through in the loose. These hurricane methods are especially useful near the line.'[17] They triumphed 15–5. Frank Mellish met King George for the second time: the previous occasion had been when, wounded and in recovery, he received his Military Cross. His ragged army uniform gloves let him down:

> A great weight was on my shoulders and I felt sure he would judge and size up South Africa by the way I comported myself . . . His Majesty put out his hand to greet me and I shot out mine and all four fingers and thumb left their cramped cubby-holes and shot out also . . . he was convulsed with mirth and if he did say anything, it was lost on me entirely.

A year later, on the pitch at Twickenham, they shook hands again, without gloves: 'You and I have met before. Let me think. Ah, yes, the Palace, was it not? I think you made me laugh.'

This was Spring Offensive time in the last four seasons. On 9 April 1917, the Battle of Arras, involving troops from all the combatant rugby nations, had opened; it was the day that Scotland's Tommy Nelson died. The same day in 1919 was also the anniversary of the death of All Black Hubert 'Jum' Turtill, left behind by the Originals but capped once against Australia in 1905. He had then toured Britain with the professional League side derisively termed the 'All Golds'; banned for life from Union, he came to England in 1909, ran a pub and played League for St Helens. He joined the Royal Engineers, survived Ypres, the Somme and Passchendaele, but finally took a hospital pass from a shell at Festubert in 1918. As for the men who survived France to earn selection for this new rugby revival, they might say (albeit improbably) with Robert Browning, 'Oh to be in England now that April's there'.

A victory for New Zealand against Australia at Bradford on 9 April would leave them unbeaten and clinch the King's Cup outright. The game seemed a foregone conclusion, especially after an earlier NZEF double when both Southern Hemisphere First and Reserve XVs met on the same February day at Richmond. But this time the improving Aussies were hitting their straps and had other ideas; a curiously tender Achilles heel – when it comes to crunch knockout ties – would first be exposed in the otherwise impenetrable New Zealander hide. Australia's team also included the much-travelled and decorated Lieutenant Danny Carroll, 1908 Wallaby and Olympic champion, and dual-country rugby internationalist, a 'ringer' drafted in from the US Army. He already had one try to his name from the Canadian rout.

Australia's 6–5 win in front of 7,000 people who were, in Goddard's view, 'treated to the finest game of the series', was not only a highly satisfying end to their campaign, but forced their opponents into a final decider on 16 April against the Mother Country at Twickenham. The Australian forwards outplayed their vaunted opponents in Bradford, with Lance Corporal Thomson and Sergeant Egan crossing for unconverted tries. The expected second-half counter-offensive from the black jerseys came with a Storey try converted by Stohr, but by the whistle, Australia were again camped on the New Zealand line, forcing them into defensive heroics.

One imagines that a copious amount of ale was taken in Bradford that night; if there was any hangover, they swiftly recovered to chalk up another 460 kilometres by train to Exeter and defeat Devon just three days later, as rugby's circus moved on. Danny Carroll returned to his American regiment. The round-robin Inter Services league competition was completed and two teams had finished even on points. For those who enjoy fine dining at a league table, here it is:

1919 Inter-Services Tournament[18]

	P	W	L	F	A	Pts
New Zealand	5	4	1	58	17	8
Mother Country	5	4	1	81	27	8
Australia	5	3	2	58	23	6
South Africa	5	2	3	65	43	4
Royal Air Force	5	2	3	37	69	4
Canada	5	0	5	3	113	0

Endgame

A band of angels coming after me
Coming forth to carry me home.

The stage was set for a crowd-puller at Twickenham, lately a horse
paddock, now the theatre of rugby dreams. A ticket for one of the
best seats in the prosaically named 'Stand B' (East) cost the princely
sum of six shillings (30p). On 16 April, it was too a dream confrontation:
the Mother Country hosts against the indomitable New Zealanders.
Again it might seem that television scriptwriters were at work before
their time.

The alternative narrative, nicely interrupted by Australia, would have
seen the Silver Ferns crowned King's Cup winners in Bradford, with the
British Army team left to play a hollow rubber against the South Africans
at Twickenham three days later. For their pains, on the day of the final,
those pesky Aussies found themselves far to the west in Plymouth, where
they defeated the Royal Naval Depot.

Even the British weather relented for the Twickenham showpiece.
Four days previously, the New Zealand B team had played Coventry after
heavy rain had turned the pitch into a quagmire memory of Flanders;
Corporal Tureia was unable to lift an attempted conversion kick from
the mud. Now an exciting game was in prospect in fair conditions. In
those amateur days, of course, it was taking part in the competition that
mattered, not the winning. But no one had told the New Zealanders that.

On Ryan's team were five mates from that last All Black Test in
Sydney of 15 August 1914. Dick Roberts of Taranaki had captained the
All Blacks; as Rifleman R.W. Roberts of the NZ Rifle Brigade, he would
now be the team's try ace, crossing the whitewash seven times in the
tournament, and a crack-shot with the boot too, with five conversions.
Private Michael Cain of the Otagos was again in the pack. One forward,
listed as plain Sergeant Arthur Wilson was, more fully, Nathaniel Arthur
'Ranji' Wilson; his nickname derived from the Anglo-Indian cricketer
Ranjitsinhji. He was born in Christchurch to a New Zealand mother

and West Indian father, and was an All Black from 1908 to 1914; his name would later make another dark mark in rugby history, but not by his own doing.

Sapper Jim Bruce and Corporal Jackie O'Brien, Auckland and Divisional Signals, at full back (but wearing number 1 in the upside-down manner of a Southern Hemisphere nation) toured but did not play that last Test. With Doolan Downing and Jim McNeece, whose bleached bones now lay scattered on the arid slopes of Chunuk Bair, they had all dashed off after their victory to catch the steamer home before the wartime curfew closed Sydney Harbour. We can guess how Ryan's motivational team talks went.

The Mother Country had stacked the deck for the tournament, with twenty-two of their twenty-eight squad players being internationalists, all from the officer class. Only one who made the selection for the New Zealand game, CSM Jones, was not an officer. Twelve of the side for this final game were full caps and they included the two try-scorers from England's 1914 victory over Wales by the 'small and artistic margin of one point',[1] 'Bruno' Brown and 'Cherry' Pillman. Back then they were young rugby players at Blackheath FC, now they were warriors who had seen the worst of war.

Brisbane-born Rhodes Scholar and RAMC surgeon, Lieutenant Colonel Leonard 'Bruno' Brown, MC, won eighteen England caps over eleven years on either side of the conflagration. From his debut with Jack King (and alongside Pillman) at Swansea in 1911, he made a huge impact on the international game during his long career. He captained England against Wales in 1922, represented NSW on the RFU committee 1922–49, chaired the Dominions Conference in 1947, and obtained International Board status for Australia, New Zealand and South Africa. He was RFU President in the 1948–49 season and helped found the Australian RFU on 26 November 1949. Did his outlook spring from his birth or six games in the King's Cup?

Photographic omens did not bode well for his survival to perform these good works: in England's line-up for both the French and Scottish matches of that 1914 season, he sits flanked by Poulton-Palmer and Francis Oakeley, both killed in the first year of war. Three more players from Edinburgh would die early: 'Bungy' Watson in the North Sea, and two Durham school mates, Dingle at Gallipoli, and the last, Alfie Maynard, at Beaumont-Hamel in November 1916, just after 'half-time' in the Great War for Civilisation. This tells of the energy with which rugby players rushed early into the fight: Brown was one of only three Calcutta Cup forwards, with Pillman and Joseph Brunton, to survive four years of war to play together again for the King's Cup. Six souls from English rugby's last peacetime hurrah of April 1914 in the Grand Slam over France would 'always have Paris'; even if four had no grave.

Charles Henry (so 'Cherry', naturally) Pillman, an exciting wing forward for Blackheath, made his England debut under the captaincy of Adrian Stoop, on the day Ben Gronow kicked off at Twickenham. In the pack with him was fellow debutant Leonard Haigh of Manchester, who was late to rugby after school, late to his first cap at 30 and too late for active service, sadly dying of pneumonia while in training with the ASC in 1916. Cherry, like Brown, won eighteen England caps, and toured South Africa with the British tourists under Dr Tom Smyth in 1910 (with William Tyrrell, Scot Eric Milroy and 'Bristolian' Tom Richards). The hard sun-baked ground suited his turn of speed; he scored fifty-nine points until injury interrupted his tour. But he returned with a match-winning performance – playing at fly half – in the second Test against the Springboks at Port Elizabeth. Boks skipper Billy Millar commented, 'If ever a man can have been said to have won an international match through his unorthodox and lone-handed efforts, it can be said of the inspired black-haired Pillman'. He returned to Britain as leading scorer with sixty-five points – six tries, three penalties and nineteen conversions and resumed a similarly free-scoring England career.

In 1911, he crossed the whitewash twice against France, but was over-shadowed by Douglas 'Daniel' Lambert's record twenty-two points (the hulking speedster Lambert was a bête-noire to the French, having scored five tries on his debut against them in 1907). Cherry was almost ever-present for his country until a bittersweet moment in 1914. Against Scotland (in what turned out to be his last game) he broke his leg and was replaced for the finale against France by his younger brother, Robert. This was Robert's only cap: the war would not only interrupt his rugby career but would cut short his life, in July 1916 near Ploegsteert, where his captain of the day, Poulton-Palmer, already lay in his grave. For Cherry Pillman, never would a broken leg be suffered with such mixed feelings; if you had to lose your England place, you would want your kid brother to take it. Captain Pillman, MC, of the 4th Dragoon Guards would find some little consolation in knowing that Robert had not only died for his country, but played for it too. Lambert had also died in France, with the Buffs at the Battle of Loos in 1915, shortly after marrying his childhood sweetheart. He left a son who neither knew him, nor was able to cry at his father's grave: Daniel's remains were never identified. How many of these memories welled up at Twickenham for the boys who lived?

Full back Barry Cumberlege, who taught Wakefield a thing or two, was the 'first' new cap for England after the war. If we accept the numerical/alphabetical system currently in vogue for heritage and shirt-embroidery reasons, his England 545 cap on 17 January 1920 came after a six-year interval since the debut of 544 Alex Sykes in pre-war Paris. Eleven brand new caps were added that day against Wales at Swansea – a sign of war's impact – with Jock Wright being number 555 by virtue of his surname. William Wavell Wakefield, with his full complement of initial Ws, just pipped him to 554 that day.[2]

Lieutenant Charles Usher of the Gordon Highlanders was the first serving soldier to captain a national team when he led Scotland in 1912. He was now one of four capped Scots to turn out for the Services team, with Gallie, Sloan and Laing. He had spent much of the war as a guest of the Kaiser at Bayreuth, where he 'did a great deal to keep up the spirits of his fellow-prisoners': 'He conducted a gymnastic class every morning, encouraged games, taught Highland dancing and even gave instruction on the bagpipes.' Membership of the escape committee doubtless boomed, as his co-prisoner Lieutenant Dobson, RNVR, observed: 'It was an open question whether this last form of sport could be considered a benefit to the community.'[3] Usher would resume his Scotland rugby career after the war, winning a total of sixteen caps. On the matter of the pipes, the record is thankfully silent.

Wales were represented by Clem Lewis at stand-off, Bill Havard and Charlie Jones. Clem Lewis joined the 16th Welsh Regiment (Cardiff City) while it was being raised in late 1914. As Lieutenant J.M.C. Lewis he was wounded at Pilckem Ridge on 31 July 1917, as Passchendaele kicked off. Charles William Jones was, in boxing terms, a comeback kid: an Old Contemptible from the pre-war Regular Army, he was so badly wounded at Mons in August 1914 that he was invalided and attached to the British Mission in New Mexico. He later joined the army gymnasium staff as an instructor at Portsmouth and won three Welsh caps in 1920, and seven for the army between 1920 and 1923 – the first non-officer to play – whilst also playing for Newport and Leicester. Captain Reverend Bill Havard, MC, of Llanelli, chaplain to the 10th South Wales Borderers and the Brigade of Guards, was a late rugby convert. A Swansea Town amateur centre forward before the war, he won his rugby Blue in 1919 in a game surely guided by divine providence: a last-minute injury replacement, he switched from the pack at half-time to replace crocked full back Waldock and converted Gerald Crole's try. Truly is there more joy in heaven over one sinner who repenteth. He won his sole Welsh cap in April against this same NZ Services team and later became Bishop of St David's.

One unsung member of the side made a significant, if unwitting, contribution to our perception of the Great War. Major Philip Henry Lawless, captain of Richmond, enlisted in the Artists' Rifles in October 1914, was commissioned in the 18th Middlesex in 1915, served on the Somme and at Salonika, and was awarded the MC in 1918. He was 'capped' not by England, but four times for this Mother Country team. He reported on rugby and golf for the *Morning Post* and the *Daily Telegraph*. More dangerously at Remagen in 1945, he was covering the Americans crossing the Rhine into Germany when he was killed by enemy fire.[4] His daughter Pamela married Peter Faulks, who had won an MC fighting in Tunisia; their son Sebastian wrote the novel *Birdsong* in 1993, and opened eyes anew to a conflict that had faded from view.

In a close game, New Zealand forward power prevailed in front of 15,000 spectators including a proud Prime Minister William Massey. He had seen his country through wartime and now found it emerging as a sporting power and a new voice in international affairs. He was in Europe as a statesman, attending the Paris peace conference which would set a course for the world's future; at Twickenham he was as nervous as any Kiwi rugby fan:

> 'Old Bill', as he was affectionately termed, went into the New Zealand dressing-room at half-time, and wore a worried look. Things had not gone too good for the New Zealanders, and Mr. Massey approached one of the husky forwards and urged him to 'do his best for New Zealand; the people back home look forward to success.' There came an unexpected reply: 'Leave 'em to us, Bill. Politics might be your game, but this is our picnic.'
>
> In the second spell the New Zealanders used steam-roller tactics and gave the clever English backs no chances. After the final whistle Mr. Massey once again visited the dressing-room, but this time he wore a triumphant smile. His friend, the husky forward, was taking a shower. Mr. Massey grasped his hand, shook it with great fervour and stood there completely oblivious of the fact that the shower was on and that he was being drenched.[5]

Singe and Ford scored tries for New Zealand and Stohr kicked a penalty in a 9–3 victory. The Mother Country's points came from a penalty by Cumberlege.

New Zealand might reasonably now have expected to receive the King's Cup for their labours. But this tournament was stage-managed to celebrate Allied unity, and the French could hardly be excluded without diplomatic incident and gross insult to the 1.4 million *poilus* who had given their lives. So the New Zealanders thus far had only earned the right to represent the 'Armies of the British Empire against the French Army'. French rugby confidence was growing: they had acquitted themselves well on their home ground against Anzac and Australian Trench Teams and proved themselves worthy to be invited to the party. Twickenham would host the game again, so the long road trips were over for the New Zealanders. After typically thorough preparation, a legacy from the Originals, Ryan led his men back to the fray once more. In a coda to the main tournament, they faced a side that was short of international experience (and of one eyeball), but long on nicknames, and full of promise for France's rugby future.

Their *équipe* was captained from outside half by Philippe 'Struc' Struxiano, a Stade Toulousain player who had been capped twice in 1913 and would win five more in 1920. He had also been a substitute for the French soccer team. As a cyclist in the 83e Régiment d'Infantérie, he was seriously wounded at Souchez, north of Arras, in 1915, and did not return to service until April 1918, not in the trenches but with the Air Force at Avord in central France. His half-back partnership was somewhat improvised, as Lieutenant Jean Domercq, a banker's son and tank commander from Bayonne, normally played back row, where he was capped against Ireland and Scotland in 1912. But he had learned his trade at Harry Roe's Aviron Bayonnais academy where forwards played like backs.

Several players as yet unattached to clubs were shown as belonging to Association Sportive de Chauffeurs d'Artillerie (ASCA) Sathony; they were 'artillery drivers' from the military camp outside Lyon, equivalent to Major Stanley's ASC (Motor Transport) unit. The forwards featured Sergeant Major Fernand Vaquer, known as 'le Maréchal', who would win three caps in 1921 and 1922. He remained a career soldier, hence the nickname, and became a legendary figure in Catalan rugby for sixty years, playing for both Perpignan teams (winning the 1921 French championship with L'Union Sportive Perpignan), both Toulouse teams and Roussillon. Sous-Lieutenant Robert Thierry from Racing Club played for his country four times in 1920 despite losing an eye. Capitaine Pierre

Pons, a prop and hooker for Stade Toulousain and AS Perpignan, won half a dozen French caps by 1921 and gloried in the enigmatic nickname of 'La Joconde'. As with Leonardo's original Mona Lisa, no one knows why; he became director of Toulouse's veterinary school, but this offers no clue.

One rising star was Private Aimé Cassayet-Armagnac, whose name predictably proved too much for the English programme printers. This lock and number eight played for the 1920 champions Stadoceste Tarbais, with Jean Nicolaï, another forward and future wine-merchant; he amassed thirty-one caps until 1927 when he died, still young at 34, of a sudden illness on the day of the French rugby cup final. Aimé had spent almost the entire war in a German prison camp, and was itching for some action. Of the others, Soldat Soulié would win nine French caps and Private Desvouges one. Sergeant Mazarico at full back, wing Lieutenant Loubatié and forwards Major Dillenséger and Sous-Lieutenant Galliax have left fewer traces.

In the centre, Sergeant Félix Lasserre, another from the Aviron Bayonnais championship team of 1913, and known as 'René' or 'Poulet', later played for Cognaçaise and Grenoble. He was a fighter pilot and later café owner and cognac distiller – all things considered, a good man to have on the team. In 1921 he became the first player to be selected for France both as a forward (flanker) and a threequarter, thanks again to Roe's *manière Bayonnaise*. Soldat René Crabos, also in the centre, played seventeen times between 1920 and 1924. Sergeant Major 'Le Roi Jean' Etcheberry, still only 17 (very young for a king and sergeant major, but promotion came rapidly with the high French casualty rate) was another versatile winger who converted to a forward as he put on age and weight. This metalworker from Boucau, near Bayonne, played after the war for SA Rochefortais, Boucau Stade and US Cognaçaise. Along with Lasserre and Cassayet-Armagnac, he would play against the USA at Colombes in 1924. He earned himself sixteen caps in a long career, including two in 1927 against, of all nations, Germany. Such is rugby's power to forgive, forget and move on in search of a good contest.

Royalty was out in force on 19 April, with King George bringing all four princes, along with dignitaries from the rival countries, Field Marshal Haig, the nation's garlanded saviour, and Chief of the Imperial General Staff, for good measure. Before the game kicked off, the king stepped forward to present his cup to New Zealand skipper James Ryan. The French were left under no illusion that they were a *digestif* after the main banquet at the triumphal Imperial house party. *The Times* was in no doubt of the game's greater meaning:

> It was more than a mere football match; it had more the character of a national festival at which the presence of the King and his four sons, Sir Douglas Haig, Sir Henry Wilson, the French Embassy staff and the High Commissioner for New Zealand gave special significance . . . it was a true 'Victory' match.[6]

The military contest was refereed by Major J.E.C. Partridge of the Welsh Regiment, who was, appropriately enough, the senior officer on the field. His rugby credentials we have seen: this Newport player and Boer War veteran stayed on in South Africa after the fighting and played for them against the touring British (and Louis Greig) in 1903; he played the All Black Originals in 1905 when with Blackheath (the club fielded twelve internationalists, but still lost by thirty-two points). He then led the founding of the Army Rugby Union in 1906, was a Barbarian regular for years and played the wartime charity matches including – ironically for the Welsh-born 'Birdie' – their first 'international' when they surprisingly beat Wales in 1915, with Edgar Mobbs at the helm.

Sadly on this momentous Twickenham occasion in the brave new world of 1919, he played to the British officer stereotype by controlling the game poorly. When the final whistle of the King's Cup blew for 'no side', the match ended in another New Zealand victory over France, 20–3. A pattern was set for their next two Rugby World Cup Final reunions, both at Eden Park. Not for the last time, a New Zealand team could claim to be rugby champions of the world. At the time of writing they still are.

A final celebratory dinner was thrown for all combatants. Many, like Frank Mellish, had already handed in their army kit to the quartermaster. They all got noisily demob-happy: 'The evening ended in a never-to-be-forgotten banquet at Oddedino's when I sat next to the brilliant French wing three-quarter, Jauréguy.'

Young Lieutenant Goddard from Australia expressed the views of all parties when he concluded his report of the tournament:

> The presence of the four Dominion teams in this contest was a splendid thing for Rugby in England . . . this great contest did more in a month to bring it back to its pre-war popularity than the ordinary club games would have done in a couple of seasons.

He might have added that the subsequent regional tours by New Zealand and Australian XVs and Reserve teams did even more to revive enthusiasm. They took their brand of attacking rugby to the green and pleasant fields of grass-roots clubs throughout England and Wales, which had been starved of competitive rugby since March 1914. From Ebbw Vale to Bradford, the New Zealanders racked up thirty-six games, and from Penzance to Ogmore Vale and Maesteg went the Australians: their Reserve side met formidable Llanelli three times, taking the first game but losing the rubber, a reminder of defeats by Welsh clubs in 1908. The New Zealand touring side included 'Ranji' Wilson and Māori Pioneer, Parekura Tureia, bringing back memories of the first Māori tourists, now thirty years past. It was springtime again for rugby: New Zealand's winning team went to Swansea and then played in Paris, Pau and Toulouse in May. During the King's Cup tournament the South African High Commissioner, W.P. Schreiner had invited them for a six-week tour of the Union to break their long journey home. The political wrangling over vice-captain Wilson and Tureia came later.

The RFU, emboldened by the success of the King's Cup, reasserted its authority over the game. Welsh proposals for minor reforms of amateur regulations were easily rejected and New Zealand's more forceful approach was rebuffed. The Empire had struck back against leadership challenges, but the RFU's attitude to the game remained insular rather than international. The boom in the domestic game and England's soaring success under Wakefield with Grand Slams in 1921, 1923 and 1924 created a complacency which would be rudely upset by the returning All Blacks in 1925, who brushed away all comers to earn their 'Invincibles' title.

Wavell Wakefield pointed out the overriding positives of the King's Cup, which, to his mind, was

> . . . a splendid opportunity during the transition period, while men were waiting to be demobilised or to be returned to their Dominions, to get Rugger started and also to see something of the best players from overseas . . . it was unique in Rugby history for footballers representing so many parts of the Empire to play against one another.

Australia's Goddard too sensed the unique moment for his countrymen and was grateful for the opportunity, with blithe understatement and an endearing absence of irony, in his swiftly published report:

> We in Australia are a long way from 'the hub of the Universe'.
> Ordinarily it costs a whole lot of money and takes many weeks
> of travel for an 'Antipodean' to reach England. But the past five
> years have caused so many changes and upset things to such an
> extent that between two and three thousands of us have not only
> seen England and the Continent free of cost, but have been paid
> for doing so.

Wide-eyed with enthusiasm, he does not trouble with the human cost
of their jaunts to Fromelles, Pozières and Amiens. ('Oh, that? Yeah, no
worries, mate.') But as with the Empire, so with rugby union, and a
moment passed: the exhausted relief of victory in war and an adrenaline
surge of conquering euphoria only masked a gradual but relentless move
away from Britain as its heart and hub.

A precarious peace broke out between victorious rugby nations in the
aftermath of war. The renewal of the inflexible RFU stance was hardly
on a par with the vindictive reparations of Versailles, but it did not help
the game's development. If there had been any doubt since the 1905
'Originals', it now became clear this was no longer Britain's game to own.
The absence of invitations to tour the heartland meant that the distant
Dominion powers turned away and formed new rivalries, notably that
between All Black and Springbok. Even neighbouring France, frustrated
by a largely self-inflicted running battle with its Five Nations partners,
turned away into the outstretched arms of Germany – almost unthinkable
after the bloodbaths of Verdun and the Chemin des Dames. Those arms
did not wrap warmly: the recent foe and new rugby opponent would later
drive France into the ground in a political and military spear-tackle of
crushing Nazi savagery.

In 2015 the William Webb Ellis Trophy has come back to Britain in
time for the tournament. As an international envoy for rugby, it has made
an epic return journey through emerging rugby nations which would
impress even the much-travelled Tom Richards and Blair Swannell. The
King's Cup trophy remains in New Zealand; the three arms of its Defence
Force play for it with passion each year. It may be out of sight for most of
the world, but it should not be out of mind.

In this year of rugby celebration, amidst four years of centenary
commemoration of war, we must remember what it stands for, and the
sacrifice that made it possible.

Aftermath and Recovery

Under the bludgeonings of chance
My head is bloody, but unbowed.[1]

It was time to go home.

Rugby's cup from the king may have run over in the euphoria of 1919, but choppy waves on the long voyage home in peace spilled much of its precious wine (that's enough of that metaphor). After the symbolic sporting celebration at Twickenham of Allied and Empire unity, and the implicit canonisation (or at least a knighthood) conferred on rugby for its contribution, Rugby union's post-war recovery was vigorous. But seeds of discord sown both at home and abroad germinated. Political tensions had surfaced, which would be further fed by popular narratives of high-handed British incompetence emerging from Gallipoli and the Somme that only seemed to reinforce the touring experiences of All Black and Wallaby in the first post-war decade. As mighty a force as rugby is, it could not mend the widening fissures in Imperial relations, only paper over the cracks.

In its English homeland, the red rose bloomed under the vigorous back-row play and assertive leadership of Wavell Wakefield, with three Grand Slams by 1924. They could not, however, overcome the might of the 1925 All Black Invincibles, even when these were reduced to fourteen men at Twickenham by Brownlie's sending off. The British game boomed with a new-found confidence as the professional middle classes and public schools further consolidated the war-winning game as their winter sport of choice. In the 'Great War for Civilisation' rugby had done its bit and would now reap the spoils of victory. Rugby carefully built its creation myth during the 1920s and seized upon the anniversary of Webb Ellis's moment of fine disregard to celebrate in style. Wavell Wakefield was an automatic selection for the historic Centenary Match at Rugby School in 1923, when a joint England and Wales side played Scotland and Ireland for the first time.

In another symbolic act, perhaps inadvertent, every soldier with a rainbow-ribboned Victory Medal pinned on his chest also owned a piece of that victory – in his own name, which was engraved on the bronze rim. Curiously, other ranks received theirs automatically while officers had to apply – a clerical nicety, but perhaps an early indication of a decline in deference. Although a welcome fit for heroes was rarely forthcoming, the demobbed private wanted his share of the spoils and would increasingly agitate to ensure he got it. The war had done much to shake the already fragile foundations of traditional British society. Estates crumbled and were sold to pay onerous death duties, and the landowning classes yielded the last of their economic grip to the industrialists and professionals. Deference had been challenged, if not banished, by the enforced parity and proximity of trench life. This was as true for individual soldiers as it was for entire dominions, who now had more of a say and less need to defer to the Mother Country. To some degree, the 1920s in Britain saw a determined drive to restore the old order and values. In the background lurked the spectre of Russia's 1917 revolution and the murder of its Romanov royal family. The hierarchy of God, King and Country was threatened and the rise of the working classes was viewed with suspicion, even fear, by the establishment, with the General Strike of 1926 seen as tantamount to bloody bolshevism.

The development of leisure and sports was symptomatic, as 'bread and circuses' must be provided to keep the working class millions happy. That opium of the masses, association football, grew unstoppably. So the middle classes took the view that, if you can't beat them, then choose another game. Rugby in England and Scotland spread its public school roots to become the ball of educated, professional suburbia; Welsh rugby, on the other hand, consolidated its working-class appeal and increasingly aligned the country's national identity with the game, worshipping a trinity of 'Pit, Pitch and Chapel' with deep fervour. As the forces of reaction responded, many more advances made in wartime were reversed. Women had worked, won the vote and successfully played wartime football (but not rugby, to my knowledge). But men returning from the front wanted their jobs back – and their balls – and women's sport returned to politeness and the tennis lawn.

The revival of rugby was a reassertion of pre-war values, never more so than in the talismanic meetings of its most august institutions. The first Varsity Match after the war was marked by an exchange of gentlemanly behaviour which recalled the chivalry of medieval jousts, let alone Edwardian Albion or Pall Mall club land. Oxford's Eric Loudoun-Shand, a Scottish internationalist before he won his pre-war Blue, and a wartime

Barbarian with Mobbs, wanted to play again for his university. There was one small snag: he had graduated in 1914 and was no longer *in statu pupillari*. But this was a detail to a man with an MA Oxon and an MC with the King's Royal Rifle Corps.

He addressed his dilemma to the Cambridge captain, J.E. 'Jenny' Greenwood: they were Dulwich friends in its 'Famous Five' of future internationalists in an unbeaten school XV of 1909 that included Cyril Lowe, fellow Scot Grahame Donald and Irishman W.D. 'George' Doherty. This gang of five also played in the 1913 Varsity Match: more miraculously, all five survived war. Six years later – and the worst part of a million men dead – Greenwood had the prerogative to deny Eric's request. He of course declined to exercise it: the two played as opposing skippers, once again in front of the rugby fanatic King George. Whether the monarch actually saw any play remains a mystery, as Queen's Club, with its notorious Kensington micro-climate, was fog-bound for the entire match.

If this seems less of a restatement of values than a reconnecting of the old-boy network, there's a painful twist: Loudoun-Shand played the match with an arm so badly damaged by his wartime wounding that it eventually had to be amputated. The storyteller in me wonders if that is why the only photograph shows the king firmly shaking Greenwood's hand, while Eric holds back. Or is it simply that Cambridge bookended their empty wartime rugby trophy shelf with another win, by 7–5 that December day and Greenwood, the victor, shook hands first? (Of course it is.) The resilient Loudoun-Shand had 'previous' as a wingless wonder, as noted by Henry Grierson who, with Greenwood, played against him in the 1910 Freshmen's Varsity Match: 'Eric Shand had two fingers broken early but played on and told nobody. But that's the sort of lad he was and is.' From that game also, wistfully summoned from an age of innocence, Grierson recalled 'little H.W. Thomas of Wales who was killed in the War, and P.C.B. Blair [Scotland], also dead.'

In the autumn of 1919, London Scottish, in common with other clubs, prepared for the resumption of the domestic rugby calendar. Of those who had played for the club before hostilities began, only twenty-nine reported for duty. A club which had once easily fielded four teams now lacked the playing strength to make up two full XVs. In time, new recruits came along, as they did every year. Frank Deakin, who played with Poulton-Palmer in that last game at Nieppe, helped re-establish Moseley following the inactivity of the war years and a bad patch after hostilities ceased; when Moseley celebrated its centenary in 1973–74 he was still there. But the losses for every club, and for millions of families, were hard to bear.

Fittingly, in the new era of peace, the post-war Five Nations series resumed diplomatic rugby relations between Scotland and France, played with an appropriate sense of new beginnings on New Year's Day 1920, at the Parc des Princes. War had bizarre side-effects: nineteen players were debutants, hard proof of the ravages that bomb and bullet inflicted on pre-war selections. Every player on the field had his personal war story, even Scot Charlie Usher, who spent most of it behind the wire of a prison camp. The Scots fielded Usher, Sloan, Gallie and Laing from the King's Cup Mother Country side, as well as Thom and Crole, like Usher a wartime prisoner, from the RAF team. The French selected eight soldiers from their King's Cup side, ample evidence of the new synergy of rugby and military.

The thirty players on the pitch could muster only fifty-five eyeballs between them, as fully five men had one eye missing from the war: flanker Jock Wemyss, lock 'Podger' Laing and at scrum half, Jenny Hume for the Scots; flanker Robert Thierry and prop Marcel-Frédéric Lubin-Lebrère for the opposition. After Hogmanay the night before, it was a small miracle that Wemyss, Hume and Laing could see at all. Just as remarkably, one-eyed Laing kicked between the posts to convert Crole's try for a 5–0 victory. The tie was christened by the French press *'le match des borgnes'* – talk about leaving it all on the field for your team; if the two sides got blind drunk at the post-match banquet in Paris, then surely five men were kings in that land. Two Cyclopeans, Wemyss and Lubin-Lebrère would have a famous rematch in 1922, officiated by former England lock, Harold 'Dreadnought' Harrison, which curious tale is best-told in John Griffiths's perennial stocking-filler.[2]

Two weeks after the Armistice, the Welsh Football Union declared that 'all clubs are now at liberty to arrange Inter Club games'. Welshmen could once again feast on the bread of heaven after four years of famine. Field Marshal Haig even granted leave to several Welshman to allow them to play the New Zealanders in two unofficial games over Christmas. Official Test rugby returned to Wales as early as April 1919. After victory over France at Twickenham, NZ Services entrained for Swansea, enticing a crowd of 35,000 to take Monday off work. There was WFU muttering about guarantees that the New Zealand soldiers were amateurs, 'just as though it matters a damn whether they are amateurs or professionals when they have come all this way to fight and die for us', protested one officer in *Truth* magazine. As far as the Welsh were concerned, this was the All Blacks, back after fourteen years: six of the NZ team had Test experience and they wore the black jersey to prove it. Wales awarded official caps against this military side and fielded thirteen uncapped players, a sign of either wartime tragedy or further WFU comedy. Their whole XV had played in a game between a Welsh XV and 38th (Welsh) Division only two days earlier.

Memories of 1905 added edge; once again a single score made the difference. New Zealand shaded a poor match, two penalties to one, by 6–3. But international rugby was back in Wales. The next would be in 1920: at Colombes, before the French game a huge wreath was dedicated 'to players who fell in the war for freedom'. Players and officials later visited the open wound of the ravaged Somme battlefield on a Thomas Cook's tour.

Ireland's uneasy peace had been broken by rebellion in 1916. There would be another war, this time between Republicans and Britain, after Sinn Féin won a landslide election in December 1918 and declared Irish independence. An Irish Civil War then followed. Peace would not return until after an Irish Free State was established in 1923. King George V again played a significant role, with a June 1923 speech in Belfast (written by South African Prime Minister Jan Smuts) urging 'all Irishmen to pause, to stretch out the hand of forbearance and conciliation, to forgive and to forget, and to join in making for the land they love a new era of peace, contentment, and good will'. Another rugby fan, Éamon de Valera, had already been the first president of the Republic.

Against this background, rugby only gradually returned in 1919 with Leinster and Ulster schools and universities to the fore (including a Trinity South Africans team). In 1920 a weak Ireland side bolstered by the brilliance of Dickie Lloyd only narrowly lost to England. Troubles continued and the island remained divided, at times violently so, over the century. Internationals were played alternately in Belfast and Dublin; they have now settled into a new glass cathedral where Lansdowne Road used to be. But on a handful of occasions every year, the men of its four provinces again stand shoulder to shoulder and Ireland is united by one rugby team.

The New Zealand Services team now effectively crowned as 'world's best' returned home via South Africa, where it 'was deservedly most popular, consisting as it did of keen unassuming players who played football of a high order'. The tour simultaneously gave a 'much needed impetus and fillip to the game'[3] and condoned the deep racial fault line in South Africa that inevitably surfaced in its sporting confrontations with other nations, with the Jimmy Peters incident in Devon being the first rugby example. The South African Rugby Board (SARB) discovered that the New Zealand team included Māori soldiers. They narrowly passed by 8–6 a motion seconded by Bill Schreiner, to cable his own father, William Philip Schreiner, South African High Commissioner in London:

> Confidential if visitors include Maori tour would be wrecked and immense harm politically and otherwise would follow. Please explain position fully and try arrange exclusion.

William Schreiner the elder was a liberal and believer 'in equal rights to all civilised men south of the Zambezi'.[4] He would not have had a problem with Māoris touring, thinks South African historian, Floris van der Merwe. What father thought of son is not recorded; he died on 28 June, the same day the Treaty of Versailles was signed.

Charlie Brown, scrum half and honorary Māori, captained the side in South Africa. Sergeant Ranji Wilson and genuine Māori, Corporal Parekura Tureia, both in the King's Cup squad, were quietly excluded: Tureia was reported, ludicrously, to have 'missed the steamer' to Cape Town. His name means 'to fight a battle', which he would do once more in the Second Great War. This time he was 'permitted' to land on African soil where, as a captain in the New Zealand Infantry, he was killed in the Egyptian desert in November 1941. Those eight men of the SARB did him an eternal injustice.

As for Ranji Wilson, King's Cup winner and twenty-one times an All Black, the *Natal Witness* reported with some excitement his later arrival in port at Durban (different city, different troop transport) when his team had already played ten of fourteen matches:

> The Pacific Islander, Wilson, just arrived from England, is perhaps the greatest player in the Service team and it would be a good thing if his inclusion could be arranged. He was a very popular player in the Home matches.

Ranji never got off the boat. His team played fifteen matches without him, won eleven, drew one and lost three and were praised by Percy Day, their South African manager, as 'a gentlemanly, sportsmanlike body of footballers ... Being all ex-soldiers, their team-work and team spirit were alike admirable, and they blended into a most workmanlike side', although there was some unnecessary Imperial snobbery about the team 'being composed mainly of men of the rank of sergeant'. One is reminded of how well the SARB got on with England's RFU Committee – they were both sleepwalking through a world radically changed by war. Nonetheless the *Cape Times* concluded:

> The value of their visit will be reflected in our football ere long . . .
> and this will be to the advantage of the game, for theirs is more
> enterprising than ours . . . that their forwards are magnificent in
> attack and in defence is undeniable – they have taught us almost
> more than we can hope to learn.[5]

More good came 'in a great revival of rugby in South Africa, and schools that had previously played the Association game intended to take up Rugby'.[6] In a final farewell on their return home in October 1919, the Services team, although still carrying injuries from the hard African grounds, beat Auckland 19–6. In May 1920, they reunited, this time with Ranji Wilson again, to end their campaign on a high note with a 23–8 victory over Wellington, as part of the celebrations in honour of the visiting Prince of Wales.

An official invitation to South Africa to tour New Zealand was issued in 1921 and a titanic rivalry was groined from war. South Africa would learn quickly on the rugby field; off the field, it would be long, painful and violent. On that tour they first played (and narrowly beat) the Māori. A journalist cabled home:

> Bad enough having play team officially designated New Zealand
> Natives. Spectacle thousands Europeans frantically cheering on
> band of coloured men to defeat members of own race was too
> much for Springboks, who frankly disgusted.

The players quickly disavowed their misattributed views: on the pitch there was only respect, but an unholy conspiracy of journalists and rugby politicians sparked a smouldering ember into flame. The tone was set for decades. Significantly, it was a rugby match against New Zealand – and a famous photograph of Nelson Mandela and Francois Pienaar, both in the number 6 Springbok jersey – that came to symbolise a new South Africa, as much as a new rainbow flag and an anthem in four tongues.

In Australia, the League–Union split was if anything more severe than the Northern Union breakaway in 1895. There is still today a class antagonism that breaks out occasionally into virulent correspondence.

Most of the 1908 touring Wallabies had defected on their return, taking their Olympic gold with them, and formidable administrators like Wallaby Ted Larkin did much to smooth the rocky road for the fledgling code. Remember, in 1916, Tom Richards had reflected morosely in the dugout with some Welsh drinking buddies that 'Australian rugby is professionalised and dead'. Like Association in Britain, League in Australia attempted to keep going during wartime and although celebrated Kangaroos and lesser lights fell with their Union brothers at Gallipoli and elsewhere, League was able to emerge from the conflict quicker and stronger. For Union, the casualties of war and the impact of League struck a double blow.

In November 1918, the New South Wales Rugby Union wired to its fellow unions:

> Greetings on the cessation of hostilities. We are proud of the part Rugby Unionists have played in the war. Though the war work of Rugby Union footballers was magnificent, and the game will be taken up again with hundreds of grand fellows gone to their fathers, the old game itself had to fall back in public eye, save when the schools were on the field, and it will require all the enthusiasm and business push to rehabilitate it in anything like the flourishing condition of a few years back.[7]

In 1919 the AIF military side ('the Diggers') returned home and played several matches in a bid to revive rugby at home. Their last as a team was in August at the Sydney Sports Ground when they defeated a national Australia side 22–6 to press acclaim:

> The final between the Diggers and Our Boys resulted a ding-dong struggle during the first half, but in the second spell the fighting boys . . . charged the line repeatedly, and had all the best of the game. Suttor electrified the shivering barrackers with his dashing sprints goalwards.

The AIF rugby was 'tough and vigorous', rooted in a belief in handling and running the ball, not hoofing it. This set the style for the famed Waratahs running game that finds its legacy in Australian back play today. Restarting the game in New South Wales, however, was tortuous, and was not helped by a seven-game pasting by the 1920 All Blacks, on their regular mission to grind weakened opponents into the dirt. Victoria and Queensland did not regroup until 1926 and 1929 respectively.

Then began the resurgence: 1929 was also the year when the famed green-and-gold was adopted, and a tour by the newly lionised British the following year gave a shot in the arm to Union rehabilitation. The inaugural Bledisloe Cup of 1931 sharpened the old rivalry with the black-jerseyed neighbours that had begun in 1903 in front of 30,000 at Sydney's Cricket Ground. In 1933 Wally Matthews, AIF team manager in 1919, took the Wallabies to South Africa; they lost the series but upset the form to win two Tests against the mighty Springboks. Arguably, Union in Australia has never recovered from the hiatus of the Great War and today stands as its third code in terms of popularity, after Aussie Rules and League. Remarkable tribute to the depth of sporting talent in this nation then, that the 'third string' has pulled off two World Cup wins against its global rivals.

In Italy, the infant rugby was stifled soon after its birth by a war which ravaged the landscape of the northern region, which was then rugby's cradle and is still its main playground. British expatriates in Genoa, French students at Milan University and Italian migrant farm-workers returning from France had all independently imported the game of fifteen. Two early exhibition matches were played over Easter 1910 in Turin by SCUF from Paris[8] and Servette of Geneva, a club now irredeemably lost to football in the lair of FIFA; the Unione Sportiva Milanese team, founded by Piero Mariani, played the first competitive match in *terra Italia* against the French Union Athlétique Voironnaise in 1911,[9] in their *bianconero* quarters, and another against Chambéry in 1912. Mariani was an engineer who had emigrated to France, but returned for military service. These games were all hastily organised, sparsely attended and without cohesion; the Club Rugby di Torino, hosts to that original exhibition, disbanded after a single match against footballers Pro Vercelli. After 1912, while training continued, there were no competitive games. When war came to Italy in 1915, many of the foreign mercenaries assembled for the Milanese team returned to fight for their country of origin; their French captain, Gilbert, was killed at Verdun.

Italy may advance parental claims on Māori All Blacks Jack and Charles Sciascia, or the noble Caesar Mannelli, born in Udine in rugby's Italian heartland, and laureate for the USA at the Paris Olympics. But organised Italian rugby did not really emerge until a late 1920s *risorgimento* under Stefano Bellandi, rugby player, football referee and manager at La Scala Opera House, who had played in the US Milanese team of 1911. He is considered the father of Italian rugby. Unfortunately, in its impressionable you're out on the rugby field and you get something wrong . a tackle, miss a chance to score – you can always come back et it right next time. Out in Afghanistan, you can't afford ke mistakes. Because a mistake might mean someone losing e.

nce Harry, vice-patron of the RFU and an ardent fan, was d' by the world's media to be in Helmand province, serving Household Cavalry unit; footage was beamed around the globe rrior prince, kicking a rugby ball about with his comrades. y's values, forged where men put themselves in harm's way lf of their team, can again help heal the wounds of war. In stan, Asad Ziar of the Afghan Rugby Federation says rugby is in spirit and physicality to traditional centuries-old *buzkashi*, a etween polo and rugby:

len on horseback grab a goat from a chalk circle, carry it round a pole and drop it into another circle. No touch judges or eferees. Sometimes there are teams, and sometimes there aren't. Sometimes the field is 200 metres and sometimes it isn't. Afghans are tough people and in a country where war has been a way of life for many decades, it can be said that *buzkashi* is the world's toughest sport.

gby is also a tough sport, he says, which is why it appeals to young hans. But the difference is economic: the cost of rugby is a single ball thirty players, not a horse for each player that costs upwards of £3,000. ar continues:

What we need is a pitch where we can open an academy to train players and newcomers, and organise competitions. Rugby is the newest team sport in Afghanistan and is only three years old. In the long term rugby can be a way of helping divided communities to focus on sustainable peace and reconciliation, and building international understanding and friendship.[12]

King George could not have said it better.

adolescence, his sporting child succumbed to the malign influence of Mussolini's fascists, who admired rugby's culture of physicality and 'manliness'. It rather gives the game away that rugby's first governing body formed in 1927 was called the Comitato di Propaganda. The first *Squadra Azzurra* would play Spain in Barcelona in 1929 and of course they now play with force and flair in Europe's top-tier Six Nations Championship.

In California, rugby was almost forgotten. A United War Work campaign was due to start on 11 November 1918 with a benefit rugby match, which was eventually played in late February and received only perfunctory press attention. Even the Armistice itself, initially announced with banner headlines, rapidly lost the public interest compared to the long-awaited resumption of the annual American Football challenge between Berkeley and Stanford. This was the social highlight in the week of Thanksgiving, another unique American institution which rarely travels outside its borders:

Prominent folk from both side of the bay are eager to witness the first American game played between the two Universities since 1905 . . . there never has been an attraction offered since which could hope to interest Californians as did the old Stanford–UC games.[10]

The USA's Olympic gold of 1924 was the last defiant bellow of a dying rugby species, largely consisting of converted gridiron behemoths. Stung by its treatment in Paris at the hands of the ungrateful French, American rugby finally retreated into its nation's political and sporting splendid isolation – and took its ball with it. Its vast resources, markets and consumption meant that its booming economy did not need Europe's problems, which, to misquote Rick, 'don't amount to a hill of beans in this crazy world'. Domestic sports like baseball and football overcame their own outrages (baseball had its 'Black Sox' match-fixing scandal in 1919) and created new national superstars like Babe Ruth, Lou Gehrig and Red Grange. When you have the World Series, who needs the world? When its economic boom spectacularly collapsed, America withdrew further into introspection and licked its wounds until they healed and strength returned. It took an act of unparalleled savagery in 1941, behind its back at Pearl Harbor, to draw it again into tangled and violent global affairs and another four years of war.

Caesar Mannelli's try was the last rugby score at an Olympic games. The USA will finally – if belatedly – relinquish its title as rugby returns in the Sevens format at Rio 2016. Unless, that is, we witness the mother of all rugby surprises. But its athletes are outstanding, its place in the Rugby World Cup is secure and growing numbers of exports to rugby heartlands will imbibe the culture and refinements of a complex sport, just as the grass roots of the domestic game will thrive again in America – as long as a Black eclipse does not blot out the sun. Transatlantic gridiron missions regularly fill Wembley. We must aspire in return to fill NFL stadia from Soldier Field to the Oakland Coliseum. Sorry, that should be the O.Co Stadium, sponsored and branded, as are all but six NFL stadia; what price one day the 'ACME Rugby Stadium' in suburban Twickenham? The Churchill Cup went to the USA, Ireland played in Houston (why not Boston?) and, yes, New Zealand took shock and awe to Chicago. Next we take Manhattan. American Football itself aspires to be an Olympic event, but will struggle, as the *New York Daily News* put it, in an unaccustomed style worthy of its patrician rival, in 'overcoming the current worldwide competitive imbalance that is in favor of American teams'.[11] It's in the name, guys.

North of the border, Canadian rugby struggled against its climate and vast distances, as well as the rival Canadian Football League, and the fifteen-a-side game remained confined to provincial pockets of strength. The pressure from a newly cleaned-up and resurgent gridiron game south of the border was irresistible. In a rearguard action, a Canada Rugby Union was re-formed in 1929. With the demise of rugby in the USA, it was forced to look across the Pacific. But the first official international for Canada, against Japan in 1932, had an inauspicious beginning; the team lost most of its rugby balls over the side of the ship en route, and once on dry land, both Test matches too. Rugby remained in Canada's vast wilderness until 1965 when the Canadian RFU was re-formed.

French rugby gained strength from its wartime trials against British imperial military teams. They won their first away match against Ireland in 1920 and won in Scotland for the first time in the following season, as well as doing the double against Ireland. But a violent flaw continued to disfigure their play – and the grandstand – as they took literally the dictum that 'sport is war by other means'. In 1923 in Wales, the Irish referee McGowan had to ask French touch judge Cyril Rutherford, (despite his Scots origins he was a naturalised Frenchman and a key figure in the country's rugby development) to translate his warnings to players guilty of dangerous tackles. 1924 saw the notorious Olympic final against the USA. In 1925 the France–Ireland clash was just that, with violence throughout;

the referee was attacked by spectators, [...]
Mr Baxter in 1913, which had led the S[...]
final season before the holocaust. A re[...]
1927: the Scottish referee, having disallow[...]
a regular, if unwitting, centre of controver[...]
players. In 1931, France was red-carded from[...]
offences, violent play and crowd misbehavi[...]
Asterix, not drawn until 1959, must surely ow[...]
rugby antics.

As the King's Cup was being played, E[...]
promising in his obituary volume that rugt[...]
Motherland calls again': 'Rugby Football will[...]
bending forward eager for the moment the fig[...]
"stick it", come what may.' William Massey addı[...]
Parliament in September 1919: 'I am not one of thc[...]
seen the last of war.' Sadly, just twenty years hence,[...]
indeed call again.

If the greatest and bloodiest war yet known to n[...]
some had to do it all over again in 1939. Bert Stolz of[...]
to fight in the Pacific. The charmed Australian Bil[...]
when he had no right. Others lacked his bullet-proof l[...]
who had played the 1912 Springboks, both now lieuter[...]
in the Second World War: John Berchmans Minch, R/[...]
1942 and Joseph Clune, an army vet killed in the Medit[...]
Norman Wodehouse captained England to the first of t[...]
Slams before the war. He served as a gunnery officer on[...]
at Jutland. In 1941, aged 54 and a vice-admiral in the Re[...]
convoy commodore (in charge of the merchant ships as dis[...]
commander of the naval escort). His convoy was en route to[...]
when it was attacked by U-Boats; he ordered the ships to [...]
armed merchantman, the *Robert L. Holt*, took on *U-69* in a s[...]
battle. He was never seen again.

Rugby recovered in 1919 and again in 1945, and was itself [...]
rebuilding process. The bond between the military and rugby[...]
close: in 2014, a serving soldier, Fijian-born Lance Corporal[...]
Rokodoguni, of the Royal Scots Dragoon Guards and Bath, rep[...]
England for the first time, the first serviceman to do so since Tim [...]
in 1999. On his first day in Helmand, 'Roko' saw a fellow soldier[...]
up by an IED. He told the BBC:

214

When [...]
– miss[...]
and g[...]
to ma[...]
his li[...]

HRH Pr[...]
'discover[...]
with his[...]
of the w[...]
Rugt[...]
on beha[...]
Afghan[...]
closest[...]
cross b[...]

Rug[...]
Af[...]
for[...]
Zi[...]

Rugby Remembers

They shall grow not old, as we that are left grow old:
Age shall not weary them, nor the years condemn.

Henry Allingham, one of the last two veterans to pass away in 2009, said of the Great War: 'Of course I remember. I was there. I have no choice but to remember.' We, who were not there, do have a choice. We must choose to remember.

Peace in 1919 allowed public expressions of mourning, in place of wartime stoicism and stiff upper lip resilience under the burden of personal loss. A flood of emotion was released and channelled through ceremonies, memorials and monuments. The response, both private and public, was varied and complex, particularly from fathers, in an era of order, rectitude and masculine formality. Rugby has always been a game of proud dads on the touchline, from the back pitch to the exalted stadium. Just ask Andy Farrell or Mike Ford. It is one of the many ways we connect the grass roots to the international pantheon, from under-9s to Rugby World Cup finalists.

At school I wore the same rugby colours – pale blue paired hoops on a navy background – that J.R.R. Tolkien had worn in the 1910 1st XV: he was probably a better player, his book sales may be marginally ahead of mine and the shirt had been washed since his day. My dad watched me play in that shirt. We won some games and we lost some; I was in the 1st XV and it was the best time of my young life. South African-born Tolkien, who served with the Lancashire Fusiliers on the Somme, and had lost all but one of his close friends by 1918, did not write the line spoken in the film: 'No parent should have to bury their child.'[1] That was Peter Jackson's screenwriter, possibly inspired by Herodotus, historian of ancient wars, who wrote, 'In peacetime, sons bury their fathers, but in war it is the fathers who bury their sons.'[2]

John Birkett of Harlequins scored the first ever try at the new Twickenham in 1909, following in the footsteps of his father Reg in the first rugby international of 1871. Reg Birkett had died of typhoid in 1898, so did not see his son score that day, or captain England against Wales the previous year. Sad, yes, but there was nevertheless a natural order in peacetime. War and the death of so many sons, often with the violent severing of male lineage in families, was a terrible inversion of the natural order: fathers, mired in grief, struggled to cope.

Walter Dowson's son, Humphrey, a Rosslyn Park forward, was articled to his law firm before going to war with the King's Royal Rifle Corps. In August 1915, he joined its 9th Battalion at the front after heavy losses – including Welsh wing Billy Geen – in action at Hooge. Humphrey won the MC at the Somme, but was declared 'wounded and missing' in action near Gueudecourt on 15 September 1916. Walter engaged in a correspondence of mounting despair: firstly with a friend at the War Office, to ascertain the facts of his son's disappearance and in the faint hope that he might be a prisoner; then with an officer in the Buffs, who had buried a body that might – or might not – have been Humphrey's, in a lull from battle.

The correspondence is remarkable for two reasons: a wartime postal service that exchanges four letters in as many days (and over a weekend too), and the compassion of Lieutenant Ivan Jacobs of the Buffs, who patiently tries to assist the grieving Walter with his own indistinct and traumatised memories from six months past. Dowson Senior was finally satisfied of his son's identification, and informed the War Office that his son may be declared 'missing believed dead' at 27. Humphrey's name was followed in *The Times* obituary column by Captain John Alfred Pym, 'the well-known International Rugby Football player, killed in action aged 26'. England's scrum half in 1912 miraculously returned from the dead to score two tries in the King's Cup tournament and lived till he was 78. Such misreported fatalities must have first dismayed, then given false hope to parents like Walter. Certain of his son's death, he died a year later of that mysterious but mortal condition, a broken heart.

Sir Edward Bagnall Poulton, Oxford Professor of Zoology, busied himself with a biography of his son Ronald, published in 1919. Professor Sir Oliver Lodge, another distinguished man of science, lost his youngest son Raymond in early September 1914 and turned to a spirit medium (as did Arthur Conan Doyle), who offered a precious glimpse of his son (and a few post-mortem anecdotes). His 1916 bestseller *Raymond*[3] was reprinted six times in its first year and double that by 1919, devoured by desperate parents seeking solace without a grave. John Maxwell Vaughan, father of Barbarian Charles, who played alongside Mobbs in the wartime matches, had lost both his sons by the summer of 1916. Three years later, his grief unabated, the cattle rancher and tobacco farmer put in a retrospective claim to the War Office for Charles's 1914 return steamer fare from Colombia to take up his position in the Reserve; it is a sum a prosperous man cannot possibly need. His letter is an agony of apologies, paternal pride and suppressed misery:

> I do not wish in any way to press a claim, at the outside limited to his home fare of £40, because his desire to defend his country was as great as mine & no sacrifice could be too great. He fought well throughout, for he fell leading the attack on Hohenzollern Redoubt Sept 25 1915. I have since lost my second son Capt J.L. Vaughan, MC, after fighting a whole year at Ypres and later the Somme. Having done our utmost & having no more sons of military age, I now am going to Colombia to work again in place of those two brave boys and am only too proud to have the honour of being their father. Should there be the slightest difficulty about this indemnity, I would rather you put it aside.

Like so many others, his sons' remains were never found – their names are on memorials at Loos and Thiepval. If Rifleman Jack Bodenham was waved off by his family at Barnes station in August 1915, where he entrained for Southampton, thence to France, it was the last they saw of him. Vaporised on that sunlit Saturday morning in July 1916 at Gommecourt, he left little but a name on the Thiepval Memorial and cheery letters home.[4] Of 109 fallen Rosslyn Park men forty-five have no known grave. For the next of kin there was often no body and no closure: men like Vaughan were lost in grief, while Walter Dowson lost his will to live.

Of course, women grieved too, and perhaps, without the terminal emotional handicap of maleness, were more open and direct in doing so. Grief, however, works in strange ways. In 1929, Harriette Raphael, mother of Lieutenant John Raphael, 18th KRRC (a battalion raised by his cousin), killed at Messines Ridge in June 1917, visited his grave in Belgium. 'Jack' Raphael was a brilliant sportsman at Merchant Taylors' and Oxford, with an astonishing fourteen Blues across several sports. He won nine caps for England, captained Surrey at cricket and led a forgotten 'British Isles' tour to Argentina in 1910: organised by Major Stanley, it mainly consisted of uncapped Englishmen, with three Scots thrown in for ethnic diversity. Obituaries glowed:

> A beautiful kick, a brilliant fielder and possessed of a good turn of
> speed, a fine natural player . . . On the cricket field and still more
> in the world of rugby football, a distinct personality. Everything
> he did created more than ordinary interest, his popularity as a
> man, apart from his ability, counting for much.

His mother (her banker husband died before Jack) was tireless in ensuring
her only son's immortality: she commissioned a memorial with the legend
'If character be destiny then his is assured', and had the same inscribed
on his headstone;[5] she published his unfinished coaching manual *Modern
Rugby Football*, and endowed an Oxford scholarship in his name. She
probably washed his kit too. Now in poor health, her last wish was to be laid
to rest alongside her beloved son. She knew well enough that any official
request would be denied, so went directly to the gardener at Lijssenthoek
Cemetery, Walter Sutherland. A year later, a package containing her ashes
arrived, and Sutherland knew precisely what he must do. Within minutes
the urn was buried next to Jack's headstone and the turf replaced. The
secret was only revealed by Sutherland's son George in 2014.[6]

The official response to this pent-up grieving was mercifully enlightened
and imaginative, and caught the national mood. The return and interment
of the Unknown Warrior from the Western Front provided an outlet for
shared mourning, and an eagerly grasped scrap of symbolic consolation
that the anonymous corpse could be any mother or father's lost son (unless,
of course, that son happened to die in Mesopotamia, Turkey, Salonika,
Italy or East Africa). Vast and sombre monuments were constructed to
carry thousands of names and the Imperial War Graves Commission
under Fabian Ware did its inspired work to give the identified bodies
dignity and equality in death. Kipling accompanied King George V to the
cemeteries and crafted a speech for him that contained the powerful line:
'There can be no more potent advocates for peace upon earth than this
massed multitude of witnesses to the desolation of war.' This multitude of
silent advocates for peace was quietly ignored twenty years later.

As the monuments were built and the burial plots consolidated into
neat cemeteries, the people emulated their king: there was an explosion
of battlefield and cemetery tourism. In some cases, with live ordnance
still lying around, the explosions were fatal for souvenir hunters. Those
who had served and survived returned to pay respects to friends; some
like Lieutenant A.P. Herbert, RNVR, would process the experience and
memory into poetry:

We only walk with reverence this sullen mile of mud
The shell-holes hold our history, and half of them our blood.[7]

For many the Ypres Salient was only a day away by packetboat and railway, just as it had been for the troops; the lack of high-explosive bombardment helped considerably with track maintenance and timetables. Michelin printed battlefield guides in 1919. The remarkable poem 'High Wood' written in 1918 by Cranleigh schoolteacher, Lieutenant John Stanley Purvis, 5th Yorkshires, under the pseudonym Philip Johnstone, was already looking prescient:

> Please follow me – this way . . . the path, sir, please,
> The ground which was secured at great expense
> The Company keeps absolutely untouched,
> And in that dug-out (genuine) we provide
> Refreshments at a reasonable rate.
> You are requested not to leave about
> Paper, or ginger-beer bottles, or orange peel,
> There are waste-paper baskets at the gate.

If you have endured the coach-party chaos of school visits at Essex Farm (John McCrae) or Thiepval, then Purvis's words look positively prophetic.

For the families of Dominion soldiers who remained in foreign soil, this was simply not possible. As Lieutenant Goddard had gratefully acknowledged, the time and expense of a passage to Europe from the 'uttermost ends of the earth' was beyond most Australians and New Zealanders. It was literally, half a world away. No symbolic Unknown Australian Warrior was returned from Villers-Bretonneux or Chunuk Bair, despite popular calls, and new methods of 'distance mourning' had to be devised. A multitude of shrines sprang up in Australia as surrogate gravestones, where communities could mourn their absent menfolk who had fallen. Pines from Gallipoli and poppy seeds from Flanders were taken back and planted, and what two-way traffic there was reciprocated with Australian flowers and trees. Postcards, books, stereoscopic slides and film all provided a visual link and the visits of state and national representatives, like Premier Stanley Bruce who had fought, were avidly reported in the press. Australian authorities moved swiftly to protect the use of the word 'Anzac' under the War Precautions Act. Requests came from wounded diggers wishing to name their dogs or sons (no worries, George Anzac), and widows their houses (refused). Brewers' beer labels, tobacconists' hoardings and the 'Anzac Gollywog Company' were all turned down.

American poet Moina Michael read John McCrae's poem; she sold artificial poppies sewn in France and gave the money to needy soldiers. UK ex-servicemen's societies united in 1921 to form the British Legion, and a Frenchwoman involved in the sewing project in France suggested that the Legion sell them to raise funds. 1.5 million poppies were ordered for 11 November 1921; the first Poppy Appeal made £106,000. The Legion then set up its own project, as employment for disabled ex-servicemen; in 2014, the appeal raised £40 million.

Rugby mourned its own. E.H.D. Sewell, former Blackheath player and Harlequin captain, who knew personally so many of the players who perished, published in 1919 his *Rugby Football Internationals Roll of Honour*, an exemplary record of facts and fond reminiscences. This 47-year-old armchair warrior felt conscious of not having served. His foreword describes the arrival of material from New Zealand via Vancouver just as an Air Raid warning sounds. He is forced to review the papers in a 'kind of dugout' shelter 'which lent an air of sharing, in a very safe kind of way, some of the perils they had undergone'.

Sewell's fondest words were reserved for Mobbs. Military matches in aid of a Mobbs Memorial Fund, between New Zealanders and South Africans, were played at Franklin's Gardens as early as 8 December 1917. Only eighty-five of Edgar's original 264 recruits for his D Company returned home. They marched together again for the first time on 17 July 1921 in his honour, as thousands lined the Northampton streets. His memorial at Abington Gardens is inscribed: 'TO THE MEMORY OF A GREAT AND GALLANT SPORTSMAN'.

On 24 July 1927, ten years after his death, when Field Marshal Plumer inaugurated the Menin Gate Memorial at a rebuilt Ypres with the words 'He is not lost; he is here,'[8] Lieutenant Colonel E.R. Mobbs, DSO, once again led the Northamptonshire Regiment at the head of a detachment of dead names. Amongst the 55,000 inscribed there are Billy Geen of Wales, Alec Todd of England, Basil Maclear of Ireland, and many more rugby men than can be chronicled in these few pages. His memory was further perpetuated from 1921 in an annual Mobbs Memorial Match between the East Midlands and the Barbarian Football Club, for whom it became their longest-standing fixture until professionalism made it impossible to assemble a side. It survives as an itinerant fixture between the British Army and teams from Bedford Blues and Northampton Saints.

The 1914 photograph of Mobbs with Colonel Fawcett at Northampton Barracks appears in the 1921 match programme; this time the caption shows his advancement to Lieutenant Colonel Mobbs, DSO. As his bones were not interr'd, the good that this man did was free to live after him. Tributes surround the team lists (poignantly, there is only one pre-war Barbarian, Coventry stand-off H.J. 'Dick' Pemberton) with Earl Spencer leading: 'In honouring him we honour ourselves, the town and the Regiment whose highest traditions he enshrined and fulfilled so faithfully unto death.' Claude Palmer, club chairman, acknowledged his enduring legacy to Saints:

> The glorious memory of my best friend Edgar . . . has been a constant inspiration in the reconstruction of the Northampton Football Club; Edgar Mobbs' last message in 1916 being a request 'to use very effort to keep the game going', and this has been our watchword.

The East Midlands Honorary Secretary, J.B. Minahan, went further:

> Edgar Mobbs was THE man of our generation, the greatest personality in English Rugger of modern days, and to us locally his death was a calamity. He played for the highest ideals and lifted local Rugby football out of the common rut. On the field he carried the spirit of adventure and reckless daring – in his stride it was rampant and insistent – and it seemed that enthusiasm and audacity emanated from his entire personality. But above all he possessed the compelling power – the birthright of such men – which drew crowds to his circle.

Tim Rodber, former England number eight with forty-four caps, was a captain in the Green Howards even after the game turned professional, only leaving the army in 2001 after retiring from rugby. In 2014 he made an emotional BBC radio pilgrimage to Zillebeke in search of his fellow Northampton Saints captain.

Rugby also had new beginnings and new colours in memoriam. On 23 May 1919, in Belfast's Thompson's Restaurant, Instonians was founded as the Old Boys rugby club of the Royal Belfast Academical Institution. Two teams were fielded in that inaugural year; they played in the yellow-and-black of the school with the addition of purple, as a permanent memorial to the 132 old boys who had fallen during the war.

Glasgow Accies' Honorary Secretary Macgill had lost none of his letter-writing energy and by November 1919 was busy with a planned Academy memorial and a match against Watsonians at Anniesland to fund it. In 1925, the city of Toulouse erected a heroic memorial, dubbed *L'Herakles*, in honour of all fallen French sportsmen. It featured a bronze relief of their rugby club founder and half-back star 'Maysso', the first international rugby player to die. Frank Cowlin, President of Bristol Football Club, wrote in support of the appeal of his city's lord mayor for a proposed memorial to local rugby footballers:

> There can be no doubt that victory was won by the sportsmen of the Empire, and the record of Rugby footballers is one of which all lovers of the game are justly proud. More than 300 local players are said to have made the great sacrifice. The amount required for the Bristol Rugby Memorial Ground is a substantial one, but [it] will be worthy of the city and the Bristol Club, and a fitting memorial to those men who 'played the game' but who alas! will never return.

The ground was indeed built in 'Proud and Grateful Memory' on 'Buffalo Bill's Field', a site used by William Cody's Wild West Show in 1891; a service is held at the gates of the 'Mem' every Remembrance Sunday. Bristol Rovers football club sold the ground to a supermarket chain, which happily employed images of the 1914 'Christmas truce football game' (for which there is no evidence) in its advertising to peddle chocolate bars. Yet it plans to knock down the ground for a new supermarket – you can never have too many of those.

It was not long before old comrades gathered on significant dates for regimental reunions. The London Scottish Regiment still convenes for a Hallowe'en dinner to remember Messines. In April 1926, the 15th Battery of the Canadian Field Artillery met at Toronto's King Edward Hotel; they drank toasts to the King and their thirty Fallen Comrades listed on the Honour Roll. In the aftermath of war, there were still lashings of the soldierly humour that had got them through it. The dinner menu makes for great reading, if unappetising eating:

Bucket of Blood, Shell-hole Special, Fish-guts
Mules Innards, Frozen Rabbit, McConnachie, Bully
PIE: Ypres Fish-tail, Somme Chalk, Vimy Mud,
Passchendaele Slime, Arras Pip-Squeak, Amiens Sunshine
PUDDING: Cambrai Muddle, Valenciennes Camouflage
or Mons Coal

In recent decades, it has become the norm for touring cricket and rugby teams to pay homage at the Western Front sites. During their French tour in 2000, the All Blacks planted a rose called 'Lest We Forget', bred in memory of those who never returned, at the grave of Dave Gallaher at Nine Elms, Poperinge. At Le Quesnoy they were joined by the New Zealand A team, which was also in France, a distant echo of the two touring military sides that brought excitement back to Britain's clubs in euphoric 1919.

Most of their fifty countrymen buried at Le Quesnoy Cemetery lost their lives on 4 November 1918, one week before the Armistice. Skipper Todd Blackadder recalled: 'We walked around the town [to the memorial] and we laid a wreath there. I was standing next to a Frenchman who had tears streaming down his face. He was moved by the generosity of the New Zealanders all those years ago. It's something you don't understand when you're in New Zealand.'9 So, Mr Gove, there is a little we can learn about the Great War from a Captain Blackadder. In November 2014, the Wallabies laid wreaths including native Australian flora at the Tombeau du Soldat Inconnu beneath the Arc de Triomphe. One player found a more direct line of understanding: James Horwill's great grandfather had won the DCM for saving the lives of fourteen compatriots in 1917.

One hundred years on from 1914–18, centenary commemorations are remembering those who fell, rugby players to the fore. The RFU commissioned a huge oil painting by Shane Record of the 1914 England team at Colombes: the six players who fell have their red roses 'greyed' in remembrance. In March 2014 Rosslyn Park righted the historic wrong of its missing memorial when RFU Chairman Bill Beaumont unveiled a new clubhouse plaque to its Great War dead. A commemorative match was played with leather ball, in baggy cotton shirt and shorts with embroidered poppy and under 1914 Laws. Guest appearances came on the field from former Artillery officer and RWC winner Josh Lewsey, and by soldiers of the Household Division, with a Rifles bugler to play the Last Post. At Twickenham on 11 December, in a ceremony to commemorate fifty-five fallen Blues before the 133rd Varsity Match, Edinburgh Academy was the first school to lay a wreath in tribute to its eight lost alumni.

London Scottish played Blackheath on 'Richmond turf', in a poetically licensed replay of their last 1914 fixture, in memoriam to Mick Imlah's 'Forty-five' and Blackheath's sixty-five lost members, Robert Pillman, Billy

Geen, Reggie Hands and Bungy Watson among them. The fallen players' names were worn on the sleeves of the multi-generational sides. Fittingly and more happily, Scottish sent a youth side back to France, to play in a commemorative tourney for the battles on the Aisne; this time they all came back. Representatives from Blackheath, London Scottish and local French clubs remembered their players at a ceremony on 13 September 2014 at the Monument des Basques at Craonelle. LSFC Secretary Paul McFarland, whose grandmother was engaged to John McCrae, read his famous words.

Edgar Mobbs's first club, Olney, honoured its sixteen fallen and marked the anniversary of the 'England v Scotland' recruiting game of January 1915 with two matches: current players from the East Midlands region lined up against the 1st Battalion, Yorkshire Regiment, and Olney Ladies played the Army Women's XV. Not only does rugby remember; it also moves forward.

In February 2015, prior to the 1st XV match against Widnes, Birkenhead Park commemorated the death of Park and England skipper 'Toggie' Kendall. A piper from the Liverpool Scottish Regiment, the military family to so many international and Merseyside club players, played a lament prior to kick-off. Old Whitgiftians Rugby Football Club toured the battlefields and cemeteries, visiting every grave and memorial on the Western Front of its forty players who fell, including Lloyd's broker 2nd Lieutenant Frank Benton, club captain for six seasons, who was killed in the same regiment and action as Humphrey Dowson. Charles Henman, architect of their clubhouse, never saw his work completed, as he was killed at Gallipoli with the Royal Marine Engineers. The Canadian rugby players of Vancouver Rowing Club, led by a New Zealander, will make their own pilgrimage in 2015, and tour Britain as the rugby world gathers again for the Rugby World Cup.

The centenary of 4 August 1914 fell fittingly, if by coincidence, on the 9th of Av in the Jewish calendar, in Hebrew, *Tisha b'Av*, the most mournful day of the Jewish year. At London's Bevis Marks synagogue, the date was marked with a candlelit 'Lights Out' commemoration following the *Tisha b'Av* service. A memorial plaque lists the names of thirty-nine members of the Spanish and Portuguese Jewish Congregation who gave their lives in the Great War, amongst some 50,000 Commonwealth Jews who fought for Britain. Among them was a rugby player from the Wasps Football Club, originally in Finchley, but in pre-war years at a dozen grounds in west London. Captain Robert Sebag-Montefiore, of the Royal

East Kent Yeomanry, died in Alexandria, Egypt, in November 1915, of wounds received at Gallipoli. He was 33 and one of thirty-eight Wasps on their own memorial.

There is even a newly revived club, inspired by a photograph in a Devon pub of a village team that last turned out in 1908. In 2014, Ide Rugby Football Club played its first match in 106 years, under the captaincy of Scott Voysey whose great-uncle, Private Jack Voysey, captained the original team. Conscripted at 37 to fight with the Duke of Cornwall's Light Infantry, Jack was shot in the stomach at the Battle of Cambrai, only three months after reaching the front. A letter from his widow Edith, postmarked 13 November (a week before he died), was later returned to sender, freshly marked with the stark word: 'Killed'.

Sergeant Mitchell wrote to her in 1917: 'It may afford you a small amount of comfort to know that he was respectably buried in the village of La Vacquerie.'[10] His grave was lost in more fighting and Jack is on the Louverval Memorial with over 7,000 other men from Britain and South Africa. Surely it would delight him to know that his Ide RFC has been revived as a barbarian invitation side, a 'lasting memorial through the playing of rugby, to those rugby-playing servicemen and women who were killed in serving their country 1914–1919'. Their first match on Remembrance Sunday, in aid of service charities, was against a veterans' XV; the spirit of Harry Burlinson at Old Deer Park must surely rejoice at this inspired idea conceived over a beer in the Poacher's Inn.

In a year when the Rugby World Cup returns to the cradle of the game, and where, in 1919, the first tentative but symbolic steps were made to bring together the world's nations in team sport, we have another choice. We must look to the future and deploy the wealth realised by such tournaments to cultivate the game's values and power for good. Let rugby build a pitch in Afghanistan; Asad Ziar assures us that if we build it, they will come. Let rugby forever avoid the farce of a governing body awarding its football world cup to a place where it can do little other than generate more money.

The William Webb Ellis Trophy has replaced the King's Cup of 1919. Rugby's creation myth of a day in 1823 where one schoolboy ran with the ball may be highly suspect. But it is time again to proceed with a 'fine disregard for the rules of football' and assert 'the distinctive feature of the rugby game'. Perhaps also in this year of all years, it is time to sing it out loud. In 1991, rugby's World Cup adopted as its anthem Gustav Holst's setting of diplomat Sir Cecil Spring-Rice's 1908 poem 'I vow to thee my country'. He had rewritten his own words in 1918, in response to wartime losses:

> The love that asks no question, the love that stands the test,
> That lays upon the altar the dearest and the best;
> The love that never falters, the love that pays the price,
> The love that makes undaunted the final sacrifice.

On the thin ice of political correctness, such heavy and unfashionable concepts as patriotism and religion have been questioned; we have only doubts where once there were certainties. Which is the better age? Discuss. The lyrics of 'World in Union' do not compare with the stirring original. In the 1915 centenary of the deaths of Ronald Poulton-Palmer, Basil Maclear, Freddy Turner, Ted Larkin, Doolan Downing, Pierre Guillemin, Owen Sawers, Billy Geen and thousands more too painful to count, is it not time to remember their 'final sacrifice'?

If rugby and war now share not only a common lexicon but a soundtrack too, this is a time for celebration of rugby values and commemoration of the men who held them dear. But let us also keep a proper perspective. An experience in the second war haunted 'voice of rugby' Bill McLaren: a grisly mound of mutilated corpses, victims of a massacre, unburied in an Italian churchyard. The sight changed his life at 21 and moulded his view on sport. Rugby was in his blood, he explained, 'but in the great scheme of things it really doesn't matter'. As our French Army officer said, 'Rugby and warfare share a common language, but we must remember they are very different'.

We must remember.

In Acknowledgement

Like my first, this is a work of personal passion, not of historical erudition. It does not aim to be comprehensive and readers may regret the exclusion of many worthy players and stories; if so, you have my apologies. There are more detailed books in the bibliography if you wish to delve deeper. My thanks go to Jo De Vries and Donald Sommerville for their patience and expertise in improving this one.

In researching this book, I found that national identity mattered less than being part of a worldwide rugby family, then as now. Welshmen coached French teams and played for South Africa, South Africans played for England, Englishmen for Australia and Australians for Britain and the USA. It's a circle of life where mud is thicker than blood.

I am therefore grateful to an international rugby family who have adopted, tolerated and helped me. If I have overlooked anyone, I am mortified. From England: Michael Rowe, Mike Hagger, Richard Steele and Deborah Mason at the World Rugby Museum, Twickenham. Ian Minto, James Corsan, Nigel Gooding, Colin Veitch, Paul Brennan, David Bohl, Kate Wills, Allan Fidler, Kath Middleditch, Sam Cooper, Ian Metcalfe, Graham McKechnie, Jon Cooksey, John Lewis-Stempel, Gordon Brown, Ian Watmore, Jason Leonard, Bill Beaumont, Richard Daglish, Ron Hall, John Robertson, Jonathan Bunn, Shane Record, Ben Cooper, Roy Barton, Simon McNeill-Ritchie and Patrick Casey.

From Scotland and the exiled diaspora: Hugh Barrow, Paul McFarland, Sandy Fitzpatrick, Mark Taylor, Simon Wood, Ross Cameron, Andy Mitchell, Hugh Pym, Alan Weir, Richard McBrearty. From Canada: Cameron Tompkins, Keith Jolly, Allan Willox, Doug Sturrock. From Wales: Gareth Thomas, Gwyn Prescott and Brynmôr Evans.

From New Zealand: Stephen Berg at the NZ Rugby Museum, Bettina Anderson, Clive Akers, Owen Eastwood, Alan Sciascia, Windsor Jones and Nicola Barrett at National Army Museum Te Mata Toa, Chris Clews and Susan Thomas of Ponsonby. From Australia: Gareth Morgan.

From Italy: Angela Teja, Elvis Lucchese, Luciano Ravagnani, Alberto Cellotto. From Ireland: Sharon Heffernan for her cover picture of son Fionn at Cill Dara training, Ciaran O'Mara. From South Africa: Paul Dobson, Nicky Bicket, Lady Maggie Robinson, Sir Peter Robinson, Floris van der Merwe, Tanya Whitehead.

From France: my guru, Frédéric Humbert, and from Afghanistan: Asad Ziar.

Lines from A.P. Herbert's 'Beaucourt Revisited are quoted by kind permission of the Executors of the Estate of Jocelyn Herbert, M.T. Perkins and Polly M.V.R. Perkins. The extract from 'Mametz Wood' from *Skirrid Hill* by Owen Sheers (Seren, 2005) is reproduced by permission of the author, c/o Rogers, Coleridge & White Ltd, London w11. Extracts from Greg Growden, *Wallaby Warrior: The World War I diaries of Australia's only British Lion*, Allen & Unwin, 2013, are used by permission. The extract from Mick Imlah's *London Scottish (1914)* from *The Lost Leader* (2008) is copyright the estate of the author and reprinted by permission of Faber and Faber Ltd.

In 2015 we will celebrate rugby's values with an event that has its origins in war. We also commemorate the men whose sacrifice in that war a century ago, and others since, allows us the freedom to celebrate our game. In a detail buried in the bibliography, Australian captain 'Paddy' Moran's *Viewless Winds* was published in 1939 by Peter Davies Ltd. This was Peter Llewellyn Davies, who was awarded the Military Cross in the Great War. J.M. Barrie publicly identified him as the source for the name of *Peter Pan*, although his brother George, killed with the Rifle Brigade in 1915, was perhaps more the model for *The Boy Who Wouldn't Grow Up*.

This label of 'the original Peter Pan' haunted Davies throughout his life, which ended under a train at Sloane Square. In 2013 Charles Spencer, reviewing John Logan's play *Peter and Alice,* observed that Ben Whishaw's performance suggested 'a man irretrievably damaged by his experience of war, and who has painfully and repeatedly learned that the only reason boys don't grow up is because they die'.

Indeed.

Notes

Chapter 1: On Rugby Fields the Whistles Blow

1 *Daily Telegraph*, 11 February 2013.
2 McLaren served in Italy in the Second World War, and was at Monte Cassino.
3 I am grateful here for a conversation with my friend Roy Barton; if you don't agree, it's his fault.
4 MC in Vietnam, Chief of Defence Staff 2002–05; Governor-General from 2014.
5 E.H.D. Sewell, *The Log of a Sportsman* (Unwin, 1923).
6 Gary Sheffield, *Leadership in the Trenches* (Macmillan, 2000).
7 9 October 1914.
8 Moran, Herbert, *Viewless Winds – being the recollections and digressions of an Australian surgeon* (P. Davies 1939).
9 Fuller, J.G., *Troop Morale and Popular Culture in the British and Dominion Armies* (OUP, 1991).
10 Ibid.
11 Growden, Greg, *Wallaby Warrior: The World War 1 Diaries of Australia's only British Lion* (Allen & Unwin, 2013).
12 John Lewis-Stempel, *The War Behind the Wire* (Weidenfeld & Nicolson, 2014).
13 The famous English game.
14 Henry Grierson, *The Ramblings of a Rabbit* (Chapman & Hall, 1924).
15 Lt Gen. Edward Fanshawe, who took over V Corps from his brother Hew, sacked by Haig for daring to defend a scapegoat.
16 Some 3–6 per cent of the world population died in the epidemic: 17 million in India, 400,000 in France and 250,000 in Britain.
17 *The Final Whistle,* listed eighty-seven names in 2012; twenty-two more have been discovered since; history may be in the past, but it is not fixed.
18 Gwyn Prescott's list is the best, but I have added George Pugh, Australia and Paul Fauré, France.
19 Lt F.W.C. Sawyer, Royal Engineers, killed 4 April 1917.

Chapter 2: The Last of Peace

1 Paul Rubens's song 'Your King and Country Want You' was addressed to sportsmen.
2 The August Bank Holiday was then observed on the first Monday in August.
3 R.F. Oakes in *Yorkshire RFU Memorial Book 1914–19*.
4 Unpublished memoir, courtesy of his daughter, Lady Maggie Robinson.
5 Fairbairn would die in June 1915 in a trench near Wijtschaete, Dale in a flaming kite balloon in Italy in January 1918.

6   *The Citizen*, 29 August 1914.
7   *The Citizen*, 3 September 1914.
8   Letters courtesy of Hugh Barrow and The Glasgow Academical Club.
9   *The Times*, 7 November 1914.
10 *Daily Telegraph*, 14 September 1914.
11 *The Stratford Express*, 2 December 1914.
12 Chairman of the Automobile Association and a leading Conservative politician.
13 Major Leonard Tosswill, *Football: The Rugby Union Game* (Cassell, 1925).
14 *Daily Telegraph*, 30 November 1914.
15 *Daily Telegraph*, 11 November 1914.
16 One of only eight in Scotland's 1914 Calcutta Cup team to survive.
17 Andrew 'Jock' Wemyss, *Barbarian Football Club 1890 to 1955* (Playfair, 1955).
18 Quoted by Sewell, *Roll of Honour.*

Chapter 3: Scotland

1   From 'Flower of Scotland' by Roy M.B. Williamson, The Corries Music Ltd.
2   Information from Ewen Cameron, Professor of Scottish History, Edinburgh University.
3   This ignored the rightful claim of France's Alfred Mayssonié, who died at the Marne on 6 September. By coincidence he was also the first Frenchman to leave the field injured in an international, against England in 1908.
4   The others came from George Will on the other wing. This 'flying Scot' was shot down over Arras in March 1917.
5   Quoted by Sewell, *Roll of Honour.*
6   Imlah sadly died young, aged 52, of motor neurone disease in 2009.
7   Lt Col. Lord Elcho in 1859 clothed his men not in a patterned tartan but in the plain hodden grey common throughout Scotland: 'A soldier is a man hunter. As a deer stalker chooses the least visible of colours, so ought a soldier to be clad.'
8   The first official Association Football international was therefore not played until 1872, after the first Rugby Football international.
9   He was never picked again by Scotland.
10 Robert Rhodes James, *Gallipoli* (London, 1965).
11 J.M. Findlay, *With the Eighth Scottish Rifles 1914–19* (London, 1926).
12 E.H.D. Sewell *Rugger: The Man's Game* (Hollis & Carter, 1947).
13 E.H.D. Sewell, *Roll of Honour of Rugby Internationals* (1919).

Chapter 4: Australia

1   Initially the name was just for the British tour; in America they were Waratahs, but Wallabies soon caught on.
2   Australian cricket had adopted the colours as early as 1899, its Olympic team in 1908, but Rugby League and Union not until 1928 and 1929 respectively.
3   *Daily Telegraph*, 27 Oct 1908.
4   *Daily Mail*, 14 December 1908.
5   Growden, *Wallaby Warrior.*
6   Ibid.
7   *Melbourne Argus*, 6 May 1915.
8   Moran, *Viewless Winds*. His chapter heading is 'Men, Rough Men and Rugby'.
9   Moran, *Viewless Winds.*
10 *Evening Post*, 12 June 1915.

11 31 March 1909.

12 *Imperishable Anzacs: A story of Australia's famous First Brigade from the Diary of H.W. Cavill* (Brooks, 1916).

13 Moran, *Viewless Winds*.

14 *The Referee*, 24 August 1915.

15 *Sydney Morning Herald*, 12 May 1915.

16 Growden, *Wallaby Warrior*.

17 Stuart Perry, Manly fullback 1911–14, letter from Gallipoli, 16 July 1915.

18 Michael McKernan, in *The Making of Modern Sporting History*, ed. McKernan and Richard Cashman (University of Queensland, 1979).

19 Lt G.H. Goddard, *Soldiers and Sportsmen* (AIF, 1919).

20 *The Referee*, March 1915.

21 *The Referee*, 13 October 1915.

22 Moran, *Viewless Winds*.

Chapter 5: New Zealand

1 Ian McGibbon, *Te Ara, The Encyclopaedia of New Zealand*, www.teara.govt.nz.

2 George Vesey Stewart, *Bay of Plenty Times*, 8 January 1916.

3 Keith Sinclair, *A Destiny Apart: New Zealand's Search for a National Identity* (Allen & Unwin, 1986).

4 Dinner speech at Twickenham 2006.

5 *Observer*, 2 February 1901.

6 British teams still played 'first-up, first-down': whoever got to the breakdown first formed the front row.

7 Lloyd Jones, *The Book of Fame* (John Murray, 2008).

8 Keith Sinclair, *A History of New Zealand* (Auckland, 1988).

9 *Express and Echo*, 16 September 1905.

10 Grierson, *Ramblings of a Rabbit*.

11 10 March 1906.

12 Lt Col. W.S. Austin, *Official History of the New Zealand Rifle Brigade* (Watkins, 1924).

13 *Auckland Weekly News*, 18 October 1917

14 Quoted in *Evening Post*, 12 June 1915.

15 A.C. Swan, *History of New Zealand Rugby* (Reed, 1947).

16 *Wellington Evening Post*, 12 June 1915.

17 *Wellington Evening Post*.

18 Jack Sciascia is shown as J. Hiahia in team photos of 1910 and 1913.

19 W.H. Cunningham, C.A.L. Treadwell, J.S. Hanna, *The Wellington Regiment (NZEF) 1914–19* (Ferguson & Osborn, 1928).

20 He is misreported in newspapers and books as Tupine or Turpine.

21 *London Gazette*, 14 May 1919.

22 Growden, *Wallaby Warrior*.

23 Malcolm Ross, the journalist who reported this figure, admitted he was not there.

24 *Pakeha*, a non-indigenous New Zealander.

25 *The Graphic*, 24 February 1917.

26 12 and 15 February 1917

27 Quoted in Charles Hoyer Millar, *Rosslyn Park The First Fifty Years* (1929) Four serving Chrystall brothers survived the war; a fifth died of a chill as a volunteer doctor in Malaya.

Chapter 6: Canada

1   By way of comparison, each English pitch today would have three men – or women – and a dog. I am indebted to Sam Cooper for the calculations: he does numbers, I do words.
2   McGill lead by eighteen wins to fourteen since the fixture's revival in 1974.
3   Ashley Ford, *Vancouver Rowing Club: 100 years of Rugby* (Vancouver, 2008).
4   *San Francisco Chronicle.*
5   Jack Carver, *A History of Vancouver Rowing Club, 1886–1980*, (VRC, 1980)
6   *Vancouver Sun*, 9 November 2014.
7   [Canadian Field Comforts Commission], *With the First Canadian Contingent* (Hodder & Stoughton, 1919).
8   John Maclaren, *The Toronto World*, 22 January 1915.
9   Ibid.
10   *The Times*, 14 December 1914.
11   Colonel A.F. Duguid, *Official History of the Canadian Forces in The Great War 1914–1919* (Ottawa, 1938).
12   *The Times*, 14 December 1914.
13   Royal Fusilier Maddock had retired from club rugby in 1913, was awarded the MC in 1918, but never recovered from a wound and died aged 40 in 1921.
14   Arnold Huckett's story is told in *The Final Whistle: The Great War in Fifteen Players* (Spellmount, 2012).
15   Letter reproduced in *With the First Canadian Contingent.*
16   John Prescott, *In Flanders Fields: The Story of John McCrae* (Boston Press, 1985).
17   Helmer's grave was lost; McCrae's dressing station can be visited at Essex Farm Cemetery.
18   *With the First Canadian Contingent.*
19   Letter of 29 November 1914, quoted by E.H.D. Sewell, *Roll of Honour.*
20   Sewell, *Roll of Honour.*
21   *The Province*, December 1915.
22   *Province*, December 1915.
23   *London Gazette*, 17 April 1917.
24   Thomas Nelson, Oxford Blue, Scottish internationalist and publisher, was also killed that Easter Monday on the Arras front. His friend John Buchan dedicated *The Thirty Nine Steps* to him in 1915, 'in these days when the wildest fictions are so much less improbable than the truth'.
25   *Vancouver Sun*, 19 April 1917.

Chapter 7: South Africa

1   Growden, *Wallaby Warrior.*
2   Thirty-six Springboks place it third in a table topped by Paul Roos Gymnasium, formerly Stellenbosch, renamed in honour of the 1906 Springbok skipper.
3   Neil Orpen, *Cape Town Rifles: Dukes* (Rifles Regimental Council, 1984).
4   David Parry-Jones, *Prince Gwyn, Gwyn Nicholls and the First Golden Era of Welsh Rugby* (Bridgend, 1999).
5   E.J.L. Plateneur *The Springbokken Tour in Great Britain* (Geo. Wunderlich, 1907).
6   Peters's England debut in 1906 was seventy-two years before Viv Anderson became England's first black soccer player.
7   J.B.G. Thomas, *On Tour* (Anchor Press, 1954).
8   Plateneur, *Springbokken Tour.*

9   Plateneur, *Springbokken Tour.*
10 *Cape Argus*, 14 October 1933.
11 Sewell, *Log of a Sportsman.*
12 Sewell, *Roll of Honour.*
13 John Buchan, *The History of the South African Forces in France* (Nelson, 1920).
14 See Floris van der Merwe's encyclopaedic *Soldiers and Sportsmen* (FJG Publikaties, 2012).
15 Lt Col. H.L. Silberbauer, 'Reminiscences of the First World War', *South African Military History Journal*, 1997.
16 Van der Merwe, *Soldiers and Sportsmen.*
17 He would also play in the 1919 Varsity Match.

Chapter 8: United States of America

1   *University of California Yearbook*, 1912.
2   *University of California Yearbook*, 1912.
3   *Washington Post*, 10 October 1905.
4   Roberta J. Parks, 'From Football to Rugby and Back, 1906–19', *Journal of Sport History*, Vol. II, No. 2 (1984).
5   *San Francisco Bulletin*, 11 February 1906.
6   12 February 1906.
7   *San Francisco Chronicle*, 14 February 1906.
8   *Daily Princetonian*, 18 January 1910.
9   The Olympic database gives his birth year as 1892, making him the youngest ever internationalist at 16 years 286 days. A birth certificate held by the ARU dated 1887 is more convincing.
10 *San Francisco Post*, 16 November 1913.
11 The first-ever All Black visit to Samoa in July 2015 is a stride forward.
12 Swan, *History of New Zealand Rugby.*
13 Frank Vans Agnew (ed. Jamie Vans), *Veteran Volunteer: Memoir of the Trenches, Tanks and Captivity 1914–19* (Pen & Sword, 2014).
14 T. Ben Meldrum, *History of the 362nd Infantry Regiment* (A.L. Scoville Press, 1920).
15 *The Inter-Allied Games Paris, 22nd June to 6th July 1919*, Report by G. Wythe & J.M. Hanson (Paris, 1919).
16 *The Inter-Allied Games Paris.*
17 Muhr moved to France in the early 1900s, played in their first 1906 Test against the All Blacks, and scored their first try against England. A Jew, he died of starvation in a concentration camp near Hamburg in 1944.
18 See Mark Ryan, *For the Glory: Two Olympics, Two Wars, Two Heroes* (J.R. Books, 2009).
19 *The Redwood*, University of Santa Clara, October 1920.

Chapter 9: England

1   Hinton would be President of the IRFU in 1920–21, Sir William Tyrrell in 1950–51.
2   County Champions in his last three seasons.
3   Quoted in James Corsan, *For Poulton and England* (Matador, 2009).
4   Edmund van Esbeck, *One Hundred Years of Irish Rugby* (Gill & McMillan, 1974).
5   W.J. Townsend Collins, *Rugby Recollections* (R.H. Johns, 1948).
6   Paul Jones, *War Letters of a Public Schoolboy.*

7　A.M. McGilchrist, *The Liverpool Scottish 1900–19.*

8　*Liverpool Mercury,* 3 May 1897.

9　*Liverpool Post,* 10 March 1964.

10　Sewell, *Roll of Honour.*

11　Sewell, *Roll of Honour.*

12　Chavasse, a keen rugby player at Oxford and 1908 Olympian athlete, died of wounds at Brandhoek in 1917, in an action which earned him a second VC, this time posthumous.

13　Sewell, *Roll of Honour.*

14　*The Times,* 11 March 1901.

15　*The Times,* 11 December 1905.

16　Ecclesiasticus 44, 13: 'Their seed shall remain forever, and their glory shall not be blotted out.'

17　*London Gazette Supplement,* 2 December 1918.

18　Oakes, *Yorkshire RFU Memorial Book.*

19　Grierson, *Ramblings of a Rabbit.*

20　Stanley Bruce, MC, Jesus College and Cambridge oarsman, became Prime Minister of Australia in 1923 and later Lord Melbourne.

21　Letter to *The Times* quoted by David Woodall, *The Mobbs Own.*

22　Oakes, *Yorkshire RFU Memorial Book.*

Chapter 10: Ireland

1　From 'Ireland's Call' by Phil Coulter, 1995.

2　*Wisden* shows him making over 2,000 runs in 1889.

3　*London Gazette,* 2 October 1915.

4　*Dublin Evening Mail,* quoted in Henry Hanna, *The Pals at Suvla Bay.*

5　*Irish Times,* 1 May 1915.

6　Later Reid successors included Irish Presidents Mary Robinson and Mary McAleese.

7　Grierson, *Ramblings of a Rabbit.*

8　E.A. Rolfe, *Old Bedfordians Year Book,* 1929.

9　Unpublished account in *The Final Whistle: The Great War in Fifteen Players.*

10　Henry Hanna, *The Pals at Suvla Bay* (Ponsonby, 1917).

11　The stories of Dingle and Oxland are told in *The Final Whistle.*

12　Quoted by Henry Hanna.

Chapter 11: Wales

1　D.E. Davies, *Cardiff Rugby Club History and Statistics 1876–1975* (Cardiff RFC, 1975).

2　National Archives WO 95/2561/3.

3　Owen Sheers, 'Mametz Wood'.

4　Gareth Thomas and Michael Calvin, *Proud* (Ebury Press, 2014).

5　Sewell, *Roll of Honour.*

6　Beware misreporting that he was killed at Guillemont, where King and Slocock died in August.

7　W.A.D. Lawrie, *The First 100 Years: History of Bridgend RFC* (Lawrie, 1979).

8　*Cambrian Daily Leader,* 4 February 1916.

9　Unpublished account, courtesy of Ann Gammie.

10　*Otago Witness,* 27 December 1918.

11　David Gronow, *100 Greats: Huddersfield Rugby League Football Club* (The History Press, 2008).

Chapter 12: France

1 A shield is awarded for the French championship, now the Bouclier Brennus.
2 My thanks here to Brynmôr Evans.
3 Bayonne's Stade Jean Dauger is on the rue Harry Owen Roe.
4 *Le Monde Illustré*, April 1913.
5 '*C'est à Craonne sur le plateau / Qu'on doit laisser sa peau / Car nous sommes tous condamnés / C'est nous les sacrifiés.*' ('In Craonne on the plateau / We're leaving our hides. / We've all been sentenced to die / We are the sacrifice.')
6 *Le Cri Catalan*, 16 January 1915 (author's translation).
7 *L'Auto*, 18 January 1917.
8 *The Dominion*, April 1917. Malcolm Ross, official NZ war correspondent on a salary of £1,000 and expenses, was derided for his relentlessly upbeat reports. As was Beach Thomas of the *Daily Mail* in *The Wipers Times*.
9 *Sporting*, 11 April 1917.
10 *The Dominion*, April 1917.
11 See *The Final Whistle*.
12 *Tous les Sports*, 22 March 1918.

Chapter 13: No Side

1 Général Maxime Weygand, *Le 11 novembre,* author's translation.
2 From the Latin *arma* (weapon) and *statium* (a stopping).
3 Lt Leslie Averill, letter written on 7 November 1918.
4 Jack's diary and letters survived and his story is recounted in *The Final Whistle*.
5 Goddard, *Soldiers and Sportsmen*.

Chapter 14: The Return of the King

1 Goddard, *Soldiers and Sportsmen*.
2 On 26 January 1926 in Soho; colour came two years later.
3 See www.britishpathe.com.
4 Now World Rugby.
5 *The Times*, 22 March 1919.
6 *Coventry Evening Telegraph*, 16 April 1917.
7 Lowe's England record of eighteen tries was not surpassed until 1989 by another RAF pilot, Rory Underwood. He was also (one of many) rumoured to be the model for Captain W.E. Johns's Biggles.
8 Wavell Wakefield and Howard Marshall.
9 Gareth Morgan, 'Taffy', *14–18 Journal* (Australian Society of World War 1 Aero Historians, 2012).
10 Interview with Doug Sturrock, Winnipeg, 30 July 1974.
11 *The Times*, 4 March 1919.
12 *The Times*, 7 April 1919.
13 Goddard, *Soldiers and Sportsmen*.
14 Essay in Ivor Difford, *History of South African Rugby* (Specialty Press, 1933).
15 Mellish also managed the 1951–52 Springbok tour of Britain.
16 *Athletic News*, 7 April 1919.
17 *The Times*, 31 March 1919.
18 New Zealand finished top by virtue of defeating the Mother Country.

Chapter 15: Endgame

1 *The Times*, 19 January 1914.
2 The full list can be inspected at www.espn.co.uk/scrum.
3 Lt T.J. Dobson, RNVR, WO161/95/62, National Archives.
4 Biography at www.sebastianfaulks.com.
5 W.F. Ingram, 'Our Soldier Athletes – Their Fame in Battle and Sport', *New Zealand Railways Magazine*, Vol. 14, Issue 12, 1 March 1940.
6 *The Times*, 21 April 1919.

Chapter 16: Aftermath and Recovery

1 W.E. Henley, 'Invictus'.
2 John Griffiths, *Rugby's Strangest Matches*.
3 Bill Schreiner, quoted in Dobson, *Rugby's Greatest Rivalry*.
4 *Cape Times*, 30 June 1919.
5 *Cape Times*, 13 September 1919.
6 *New Zealand Herald*, 17 October 1919.
7 *The Referee*, 20 November 1918.
8 *La Stampa Sportiva*, Torino, 3 April 1910. Not Racing Club as widely misreported.
9 The (mis)printed 1938 *FIRA Yearbook* includes the exotic but not very Italian Mac Cornac and Orinkewatez – more prosaically, MacCormac and Drinkwater.
10 *San Francisco Chronicle*, 24/29 November 1918.
11 Ralph Vacchiano, 2 March 2010.
12 Interview with Asad Ziar, CEO Afghan Rugby Federation, January 2015.

Chapter 17: Rugby Remembers

1 Theoden of Rohan, *The Two Towers, Lord of the Rings* (New Line Cinema, 2002).
2 *Histories*, Book 1.
3 Sir Oliver Lodge, *Raymond, or Life and Death* (Methuen, 1916).
4 His letters and diary until 29 June 1916 survived. His story is told in *The Final Whistle*.
5 A more Nietzschean version is used – 'Character is Destiny' – although the original was just within CWGC stipulations.
6 *Daily Express*, 27 March 2014.
7 A.P. Herbert, 'Beaucourt Revisited'.
8 General Charles Harington, *Plumer of Messines* (John Murray, 1935).
9 Phil Gifford, *Loyal: The Todd Blackadder Story* (Hodder Moa Beckett, 2001).
10 *Exeter Express and Echo*, 4 November 2014.

Bibliography

Akers, Clive & Bettina Anderson, *Balls, Bullets and Boots – New Zealand Rugby in World War 1* (New Zealand Rugby Museum, 2015)

Billott, John, *A History of Welsh Rugby* (Ron Jones, 1970)

Bodis, Jean-Pierre & Pierre Lafond, *Encyclopédie du rugby français* (Dehedin, 1989)

Bohl, David, *Sefton Rugby Union Football Club* (Serendipity, 2003)

Busson, Bernard, *Héros du Sport, Héros de France* (Editions d'Art Athos, 1947)

Chester, Rod & N.A.C. McMillan, *Centenary: 100 Years of All Black Rugby* (Blandford Press, 1984)

Collins, Tony, *A Social History of English Rugby Union* (Routledge, 2009)

Cooper, Ian, *Immortal Harlequin* (Tempus, 2004)

Cooper, Stephen, *The Final Whistle: The Great War in Fifteen Players* (Spellmount, 2012)

Corsan, James, *For Poulton and England* (Matador, 2009)

Davies, Martin & Teresa, *For Club, King and Country 1914–1918* (Soldiers of Gloster Museum, 2014)

Difford, Ivor, *History of South African Rugby Football* (Specialty Press, 1933)

Dine, Phillip, *French Rugby Football: A Cultural History* (Berg, 2001)

Dobson, Paul, *Rugby's Greatest Rivalry, South Africa vs New Zealand 1921–95* (Human & Rousseau, 1996)

Dunning, Eric & Kenneth Sheard, *Barbarians, Gentlemen and Players: A Sociological Study of the Development of Rugby Football* (Robertson, 1979)

Fox, Dave, Ken Bogle & Mark Hoskins, *A Century of the All Blacks in Britain and Ireland* (Tempus, 2006)

Fuller, J.G., *Troop Morale and Popular Culture in the British and Dominion Armies* (OUP, 1991)

Garcia, Henri, *Les Contes du Rugby* (La Table Ronde, 1961)

Goddard, Lt G.H., *Soldiers and Sportsmen* (AIF, 1919)

Greig, Geordie, *Louis and the Prince: A Story of Politics, Intrigue and Royal Friendship* (Hodder & Stoughton, 1999)

Grierson, Henry, *The Ramblings of a Rabbit* (Chapman & Hall, 1924)

Griffiths, John, *Phoenix Book of International Rugby Records* (Phoenix, 1987)

Griffiths, John, *Rugby's Strangest Matches* (Robson, 2007)

Growden, Greg, *Wallaby Warrior: The World War 1 Diaries of Australia's Only British Lion* (Allen & Unwin, 2013)

Hanna, Henry, *The Pals at Suvla Bay* (Ponsonby, 1917)

Holt, Richard, *Sport and the British: A Modern History* (OUP, 1989)

Howitt, Bob & Dianne Howarth, *The 1905 Originals* (HarperCollins, 2005)

Jones, Paul, *War Letters of a Public School Boy* (Cassell, 1918)

Lawrie, W.A.D., *The First 100 Years: History of Bridgend RFC* (Lawrie, 1979)

MacLaren, John, *The History of Army Rugby* (Army RFU, 1986)

MacLeod, Iain, *The Glasgow Academy* (GA War Memorial Trust, 1997)

Mason, Tony & Eliza Riedi, *Sport and the Military: The British Armed Forces 1880–1960* (Cambridge University Press, 2010)

Meignan, Francis, *Dans la mêlée des tranchées: Le rugby à l'épreuve de la Grande Guerre* (Editions Le Pas d'Oiseau, 2014)

Moran, Herbert, *Viewless Winds: Recollections and Digressions of an Australian Surgeon* (Peter Davies, 1939)

Morris, Frank, *The First 100: History of the London Scottish Football Club* (LSFC, 1977)

Mortimer, Gavin, *Fields of Glory* (Deutsch, 2001)

Mosse, George, *Fallen Soldiers: Reshaping the Memories of the World Wars* (OUP, 1994)

Mulholland, Malcolm, *Beneath the Māori Moon: An Illustrated History of Māori Rugby* (Hula, 2009)

Owen, Owen, *A History of the Rugby Football Union* (Playfair, 1955)

Parker, A.C., *The Springboks 1891–1970* (Cassell, 1970)

Parry-Jones, David, *Prince Gwyn: Gwyn Nicholls and the First Golden Era of Welsh Rugby* (Bridgend, 1999)

Pelmear, Kenneth (ed.), *Rugby Football; An Anthology* (Allen & Unwin, 1958)

Prescott, Gwyn, *Call Them to Remembrance* (St Davids Press, 2014)

Ravagnani, Luciano & Pierluigi Fadda, *Rugby: Storia del Rugby Mondiale* (SEP Editrice, 2007)

Richards, Huw, *A Game for Hooligans* (Mainstream, 2007)

Ryan, Mark, *For the Glory: Two Olympics, Two Wars, Two Heroes* (JR Books, 2009)

Sewell E.H.D., *Rugger: The Man's Game* (Hollis & Carter, 1947)

Sewell E.H.D., *Roll of Honour of Rugby Internationals* (1919)

Smith, David & Gareth Williams, *Fields of Praise* (University of Wales Press, 1980)

Swan, A.C., *A History of New Zealand Rugby 1870–1945* (Reed, 1947)

Sturrock, Doug, *History of Rugby in Canada* – as yet unpublished

Thomas, Clem, *History of the British & Irish Lions*, (Mainstream, 2005)

Thompson, Brian, *Leicester Tigers: A History of the Leicester Football Club* (Backus, 1947)

Thorburn, Sandy, *The History of Scottish Rugby* (Cassell, 1980)

Tonetti, Guiseppe, *Cinquant'Anni di Speranza* (La Guida Editrice, 1979)

Tosswill, Major Leonard, *Football: The Rugby Union Game* (Cassell, 1925)

Van der Merwe, Floris, *Sporting Soldiers: South African troops at play during World War I* (FJG Publikaties, 2012)

Van Esbeck, Edmund, *One Hundred Years of Irish Rugby* (Gill & McMillan, 1974)

Wakefield, Wavell & Howard Marshall, *Rugger* (Longmans, 1928)

Wemyss, Andrew 'Jock', *Barbarian Football Club 1890 to 1955* (Playfair, 1955)

Weygand, Maxime, *Le 11 novembre* (Flammarion, 1958)

Woodall, David, *The Mobbs Own* (Northampton Regiment Association, 1994)

Zavos, Spiro *The Golden Wallabies* (Penguin, 2000)

Index